The Path

Leveraging Operations
In a Complex and Chaotic World

SHRIDHAR LOLLA

The Path
Copyrights © Shridhar Lolla 2013
First Printing, 2013

ISBN-10: 1482759144
ISBN-13: 978-1482759143

All rights reserved. This book or any portion thereof may not be reproduced or used in any manner whatsoever without the express written permission of the publisher.

Published by Shridhar Lolla
#2304, Nandi Park, Gottigere
Bannergatta Road, Bangalore- 560 083
INDIA
E mail: lolla@cvmark.com

The Book is a work of fiction based on the experience of the Author. The names, characters, dates and places used in the Book are fictional and any resemblance to reality is purely coincidental. The Book also contains information that might seem prescriptive in nature. The Author can't assume any responsibility for the validity of all the materials or consequence of their use. The Author has attempted to trace the copyright holders of materials reproduced in this publication and apologize to copyright holders if permission to publish in this form has not been obtained. If any copyright material has not been acknowledged please write and let him know so he may rectify in any further reprint.

Trademark Notice: Product or corporate names may be trademarks or registered trademarks, and are used only for identification and explanation without intent to infringe.

To
My Dad Narasimha Murthy
He held my hand and I started writing
My Mom Vijayalakshmi Devi
For her silent prayers

And

My ever high performing team
Kavya, Krishna and Urgita
Home has always been my best place

The Co-creators

Adarsh Pakala
Ajay Kumar
Ajayan N
Alok Dugar
Anil Rajani
Anindya Purkait
Anupkumar Gandhi
Anurag Seksaria
Arvind Pachauri
Ashok Kumar
Asogan K
Benny Varghese
Bhupati LSR
BN Jha
BN Singh, Dr
Chandrasekar KP
Chandrasekar Rajaram
Chandu Nair
Dileep More, Prof
Dwarakanath RS
Ehsaan Khan
Gagandeep Singh
Gajanan Kshirsagar
Gautam Jain
Gopalakrishna Kuppa
Gopinath M
Govindarajan M
Hemant Kalia
Jaisimha Belagur
Jatin Seth
Javin Bhinde
John P Santhosh
Kalyanakrishnan NH
Kalyanasundaram S
Keshav Nandurkar, Prof
Kiran VVN
Kirankumar K
Koteswararao Vaddadi
Krishna GVN
Krishnasastry KV, Prof

Manikandan Murugesan
Manoj Chandan Jain
Meera Srikant
Mihir Jain
Mohan Kolhe, Prof
Mohan Pandey
Mohan Ramanathan
Moinuddin Rawoot, Dr
Neeraj Kumar
Nitin Bhadauria
Nityanand Mahale
Omprakash C
Pradeep Jeswani
Pramod Kummaya
Prasad VB
Praveen Singh
Raffi SM
Raghavendra S
Raghu Ananthanarayanan
Raghuram Kalachaveedu
Rahul Gosain
Rajeev Athavale
Rajeev Ranjan
Rajiv Singhai
Ramani Sundaresan
Ramesh Iyer
Ranganathan K Rao, Prof
Ravikumar Achanta
Ravi PS
Rituraj Khare
Sagar Ballari
Sandeep Modi
Sanjay Adivarekar
Sanjay Deshmukh
Sanjay Saxena
Sankary Viswanathan
Santosh Mavely
Santosh Patwardhan
Sanuja Vibin

Sarala M
Satyajit Majumdar, Prof
Shankar Rao
Shashidhar Shettar
Shekar Rangarajan
Shirish Agrawal
Shivaram A
Shriharsh L
Shrikant Bartakke
Siraj Ahmed, Prof
Srikrishnan Narayanan
Srinivas Thumma
Srinivasamurthy K
Srinivasu Vendra
Subbareddy V
Sudhakar SV
Sugumaran J
Sujit Kaushik
Sunil Kanvinde, Dr
Sunil Kumar Gupta
Surenderanath M
Suresh TS
Umang Gandhi
Umesh Shetty
Uttam Lal
Vaibhav Agarwal
Vaibhav Kaley
Varma KRC
Vasu KS
Veena KN, Prof
Veerkamesh V
Veerramani SV
Vibinkumar Vasu
Vikram Singh
Vilas Dholye
Vinay Baijal
Viresh Bansal
Vishwanath Belliappa
Vishwanath Edavayyanamath

Profile of Readers

Chief Executive Officer
Objective: To achieve sustainable growth.
Challenge: The industry has moved away from product and market advantage, and Operations is becoming a critical area for success. How to leverage Operations for sustainable growth?

Vice President Operations
Objective: To constantly improve response to market.
Challenge: In an ever changing and uncertain business environment, it is a constant struggle to maintain fast response time along with high quality, good flexibility and low cost. How to align operations from material warehouse to plant to distribution seamlessly?

Head Supply Chain
Objective: To provide right quantity of right products at right place at right time.
Challenge: In an increasingly complex supply chain, it is critical to prevent delays, minimize overstocks and eliminate stock-outs. How to improve co-ordination with plant and material suppliers to meet an ever changing and volatile market demand.?

Production Manager
Objective: To constantly improve throughput of the plant.
Challenge: So many disruptions and priority changes. How to avoid the trade-off between throughput and cost? How to reduce firefighting and give work-life balance to the staff?

Profile of Readers

Head Business Excellence
Objective: To constantly improve performance of the organization.
Challenge: Change process takes a lot of time and effort. How to integrate various tools and techniques? How to improve the process of improvement? How to roll out improvement programs without disturbing the ongoing operations?

Professor: Operations Management
Objective: To Prepare industry ready managers.
Challenge: Integrating Business aspects into classroom teaching. Students are well geared in technical knowledge but their managerial skills are not satisfactory. What's it like working in a manufacturing organization? Which issues are important for my students to be industry ready?

Business Consultant
Objective: To provide a solution that directly improves business results.
Challenge: With chaos and complexity around, clients are increasingly asking for tangible and sustainable benefits. How do I approach to build a capability in my clients to manage performance better?

Investor
Objective: To support organizations which solve real world problems and fulfill important needs of the society.
Challenge: There have been too much investment with too little returns. Huge capacities have been built but are waiting for effective operations. Where is the next hidden opportunity? How to increase returns without taking too much risk and investing too much capital?

List of Content Tells the Story

The Co-creators v
Profile of Readers... vi
Summary xiii

The Traditional Reaction..1

   The Trigger 3
   Reacting to Competitive Landscape.. 5
      The First Change 6
      Several Changes...7
      Interim Results 8
   Applying Traditional Tactics.. 9
      The Susceptive Tactics 10
      The Reversal of Results..10
   Meeting the Thought Leader.. 14
   The Pharma Plant: Physical Setup 18

Chasing the Numbers..23

   Betting on Intuition.. 25
   Starting with a Workable Solution... 27
   Plant Load - the Beast... 29
   Emotions are Stronger than Logic 32
   The Inevitable 37
   Mt. Kilimanjaro - Tactics for Dealing with the Unknown........ 41

Preparing for the Change...47

   Re-reading the Situation 49
      Describing the Business 51
      Visualizing the Logic of Business............................55
      The Secret to Sustainable Operations......................59
      Gazing the Environment 61
   Grasping the Problem... 66
      Taking Initiative 67
      Picking a Direction of the Problem 69
      Understanding the Bigger Problem 70
   Direction to the Solution 71
      Common Understanding......................................72

Better Understanding 73
　　　Consolidated Understanding 74
　Leadership at Work *76*
　　　Common View 77
　　　Aligned View 77
　　　Committing to Fundamentals 79

Installing the New Paradigm **83**
　Building on Intuition and Coming out of Chaos *85*
　　　Visualizing Likely Chaos in the Plant 86
　　　Making a Strategic Choice 89
　　　The Vicious Cycle 90
　　　Intervention to Create a Virtuous Cycle 93
　　　Agreement on Stock Design 97
　The War Room *99*
　Scheduling @ the Speed of Light *104*
　Aligning Upstream *108*

Nurturing the Right Behavior **113**
　Evidence of the Need for Behavior Change *115*
　The Right Behavior *120*
　Codifying the Desired Behavior *126*
　　　Scripting the Operating Rules 126
　　　Improving System Design on the Run 127
　　　Moderating the Message 130

Reclaiming the Core **135**
　Dealing with High Attrition of Talent *137*
　Manufacturing is a Core Competency *140*
　Big Opportunity but People Hesitate to Commit *143*
　　　The Hesitation List 144
　　　Setting up the Operating System 145
　　　Escalation ≠ Expediting 148
　　　Subject Note on Escalation and Expediting 149
　Reducing Dilemma by Innovating Measurements *151*

Executing the BIG Change **163**
　Connecting to the Purpose *165*
　Dealing with the Long Tail *167*

Improving the Process of Improvement *176*
   Aren't Big Improvements Overwhelming? 176
   Identifying the Weakest Link 179
   Leveraging the Weakest Link 181

Face-Off with Changeovers *187*
   Identifying and Observing Activities 187
   Separating Internal and External Activities 190
   Converting Internal to External 192
   Stabilizing the Improvement Process 193

Campaigning-The Holy Grail of Operations *195*

How do you Set Improvement Targets? *200*

The Impact *209*

The Larger Effect *212*

Consolidating the Change **215**

Business Model Innovation *217*
   The Business Model Approach 217
   Visualizing Innovated Business Model 220
   Read-out of Innovated Business Model 221
   Guidelines for Operational Excellence 225

Appendix **229**

Unambiguous Priority System *231*

Inside the Growth Curve *236*

Key References *245*

Co-creation of The Path *246*

Results of Co-creation *247*

About the Author *248*

Summary

Experts have called the current pattern of rapid and unpredictable changes in business conditions as the New Normal. In order to lead in these conditions, it is critical to constantly innovate business at *an ever faster pace*. And to obtain the desired responsive capabilities, organizations significantly rely on a process or function called operations. They are therefore under an increasing pressure to make Operational Excellence central to their core strategy.

In their aspirations to achieve superlative operational performance, organizations have often rushed to adopt a large variety of tools and techniques. However, a vast majority of attempts to cut and paste such tools and techniques has made their journey painful, exhausting and costly. Not surprisingly, over 70% of well intended initiatives to achieve breakthrough performance in operations have either stopped midway or given suboptimal results.

'The Path' presents a way to achieve dramatic growth on an ongoing basis without taking costly trade-offs and burn-outs. It emphasizes that dealing with the New Normal is not so much about running after an overwhelming number of improvement skill-sets, rather it is about *'improving the process of improvement'* itself. According to the book, an organization of a reasonable size has enough intuition, experience and logic to figure out its own way of Operational Excellence. It shows that in today's environment, an actionable approach of 'learning by doing' provides a strong option for achieving rapid, yet sustainable growth.

The book is set in an operational warzone and it describes the saga of teams in dealing with the New Normal. Since, intuition and emotions are hallmark of day to day operations, it is written in a semi story driven format and contains operational dialogues between players in the field.

Notwithstanding its story driven approach, 'The Path' attempts to provide a business solution to one of the biggest social evils: the skyrocketing cost of medicines. It derives its content from the pharmaceutical industry to which every reader is a customer. Like the great debate of global warming, the book recognizes the growing tension between drug manufacturers on one hand and governments, regulators, social media and patients on the other hand. It places non-availability of drugs at the center of discussion and pinpoints ineffective and inefficient way of doing business as a core problem to the conflict. It shows how a high availability of drugs is achieved by dramatically improving operations of pharmaceutical organizations, while lowering the cost.

From the industry domain point of view, the book is unique because it moves the popular literature on organizational effectiveness beyond automotive and engineering centric industries. By doing so, it provides opportunity to professionals to relook into Operational Excellence from a very fundamental level and then, build their own way of achieving quick and dramatic growth on an ongoing basis. In fact, no industry is untouched by the type of changes taking place due to the New Normal, although at different and varying intensity. 'The Path' is therefore as much applicable to a well matured commodity business as it is to the one in the new product intensive Hi-tech industry.

As a book, 'The Path' is also unique in the way it was created. In fact, it was co-created by over 100 professionals online. These professionals from different industries have provided insights from their years of experience in making organizations more effective. And in doing so, they have offered a direction to make quality medicines readily available and affordable to the world.

The Traditional Reaction

The Trigger

October 2006

My flight to Dubai was already late by over two hours and I was doubtful about catching the connecting flight to Johannesburg. But as soon as the airplane landed, the airline staff, adorned in their rich chocolate color suit, moved me quickly on topmost *priority,* ahead of everyone else. I needed to take the flight as I had an important meeting to attend.

The ground staff of the airline drove me around in a Land Rover to the next terminal. They rushed me through a couple of check points. Soon, I was at the door of the airplane. I walked in and threw myself into the cushy seat.

I was trying to catch my breath when someone almost shouted into my ears, "DJ!!!"

"Yes please," I said, looking at the gentleman in the seat to my left.

"Don't you recognize me?" asked a fair and bespectacled guy, a Bill Gates look-alike.

"Sorry, I am not able to…" I replied without thinking hard.

"I am Ajay… Ajay Basu!!!"

"Ajay Basu!" I looked into his eyes with surprise.

Ajay was my buddy from school and we used to connect to each other very well.

"Boy, what a place to meet you after such a long time!" I said as I kept looking into his eyes, remembering our childhood togetherness. His face had the typical smile, which I would not have failed to recognize even without an introduction. We immediately shook hands and hugged each other.

Ajay was on his way to join his family on a vacation. We reminisced about school, friends, family, career and business.

After passing out of school, Ajay did a BA in Psychology and then an MBA in Human Resource Development. Since then, making organizations better place to work has been his career objective.

I learnt that Ajay was in between jobs, having quit his current employer Reamedics, a leading Pharmaceutical Company based out of the eastern part of the region.

While we chatted enthusiastically, he shared the interesting situation at Reamedics, and the bit of his struggle in aligning HR development with organizational objectives to deliver better business results.

My experience of the Pharmaceutical (Pharma) Industry was limited to building a SCADA system for a large European company. A SCADA system, i.e., Supervisory Control and Data Acquisition system, is a real-time software system used to automate management of complex operational infrastructure, like manufacturing facility, power system network, water distribution system etc.

As a consumer of drugs, I had some idea about the regulated nature of the industry, the spiraling cost of drugs and the clamor for Generics (the low-priced version of off-patented drugs). But I did not know *the way* local pharma companies operated internally till Ajay opened it up bare during our over eight-hour travel across the Arabian Gulf and the Dark Continent. Here is an interesting account in his words.

Reacting to Competitive Landscape

Reamedics is a large generics company and a significant player in local as well as global market. However, growing competition in the marketplace, increasing government intervention on pricing and ever tightening regulations have created a lot of uncertainty in the business.

A decade ago, the market had just a few significant players. It is now fragmented with thousands of players vying for each and every part. Smaller players have started dominating not only the niche fragments of the value chain but also the low value market segment. At the same time, innovator companies from abroad have started to build upon their strategic presence and grab the high value market segment.

More recently, activism driven by consumer led forums has been growing, questioning not only what the Industry delivers but also the way it works.

With healthcare cost cornering a large part of patient's budget, governments and social organizations have teamed up to demand dramatic reduction in the price of drugs. The list of drugs under price control has increasingly become a critical point of contention between health care reformers and corporate houses. At the same time, increased awareness of patients about health as well as environment is forcing regulators to adopt tighter quality, safety and health norms. As a result, being used to hefty margins, businesses are under severe stress to break free.

At Reamedics, several quick fix initiatives were applied to deal with the complexity posed by the rapidly changing market conditions. During the past few years, new technology was implemented to automate flow in manufacturing and an ERP system was implemented across the organization to improve operational transparency. Also, specialists were recruited to crack complex products, new geographies were opened to expand reach and a new sales strategy was introduced to increase market share. But none of them gave the desired results.

By the 3rd Quarter of 2005, Reamedics had already lost quite a bit of the market share, and its bottom line was nose diving. The honchos at Reamedics were struggling to pin down the core problem linked to its poor performance.

One of the few things the Executive Council of Reamedics concerned about was the difficulty in aligning different functions of the organization towards a concerted effort to improve the situation. Most of the initiatives, which were started with seemingly strong commitments, fizzled out because of the lack of collaboration between functions.

Amongst the dominant causes of internal misalignment was the apparent regular infighting between the Sales Head and the Operations Head. The teams of sales and operations were working in silos, often at loggerheads and lacking accountability. They always had enough justification to blame each other for missed performance targets. Sales would blame Operations for not keeping its promise on deliveries and Operations would counter attack Sales for unnecessarily fiddling with priorities.

In fact, the staff of Reamedics across the supply chain was under constant pressure to deliver. Almost everyone was working overtime, but business results were showing a disproportionate negative bias. The due date performance, product availability, plant productivity, machine utilization, return on capital, inventories, work in progress and overtime wages, all were in red.

The organization lived in a strange cultural trap. Celebrations would breakout for every minuscule improvement, but no accountability existed for big slippages. Over commitments were made to clients but deliveries were grossly unreliable. It was always possible to identify some external reason to convincingly justify non-performance. In fact, during the previous two quarters, 90 percent of its key clients did not get even one delivery within the agreed time.

Too many variables seemed to adversely affect the business and the key performance metrics were swinging wildly. Nobody had any clue about the underlying control parameters. Despite its best product portfolio in the industry, Reamedics was losing its key clients.

Unable to cope up with the pressure and the back office politics, the CEO quit.

The First Change

The company promoted its Sales Head as the CEO. The new CEO had been in the industry for over 25 years, and knew every trick of the trade.

His only regret was that during his tenure in Sales, he seldom had an objective discussion with the operations team. Actually, he never understood why there were so many problems with Operations and why it could not deliver client orders in time, despite sales teams often lowering the forecasted demand.

Anyway, now that he got the opportunity and the authority, it was time for him to do his best.

Although the CEO did not mistrust the existing operational structure, he thought of straightening the manufacturing system of Reamedics. With that intention, he immediately hired an expert to build a Centre of Excellence (COE) in manufacturing and redraw the manufacturing strategy.

He took a mandate from the Executive Council to debottleneck manufacturing so that the sales team could go full throttle into the market.

Further, he did not want to be biased by his own opinion, nor wished to depend on intuition of the manufacturing team. Hence, he engaged 'Top Consult', an iconic consultant group that specialized in performance improvement. The mandate given to Top Consult was to provide strategic inputs to *double* the production capacity.

Several Changes

Top Consult brought in its talented associates, who went across the organization interviewing top-level executives.

Armed with the mandate to increase production capacity, they zoomed into manufacturing and collected enormous data from the ERP system. For the first time since its implementation three years ago, Reamedics was able to justify over $12 million investment in ERP.

Top Consult made an electrifying presentation about its findings to the Executive Council and gave a solid proposal for dramatically improving performance of the company.

The management was excited to see the truth about its organization laid bare by the well-structured and sharply analyzed presentation. It had no difficulty in understanding the reality and in agreeing with the direction of the solution. Top Consult recommended layout changes, new machines procurement, automation, new formats, new reporting structure, new metrics and new accounting rules.

Subsequently, Top Consult called the implementation team for a working session. The COE Head moderated the workshop. The implementation team drew up the plan and estimated the budget required to achieve the big jump in performance.

Then the Executive Council made commitment for the resources. There onwards, the implementation team launched Project2x; mobilizing, communicating and shaking the complete organization.

My team's hands were full with creating a new structure, recruiting new staff and driving communication about Project2x. The plants went ahead, placed orders for a range of ultra smart machines and poached the best talent from rivals at all time high compensation levels. The COE was installed as the project monitoring agency with the privilege of an 'empowered agency' (no questions asked on its decisions).

Within a week, the pharma world came to know about the changes and was overawed by the quick decisions at Reamedics.

Interim Results

Within eight months, throughput (number of pills produced per month) of its largest plant reached to an all time high level and celebrations broke out across Reamedics.

Top Consult got its check and bonus. The Reamedics story was communicated across media. The media went abuzz with 'Introduction of Advanced Production Systems in the Pharma Industry'... 'First of its Kind Manufacturing Process'... 'A Marvel of the Regional Manufacturing Industry'... 'Big Leap for Reamedics', etc. Business magazines went overboard in predicting exponential growth of Reamedics.

Reamedics' stock had already zoomed up 2X on the bourses. Investors always liked visible investment for the future, and Reamedics became a darling of the stock brokers and analysts.

Applying Traditional Tactics

The jump in the throughput of its main plant was nothing less than a miracle for Reamedics, and people were still trying to understand exactly what made it happen.

Given the mandate to produce more *from more*, increasing capacity of its infrastructure became the prime objective of Production and the tactics were worked out in great detail.

First, the production team got the best of the machines. Then it powered them with 24x7 manpower and finally conducted cross skill training for technicians.

During this period, the throughput went down. But it was understood that when one starts to chase a big target, a little dilution of daily chores is expected. And people knew that there would be teething troubles. After all, doubling the throughput is no mean mission!

As the team went after doubling the throughput, even a small hurdle would become a big obstacle to the smooth flow of process orders. A batch would fail to move ahead due to quality problem. Machines would break down often, and too often in packaging lines. People would go on leave, fall ill and quit the organization; while replacements would not be available in time. Sometimes raw materials would arrive late, and as a result, process orders wait longer than they should before being released into the shop floor.

In that year, the region saw the heaviest rainfall in 15 years. The plant was submerged in knee deep water, and millions of dollars worth dispensed materials and those under process were spoiled. The machines were saved somehow. The plant lost over 19 shifts of work on critical machines.

Four weeks into Project2x, the plant was sounded to get ready for a major regulatory audit. *The plant went into 'safe mode' of operations*. From 60 days before the audit to 20 days after the audit everything moved slow, (*typical of some 'quality controlled' companies!*).

All improvement activities were stopped, and vendors and consultants were asked to keep away from the plant. Most of the incidents, big or tiny, were closed during this period. Batches with the smallest doubt about quality were stored separately, while those languishing long for corrective actions were written off immediately. The plant became QA centric.

Also, most of the staff in manufacturing was assigned to carry out documentation work (now you do not have enough people to work on machines!). But in the name of regulatory 'Audit', all was acceptable; in fact, this has been a norm in most pharma companies. The disruption to production activities during preparation for an audit was *called a 'business continuity' need*.

The Susceptive Tactics

Following the increasing pressure to justify heavy investment and its inability to deliver any improvement in the throughput during the first four months, the manufacturing team huddled together for a renewed tactical discussion.

The team looked at products that could be produced faster, i.e. 'the fast moving products'. It understood the flow of products and increased focus on those manufacturing lines that had high capacity machines.

Luckily, the team had 'pouch line' products. Pouch lines are the packaging lines, where packaging complexity is minimal as pills are directly dropped into pouches by weight. During rush hours, you could gain significant extra capacity of the plant, just by increasing feed to pouch packaging lines. The team worked out with the sourcing department to improve feed to pouch lines. And then the team focused on products that were packed in bottles.

Thus the manufacturing team focused largely on the chosen lines while reducing its attention on products passing through other packaging lines (i.e., blister and strip lines, where the productivity was traditionally awfully low). Actually, the plant also neglected some of those drugs that took too long to coat. Irrespective of the packaging type, some of the drugs involving complex processes were classified as strictly no-nos in the shop floor.

The plant produced the fast moving products at almost twice the usual pace and dispatched them to warehouses all over the world.

No doubt its throughput doubled in the next six months. During the same time the local currency against the US Dollar depreciated by over 15%. When the impact of depreciating local currency against dollar was accounted for, it showed huge improvement in profitability.

The Reversal of Results

In the Annual Review Meeting, the story of manufacturing excellence received big applause, but the finance wizards and the bean counters did not smile.

The Path

The CFO turned to make her presentation. She showed the inventory levels at 3X times of what it was a year ago and exposed the huge trapped cash therein. Also the manpower expenses had doubled.

Customer satisfaction index fell to all time low levels, quality failures zoomed up without anybody having a clue about the root cause, three major molecules were on voluntary recall and the possibility of a ban of flagship products by regulators in prime markets loomed large!

The CEO did not understand anything, even though he tried his best. The board asked him to quit.

So, Where Did We Go Wrong?

The decision to double the throughput exerted tremendous pressure on Manufacturing to produce more pills. It actually put its capability to test, i.e., to produce 2X number of pills. The manufacturing did so, but it produced more of the products that were 'moving faster *in the shop floor*'. Other products, therefore, continued to move slower *in the shop floor*.

The disproportionate attention of the management on 'things' which moved faster *in the shop floor* in reality made performance of the slow moving products worse as they did not get enough attention.

So while manufacturing produced more of *the self-defined* 'fast movers', these products were, in reality, 'not necessarily fast movers *in the market*'. Due to this changed behavior of the plant team, a significant number of products which 'moved faster in the market' were moving 'slower and slower in the shop floor'. The skewed manufacturing tactic and behavior only added to excessive inventories that climbed to roof top in the warehouses and the distribution centers. No doubt, significant cash of the organization was trapped in non-moving inventories. While this happened, the availability of 'non-focused' drugs worsened and the overall customer satisfaction levels went down dramatically. As a result, several customers started threatening to pull out from Reamedics.

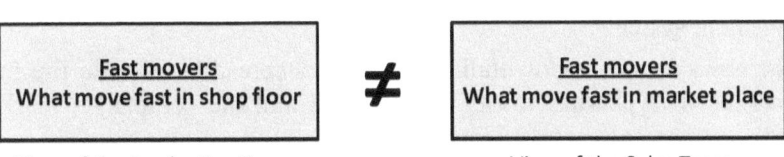

Figure 1.1 Conflicting definitions of fast movers in Production and Sales

While bonuses were liberally offered to the manufacturing staff for producing more number of pills, performance of the sales team took a beating as it struggled to sell overproduced drugs and failed to satisfy the demand of stocked out products.

Hence the drugs that were more in demand could not be serviced, while those in low demand moved faster in the shop floor and were being force flooded into the distribution chain. This further accentuated the mistrust between Sales and Operations.

The Big Change was any way in the offing. A new CEO was hired!

Mandate: Contain Cost!!

Falling into Dangerous Trap

The new CEO pushed sales staff to clear the inventory at the first available opportunity. Massive write offs and expiries were undertaken. For Reamedics management, numbers became sacrosanct. A hawkish measurement system was introduced and people were asked to deliver as per the targets.

Strict discipline was enforced across workplaces. Office entry and exit times were closely analyzed, and salary cuts for each 30 minutes deviation was imposed.

People found themselves being watched and were reminded of the proverbial 'Big Brother is Watching!' ('1984' by George Orwell). Worker unions revolted, forcing the management to compromise and pay a hefty compensation.

The staff of Reamedics assumed cost cutting as its prime responsibility. People were being measured on how much cost they cut than on how much revenue generation they could influence. Thus, the fundamental principle of business was inverted. At one point, size of paper teacups used in the canteen was cut to half and air conditioning in offices was cut off.

Hiring was frozen, vendors were squeezed to the last penny and managers demonstrated austerity by taking salary cuts. More people left the company than expected and returned to their pervious organizations. Robust processes were abandoned and people lost faith in the management system.

The news about the downfall of Reamedics spread like a wild fire in the market. The pharma world was shocked and the company's stock tanked!

After narrating the affairs at Reamedics, Ajay took a deep breath and said, "So you can imagine the amount of stress the organization went through."

"It sounds like a turbulent business story," I said, running fingers through my hair.

Ajay said, "Yes, it is a sort of. However, the company is now turning back to better days, with some real soul searching."

I jumped up in disbelief, "Oh, really!!"

"I am optimistic, after all it is a living system and it does have some resilience to bounce back," he said cautiously.

"Of course, there are too many deep rooted conflicts in Reamedics that must be resolved to bring the organization back to a healthy and stable situation. Till recently, managers were too comfortable and *all inefficiencies were covered up by the high margins of the Pharma Industry*. Now that the bottom line is thinning down rapidly, people are trying to react. There is also a lot of stakeholder activism. I guess that the system will clean up itself," Ajay concluded the saga of downfall at Reamedics on an optimistic note.

Time seemed to have ticked away faster during our conversation. The cabin crew kept offering us a wide range of delicacies and drinks that were the hallmark of the airline. I was tired but Ajay's company kept me awake.

It was not long before the airplane started preparation for landing. As it landed at the airport, we got up and walked out together and promised to meet back home.

Meeting the Thought Leader

The next day, when I woke up in the cozy suite at the Marriott in Jo'burg, Ajay's description of Reamedics was still fresh in my mind. It left me frustrated over the way organizations behave and complicate things. Soon the realization dawned on me that perhaps not everybody would act the same way.

During the session on entrepreneurship, for which I was here, I was introduced to George Blackwell. He was a thought leader for the Pharma Industry and had built the most respected advisory, the Rx-Strategy. Active across the globe, he was involved in transforming large generics companies in dealing with the increasing turbulence in their businesses.

George was waiting to start an engagement shortly and he wanted me to work with him. He invited me for a discussion during the weekend, which I couldn't refuse. To meet him, I flew down to Cape Town.

While cruising in the Sea, off Mouille Point on his luxurious yacht, I shared the story of Reamedics.

After hearing me out, George asked, "So, what do we see here?"

Without waiting for my response, he said, "DJ, there is a traditional tussle between Operations and Sales. Managers, based on their backgrounds, take sides and create win-lose games."

He continued, "Most of the managers are trained to lead *investment-based growth* (i.e. make more money from more money), which defies fundamentals of entrepreneurship and is not sustainable. They invest heavily in expansion and then go on cost freeze; to the level that it threatens company's survival."

"Yes, larger the capital budget you are entitled to, more powerful manager you are," I quipped.

He nodded.

A gentleman came in a colorful uniform with a tray in hand and wished me. I reciprocated the greetings with a smile. He carefully laid out glasses and a bottle of Nederburg vintage wine on the table.

As he retreated, George slowly poured the wine into the glasses, passed one to me, and we said, "Cheers!"

Sipping the wine slowly, he leaned back on the chair and said, "Despite decades of history, pharma companies continue to operate under inappropriate assumptions. They continue to assume that *more production can be obtained only from more physical assets; and anything that can be produced, is considered sold.* They continue to produce more than actual demand to justify their productivity targets. And then write-off large quantities of drugs that are left to expire."

"Yes, when they do that, they produce what they want and not what the market needs," I added.

"Indeed! This they do while millions of people die due to non-availability of essential drugs... Companies make huge money in one year and then suddenly slide into poor performance the very next year," he said.

"But most of the profitability numbers are manageable by current accounting rules. It is quite possible to hide such wild fluctuations in performance and keep stakeholders unperturbed." Perhaps, I was too much aware of such manipulations.

"Quite possible in a short term! One year they reward people for high performance and the very next year they allow the threat of layoff to build up. It creates a sort of internal instability. No doubt, a critical parameter for this industry, i.e., trust of employees in the management is at all-time low levels."

"And then organizations announce corrective and often, *reactive* measures to retrieve lost ground. Whether companies measure it or not, trust of even consumers in the dealings of the Pharma Industry has never been worse."

He paused and then said, "Companies then hire consultants and start transformation exercises. Unfortunately, now this is happening too often. Sometimes I hate engaging with some of my clients who hire me as a consultant only to clean up the mess that they keep on creating."

"Yes, sometimes it does hurt," I said.

"DJ! Things go full circle, year after year. Somehow managers who work with a short-term view reconcile to this situation and take it as a way of life. Industry experts too stonewall it with catch words like 'economic cycle', 'industry cycle', 'this is the way it is done', 'pressure of regulated environment', 'economic down turn', etc. This is pathetic," said George.

I looked at him and said, "Isn't all this because of the high margins in the Pharma Industry? And perhaps its business model is too much centered on R&D and doubtful sales practices?" I wanted to validate if all roads led to Rome.

George said, "Yes indeed, and possibly this model is the reason for current problems. Even today, there is hardly any other business with such high margins. For Innovator Companies, the margins for some of their products are over 90% and often their operating expenses are very low. As a result they virtually operate like a service company, where any additional sale directly reflects into the bottom line. Thus, having a patented drug with long-term exclusivity is a gold mine (block buster). After R&D, since your marginal costs are low, it makes sense to drive business through *whatever way sales can be driven*. It is a different issue that extreme practices in sales have fallen prey to the watchful eyes of social media, regulators and even patients."

"But this may not be the case with companies that are mainly in the business of Generics," I said.

He looked at me and then said, "In reality, it is the same case with generics companies too."

He clarified further, "You would find that most of the generics companies are from emerging markets and do big business in developed markets. These companies, due to cost advantage in operations and development (re-engineering), enjoy no less margins on purchase power parity (PPP) basis. Indeed, flagship products of leading generics companies have over 90% margin. Hence, here too the business model is development and sales centric."

"I see!" I said and then added, "But the law of average across the product portfolio would level down such margins."

"Yes, I agree with your observation… In one way, companies try to gamble on a few products at the cost of over 95% of their portfolio. This practice has now become dangerous…since the reality is changing rapidly. The productivity of R&D has reduced dramatically. Most of the discoveries of 1990s are on the verge of losing patent protection. In fact, several Innovators are moving into Generics space, making the life tougher for pure Generics companies. Hence, whether it is a new molecule for Innovators or new generic drug for others, the probability of hitting high margin products is dramatically reducing and becoming unpredictable. The pity is that despite the changes in environment, pharma companies are still working in their old business model. And hence they are into all sorts of seemingly complex mess of their own creation. Actually, running their business in such a situation highlights long ignored inefficiencies in their Operations," said George.

"Oh! So we see the effect of this untenable business model on inefficient operations. By the way, is somebody trying to leverage operations?"

George looked at me and then turned to fill up his glass. But he waited and said, "Yes, there is one organization that had actually taken up initiatives in *Operations* to deal with uncertain business environment.

However, the management hardly knew what it takes to improve operational performance in a sustainable way."

He stared into my eyes and said, "By performance improvement, people first think of a number in millions of dollars or millions of pills, as a target."

As I emptied my glass, he refilled for both of us.

"We pretty much saw its impact at Reamedics." I said, as I lifted the glass to my lips.

"Actually, it is deeper than achieving numbers!" he stressed and said, "Numbers are to be driven by doing something else that is core to the company's culture, and you can make mistakes there."

George continued, "Since you shared with me the situation at Reamedics, let me also take you through what happened at this company, which is in the same space and of almost the same size. I will describe the case, where people identified a part of the problem and started working on improving operations to deal with the situation in hand..."

Then, he stopped and said, "Before we look into the situation of this company called Pharma One, let's know the inside setup of a typical Formulation Plant of a mid-sized pharma company."

The Pharma Plant: Physical Setup

A pharmaceutical Formulation Plant has several distinct production areas. It manufactures hundreds of stock-keeping units (SKUs) in batch production mode. In one area technicians blend APIs (Active Pharma Ingredients, the drug) and other key materials (called Excipients) in stainless steel equipments. The blend is then compressed into tablets of sizes based on the required potency in rapidly rotating machines. Sometimes blends, when transformed into pellets, are used for filling into capsules.

Subsequently, depending upon their drug release pattern, tablets are coated or left uncoated. The pills undergo manual inspection or automatic sorting to weed out bad ones. These are then sent to packaging lines to pack them in different multiples of pills in blisters, strips, bottles or pouches.

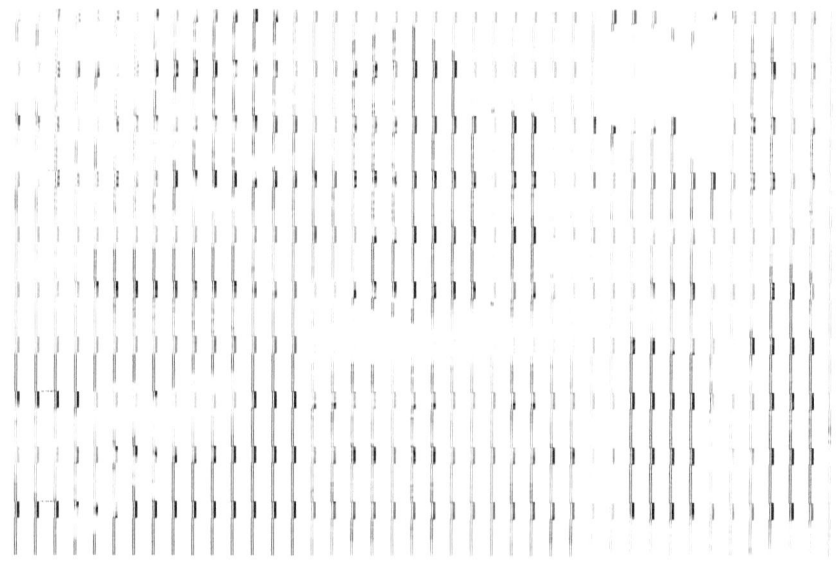

Figure 1.2 Representative products and their packaging from a pharma plant

In some plants, there are production lines for injectables, gels, lotions, ointments and liquids, which follow a manufacturing process that is closer to continuous process and differs significantly from the manufacturing process of tablets and capsules.

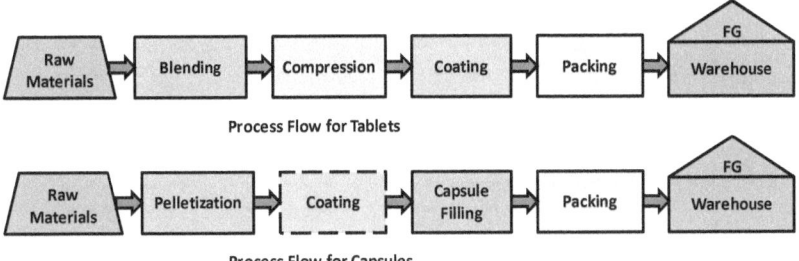

Figure 1.3 Process Flow for Tablets and Capsules in a Formulation Plant

Elsewhere, people from QC (quality control) collect samples at different stages and take them to laboratories to analyze the quality parameters. In the meanwhile, QA (quality assurance) teams keep visiting production rooms to check compliance with the cGMP (current Good Manufacturing Practice) guidelines.

There are specific areas with qualified people poring over a large number of documents and checking if what is written is done and what is done is written. In an overly protective organization, a batch record can run into more than 300 pages containing manually written, printed, annexed, pasted, stapled, signed, dated and reviewed pages. A plant producing around 500 million pills could have more than 600 such records to generate per month.

Drugs are made in a controlled environment. The complete facility including warehouse is atmosphere-controlled. There are strict dress codes for working in the plant. Generally, Engineering and Utility staff members have more than enough work in fixing equipment breakdowns.

More than one room is needed for storing tools and spare parts of equipments. A huge warehouse is spread across several million cubic meters of air conditioned space for raw materials and a still bigger one for packing materials. At the end, you would find finished goods warehouse that often runs out of space. People busy in moving batches from one place to another are ubiquitous.

A plant is normally designed based on product or process, or a combination. There are dedicated interconnected compartments called modules, where if one batch is released at blending, the end product comes out without any intermediate change in schedule. For others, there are discrete rooms for doing different operations. The space for placing material in front of an operation is limited, and hence, dedicated hold areas are created, where materials of different intermediate stages are stored.

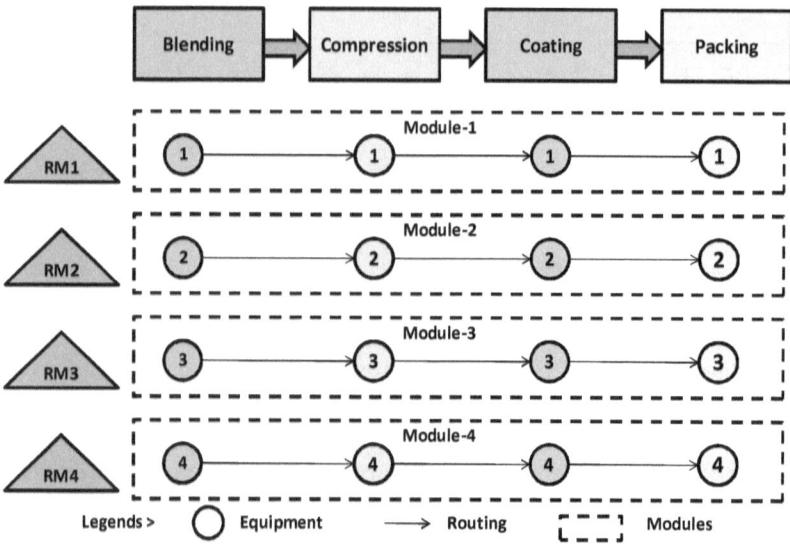

Figure 1.4 Routing of batches (Tablets) in Modules

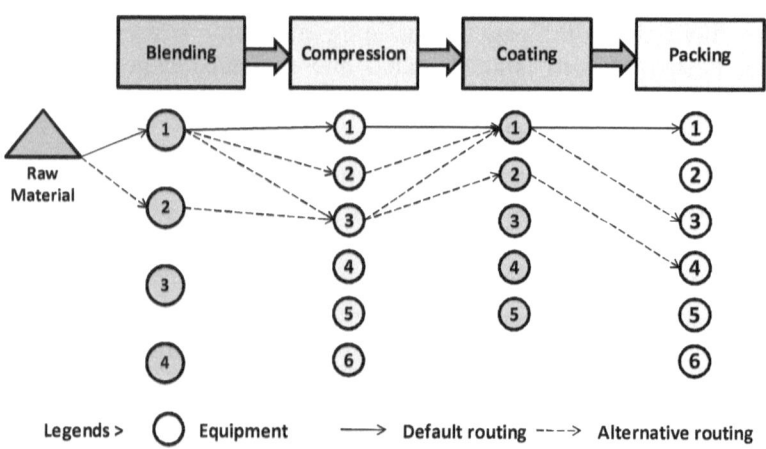

Figure 1.5 Routing of a batch (Tablets) in Suites

In most of the pharma plants, formulation is a human intensive process. People move huge amount of materials, lift and place containers, change over machine parts and do setups. They operate, monitor and maintain machines; and clean rooms and machines, keeping them clinically spotless. They document, review and approve huge amounts of batch related data, carry out chemical analysis, plan and expedite process orders; and above all, prepare for and manage regulatory audits.

Some product families have tens of SKUs because of differences in active ingredients, concentration, packing scheme or geographical differences. Swings in the monthly volumes and the mix of products make it further difficult to pinpoint productivity problems. Pharmaceutical production is about batch manufacturing in a highly regulated environment; and since it takes time to validate changes in form, process, equipment or size of a batch, it offers unique challenges to improve flow of process orders in the plant.

Chasing the Numbers

Betting on Intuition

Then, George spoke thus:

Pharma One, the #5 pharmaceutical company by market share in the region, has one of the biggest manufacturing facilities in Asia. Three years back, its main plant was producing around 500 million pills every month. Its staff was working hard, 24x7. People were always running around and *nobody ever had any time to sit back and relax.*

Pharma One's supply chain resembled that of an FMCG company, Figure 2.1. It had regional and international warehouses that fed into distributors and through them into retailers.

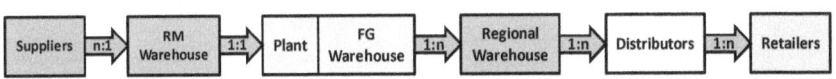

Figure 2.1 The Supply Chain of Pharma One

Despite the best efforts of its staff in the plant, a significant number of SKUs regularly stocked out. It often caused failures in meeting the supply due dates committed to the customers. This had led to constant bickering between Sales, Delivery and Production. Whenever Sales chased an SKU, Production would process it on priority. But in the meanwhile, other SKUs would stock-out. And when the other SKUs were worked upon, the first one would go out of stock.

For starters, Figure 2.2 presents visual representation of possible situations of stock level for an SKU at a given location. The height of the rectangular box represents the desired target level of stocks. The shaded area in the rectangle represents 'stock in hand'; a fully filled rectangle represents a 'full stock' situation, while a blank rectangle represents a 'stock out' situation.

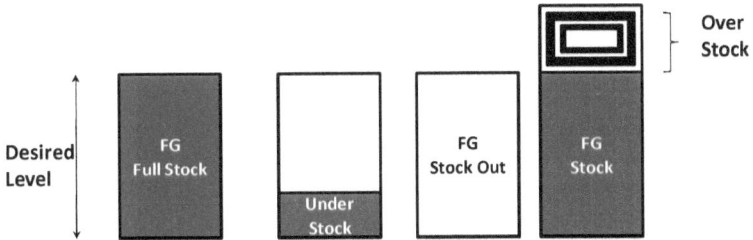

Figure 2.2 Visual representation for possible situations of stocks

Internally, staff members from different functions were constantly under a tug of war. At the same time, the dwindling business performance during the past few quarters weighed heavily on their shoulders to improve reliability of deliveries.

Intuition of people hinted that there was something wrong with the desired level (target) of stocks in the distribution chain. It was also felt that perhaps everything was not well with the capacity of the plant. There were certainly some difficulties with the plant in meeting the dynamic demand of the market that kept changing both in scale as well as scope.

Starting with a Workable Solution

One day, the team of Pharma One got together to thrash out the problems. It reviewed its distribution and manufacturing architecture in great details.

Upon reviewing the trends in sales and production, the sales team claimed that it could actually get 50% more customer orders if Production delivered enough. Not to be cornered, the production team accepted the challenge and agreed to work out a way to capture this opportunity.

At the end of the day, the operations team (consisting of teams from sourcing, manufacturing, delivery planning and distribution) came out with a revised design of stock levels in the distribution chain. It led to changes in the desired stock levels for SKUs across the distribution chain. The new 'desired' (target) stock levels at the plant warehouse were based on an acceptable estimation of demand and capability of the plant.

Figure 2.3 A generalized expression for estimating desired (target) stock levels

This general expression was based on the logic that if fully filled, the stock must last till the time a process order travels from its initiation to the warehouse. Similarly, the desired stock levels at downstream warehouses were estimated.

The design of the distribution system was contemporary; hence it presented a new reality. Some SKUs, which were in demand and had faster consumption pattern, desired higher levels of stocks. As a result, the gap between 'desired' stock levels and 'actual' stocks in hand for these SKUs widened, Figure 2.4.

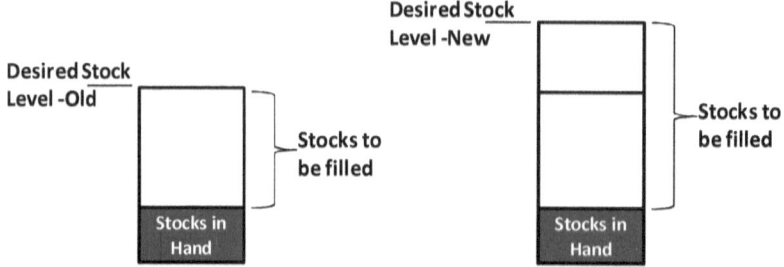

Figure 2.4 For some SKUs, the desired stock levels increased, increasing the amount of stocks to be filled in.

Before the stocks were redesigned, stocks of many SKUs were neither available in the warehouse nor enough process orders for them were present in the shop floor. Surprisingly, a vast majority of these SKUs were in great demand, e.g., see SKU A and SKU C in Figure 2.5.

On the other hand, other SKUs which were not in good demand were in abundance in the warehouses as well as everywhere in the shop floor, as if they were very urgent, e.g., SKU B and SKU D.

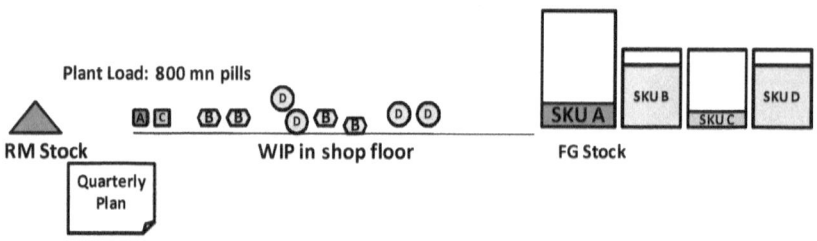

Figure 2.5 Orders for SKUs (SKU-A and SKU-C) with too less a stock than desired were hardly released into shop floor. While orders of those (SKU-B & SKU-D) with comfortable stock levels flooded the shop floor.

Thus, the analysis and reworking of the stock levels revealed that the plant was obviously running out of priority.

Plant Load - the Beast

The team stuck to the core concept of supply chain: in order to *reliably* deliver drugs to the clients, there must be a high availability of stocks in warehouses and distribution centers.

The redesign of stocks increased the 'desired' levels of stocks for a significant number of in-demand SKUs that actually had low 'stocks in hand'. It was natural that immediately new process orders were initiated to bridge the gap.

Initiation of additional process orders led to nearly 2 times the number of process orders in the system than those existed before the stock redesign. It was equivalent to around 1600 million pills instead of the usual 800 million pills, as shown in Figure 2.6. Although the team was expecting some increase in the load on the plant, the reality was way off.

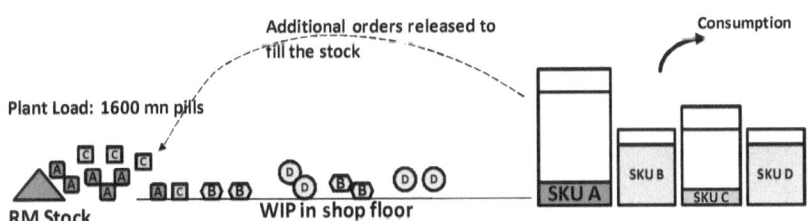

Figure 2.6 Resizing of targets for stocks dramatically increased the load on the plant.

Definition-Plant Load

Plant Load is the work waiting to be completed by a plant. Only when the existing work is completed, in a sequential flow system, additional work could be taken. If the load on the plant is high, any new work will take proportionately longer time to complete.

In the operational language of the shop floor, Plant Load is the number of manufacturing orders (or an equivalent number of manufacturing units) a plant currently has to work on. Only when the existing load is processed, could the plant intake new manufacturing orders into the shop floor. And hence, any new order will take too long a time to fulfill a demand, if it is queued behind an existing long train of orders.

Delays in fulfilling new orders beyond a time can jeopardize the ability of the plant to respond faster to changes in demand, increase stock-outs and even prevent it from meeting standard supply lead time. Hence, plants want to reduce the load to a reasonable level.

Although, the load on the plant was too high, the Pharma One team seemed committed to achieve higher availability of its products at the stocking points. It became clear that the plant must fill the gaps in the stock levels of several SKUs, while simultaneously meeting the ongoing consumption by the market, Figure 2.7. The team then felt that the plant was required to deliver drugs at almost double the earlier rate of production.

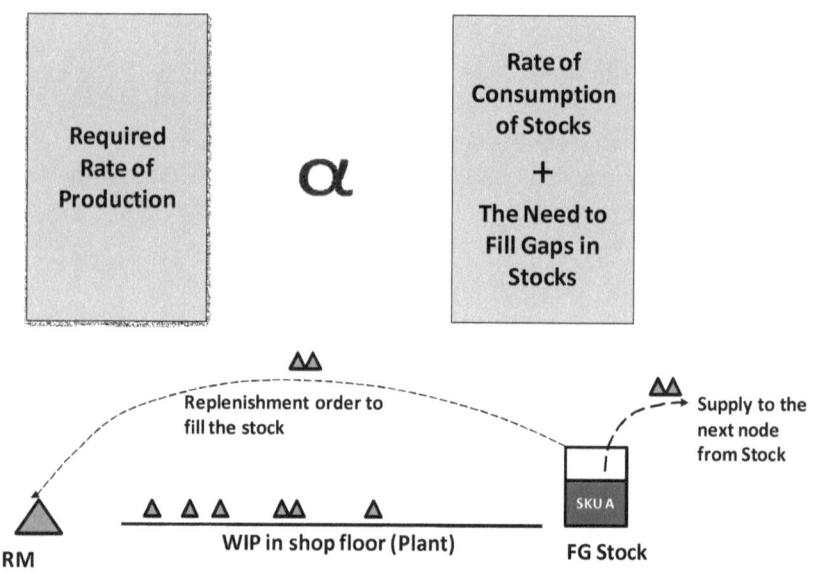

Figure 2.7 The plant was forced to supply pills to fill the stocks while simultaneously meeting the daily demand (consumption from the stocks).

Subsequently, the Operational Committee of Pharma One met and the Plant Head was *asked* to respond to a load of 1600 million pills. He was *convinced* to accept a steep increase in production target.

By accepting a challenge of dealing with a load of 1600 million pills, the plant went on a massive operational improvement program.

The plant recruited additional staff across levels - technicians to managers and trained people on multiple-skills. It relaxed the rules of capital expenditure to raise throughput and procured extra raw materials to protect utilization of the plant.

In due course, the plant indeed increased throughput significantly, and in one particular month, it produced almost 900 million pills crossing the historical monthly average of around 500 million pills by a huge margin.

It took 12 months for the production to take a seemingly sustained lead over the flow of incoming orders. *Buoyed with enthusiasm, the plant reset its monthly throughput target to 900 million pills.*

Thereafter, stocks for quite a few SKUs (the plant served around 1150 SKUs) were filled to the brim. During that period, monthly throughput of the plant was varying in the range of 600 to 750 million pills. The sales did seem to increase a bit, though the main reason for this was disputable.

Production thumped its chest claiming an unassailable lead over Sales and presumed to have closed the competition between the two functions once for all. There was tremendous pressure on Sales to keep its promise to increase revenues. The sales team felt appropriate to revise its forecast and started preparing for a sales drive to increase demand.

While the stocks were being filled and consumption was taking place, what happened to the load on the plant?

Since capacity of the plant was increased by expanding resources, for a while stocks in warehouses reached good enough levels to take care of any reasonable fluctuation in demand. As a result, most of the process orders placed on the plant were for replenishing those consumed from the stocks. Thus, the load on the plant was mostly due to consumption from the stock, Figure 2.8.

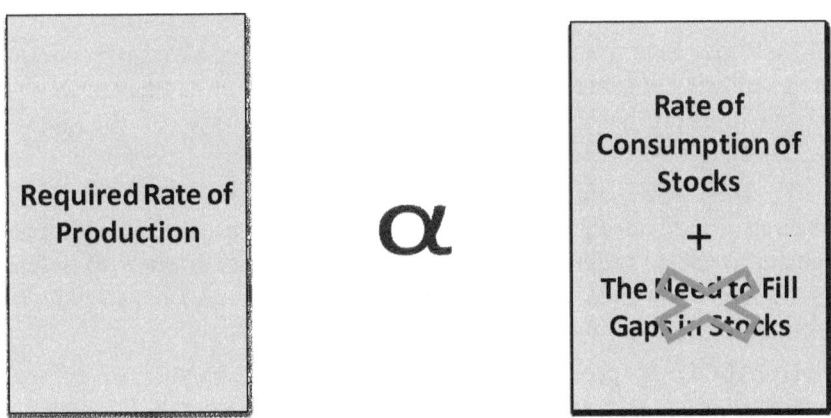

Figure 2.8 Once the stocks were well filled, the need for the plant was mostly to produce as per consumption from the stocks.

Very soon, the load tended to decrease gradually to lower levels. It went down from 1600 million pills to 900 million pills, and it was all set to go down to 600 million pills.

Emotions are Stronger than Logic

Unbridled Emotions

The new monthly target of 900 million pills was a matter of pride for the plant and it was important for its staff to defend it by all means. When the plant load fell below 900 million pills, uneasiness started creeping into the plant team. Managers foresaw that the plant would not be able to produce 900 million pills in the following months if enough process orders were not created, Figure 2.9. It would, of course, hurt their metrics. Further, if the process orders were fewer, people would have less work and would sit idle.

Figure 2.9 A good level of stocks in hand leads to production only as per consumption

Staff members from sales and delivery were scared about returning of the plant to its old inertia and losing the momentum it had gathered with so much effort. Of course, they were also skeptical of the plant's capability to be ahead of market demand.

To keep the plant busy, the delivery staff artificially raised the 'desired' stock levels of several SKUs, thereby triggering additional demand (process orders) for production. In any case, in order to defend its high performance levels, the production staff was begging to be allowed to produce beyond the actual consumption levels.

Everybody in production and delivery teams wanted to achieve personal targets and justify good work. So, by disrespecting the natural demand of the market, *undesired* orders were unabatedly released into the plant month after month. Various '*official*' reasons were offered in justification; like, expectation of higher demand, seasonality effect, freeing of coating machines, revalidation of batches, trial batches, cost improvement programs, productivity improvement, etc.

Further, in a Quarterly Review Meeting at that time, the Manufacturing Head took a personal target to produce 200 million pills of an anti-inflammatory drug. He gave an open diktat to the plant, "If there is no batch to work upon, then create new *internal orders* and produce them, not a pill to be short of 200 million!"

What's the cause of this unreasonable behavior?

People had never been in a situation of idleness, even during the previous years when the throughput was less than 500 million pills per month. They had never imagined a situation of the capability of Production surpassing the demand created by Sales. They were mentally and behaviorally not prepared for such a healthy and 'good' situation. Being overwhelmed by their achievements and uncontrolled exuberance, people created additional work (process orders) to justify some or other thing, even though it did not benefit the company.

Of course, the Plant Manager won't let machines and people idle, since one is paid to always keep machines and people working.

When people think about work in a plant, they mean 'always work'. Leaders come early to office and leave late for home; they try to set examples (*sic!*). They also come during holidays and weekends, and take pride in telling people how important it is for them to be visible and look hands-on. In turn, they create for themselves and their colleagues a rather unbalanced work and family life.

What happened subsequently?

The staff in the production and the delivery did a real good job. They worked hard, and under strong executive intervention, filled in the stocks and released substantial manufacturing capacity. At a plant load of about 600 million pills, they had demonstrated that manufacturing was indeed ahead of sales by at least 30% (it had 30% *free capacity*).

However, *undesired* orders continued to be released into the shop floor. The plant produced and dispatched month on month an excessive volume of pills. Monthly meetings often saw rave reviews of improved production volumes. The world outside Pharma One was abuzz with stories of manufacturing success of its leading plant. The manufacturing in-charge at the plant got regional award for productivity improvement and earned a well deserved promotion on an unprecedented performance.

Good Intention Alone is not Enough!

Within one year, several things changed. The mix of products (scope) shifted dramatically. As a result, products that were in demand earlier lost their volumes, while others for which demand went up were not so easy to produce. Even the expectations of customers grew significantly. In order to get new orders, all types of commitments without adequate oversights were made to customers. New products found greater presence in the portfolio and complexity of operations increased.

Often, more than reasonable fluctuation in the demand caused stocks to deplete quickly, forcing release of a flood of process orders onto the shop floor. Such spikes often caused havoc and delays in the plant. Sometimes it did give a feeling that the plant did not have a smooth flow and consistent control on availability of drugs.

Since the plant was chasing numbers, efficiency factor dominated its actions. It got into a compromised monthly routine. In the first 10 days of the month, the shop floor would produce strictly as per market demand; but somewhere in the second half of the month, the pressure to meet the production target would weigh heavily in the minds of the staff. And, in a rush, what could move faster in the plant would be pushed. This often led to several products with good demand left by the side for several small and big excuses. Also, the pressure of defending monthly target outweighed the attention needed to resolve issues in the shop floor and deal with the changing demand from the market.

Thus by releasing *undesired* process orders, the team preferred easy-to-produce SKUs. SKUs which were tricky and waited for certain decisions, actions or investigations were held back. As time moved ahead, a number of process orders were left neglected in the shop floor for over 100 days, and they were on nobody's radar, Figure 2.10.

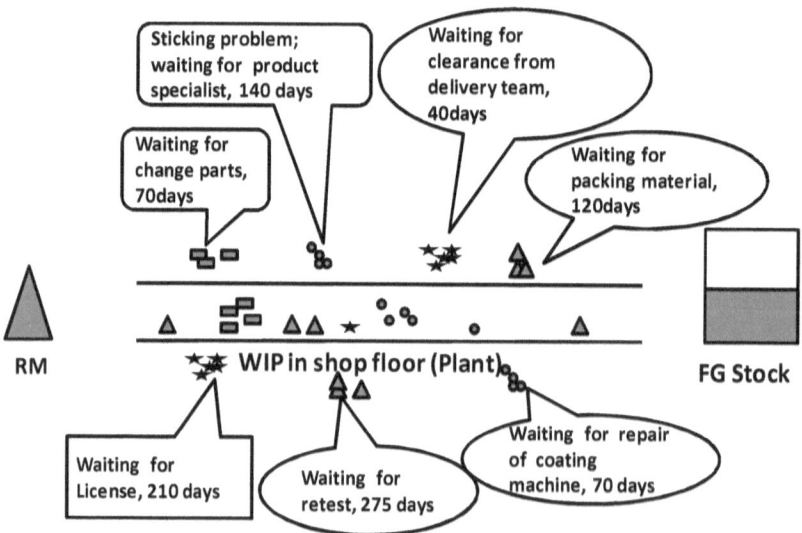

Figure 2.10 A major part of the increase in WIP was due to batches waiting for actions

It was not very long before excessive number of batches flooded the shop floor and the WIP (work in progress) increased dramatically.

More WIP meant more chaos, more mistakes, poorer attention and more defects (*TQM tells us!*)[1]. Actually, when the load on the shop floor goes beyond a level say, approximately 80% of the normal capacity, it creates a lot of chaos. The delay in delivering a process order amidst chaos is just like the delays you face while driving on a road with heavy traffic. As a result, the response time of the plant stretches dramatically.

The load on the plant at Pharma One had already shot up well above 1400 million pills. As a consequence of the load and the poor quality of WIP, the response time of the plant slowed down.

Even though stocks of some SKUs were filled to the brim, the response time for meeting changes in market demand or for taking advantage of any sudden market opportunity became very slow. Gradually, the ability of the plant to maintain healthy stock position of even easy-to-produce SKUs deteriorated.

The sales team was very quick in sensing the signals of deteriorating situation of deliveries and it promptly throttled its expansion plans. It was not ready to create new demand and face embarrassment when the existing demand itself was becoming difficult to fulfill as committed.

Since the 'diktat' was to defend the new production target *somehow*, people produced *anything and in anyway*. In turn, an increasing number of products stocked out and their response time increased substantially. The impact of the long lead time of orphaned orders, which were genuine process orders and which the customers were waiting for, continued to further hinder the overall lead time of the plant.

In fact, it was a small team of management trainees, who, as a part of its study, presented the analytics on deteriorating situation of the shop floor to the management. Immediately managers were seen running around 24x7 tracing and pushing those process orders that were neglected for a long time. The reaction was too late and symptomatic. The customer satisfaction index, in the meanwhile, fell to all time low levels and key clients had started deserting Pharma One.

The staff at Pharma One was exerting itself with good intentions. However, by 24th month, the plant ran into an inventory level of 210% of what sales off-take and manufacturing speed would justify.

The performance of its main plant and the spillover effect on other plants had significantly dented the consolidated performance of Pharma

One. When the time for Annual Communication Meet came, even before company results were made public, there was sudden numbness amongst senior executives. Based on the preliminary operational results, the reasons were more than obvious. This time, the CEO cut short his presentation and handed over the dais to the CFO. The CFO was not smiling.

What everybody saw was a bloodbath. Everywhere, the company was in red. The cost of goods went up by 70%, cost of manpower by 60%, depreciation by a whopping 175% ... while sales in volume went up YOY by a meagerly 5%.

There was no place to hide, even though Pharma One was in a high margin business. It somehow managed to roll out one Para IV drug.

People felt that the CFO was on his way out for the lack of oversight and for not containing the cost. They also found that 30% of their raw materials and 40% of their finished goods were due for expiry in the next quarter and that there was no consumption prospect for them. *The company, in an obvious 'blindness', had over flooded its plants and distribution chain without adequately aligning with the market and timely opening up its sales capacity.*

Choosing wrong path at wrong time...

As a result, the Annual Communication Meet was kept to just one and half hours, than the traditional half a day of pomp and show.

People had work cut out for them. The CFO had set the agenda and wanted to see the cost cut by 30% in the next quarter, by whatever means possible. He was more than assertive and literally shouted, "Cut staff, cut salary, cut benefits, stop recruitment and freeze CAPEX..., across board." The sales team was asked to liquidate the inventory and contain the expiry, at whatever discount it felt like offering.

Everybody went back with their homework and huddled in groups, working on spread sheets to see how some numbers could be improved. The HR department became central to all these activities.

For the Vice President-HR, how to communicate the bad news was a challenge. She knew that the Pharma Industry was already suffering from severe scarcity of resources; and how difficult it was for her team to snatch talent from competitors, just a few quarters back. She had managed to recruit some of the high level resources with over 100% increase in pay packages. And now, chucking them out even before they started delivering results was difficult to digest, but she needed to do the job of cleaning up and communicating the bad news, anyway.

The Inevitable

While George narrated the debacle at Pharma One, I did not realize that the sun had already slipped into the horizon. Far off along the coastlines, lights had switched on and the skyline twinkled. We were deep into the sea and George's crew was preparing the deck for the banquet.

"Where is Pharma One today?" I asked him.

He said ruefully, "It is Down and Out! Immediately after the Annual Communication Meet, its manufacturing head resigned and migrated to a big pharma company. His exit was followed by the exit of additional 15 senior managers."

"Sometimes people move out in herd," I commented.

"Yes, especially when the core of the organization is not strong enough. Perhaps, there were too many opportunities around as well, as almost every big pharma company was on a massive expansion mode," George said as he refilled my glass.

"How did the staff cope with the terrible disturbance?" I asked.

"Actually, people lost the enthusiasm and the camaraderie to work. Talented people found a way out easily and the HR department had no time to persuade them to change their decisions. The complacent ones remained behind, dramatically bringing down the overall quality of management," said George.

"A very tough situation!"

"But Pharma One continued to operate in a ferocious cost cutting mode, and life was never the same again." He looked at me with pained expressions on his face. He took a sip of the wine and pressed his lips in, to relish the taste.

"How far could it hold its market position?"

"Not at all, its ranking by market share fell from #5 to #11, within two years," said George.

And then he continued, "The panic in operations led to severe degradation of work standards. Pharma One increasingly faced product quality problems; and stricter regulatory norms forced costly drug recalls. Four of its prime drugs (making 73 SKUs) were banned for over a year by the regulatory authorities. Clients started looking out for alternative vendors, and five major retail chains from abroad severed the longstanding relationship. As it is a norm in the Pharma Industry, the competitors immediately reaped the windfall."

"What was the response of the shareholders?" I asked to know the situation in the boardroom.

"Very reactive... Within a year, the owner sold out a large part of his stakes to an innovator company and virtually exited the business. The new board came in and made sweeping changes all across."

That was terrible. I thought that there must be others who cared about the organization, and therefore asked, "During the whole episode, did not anybody ever ask why the company landed into such a situation?"

"Nobody cared a bit. Nor did anybody question assumptions, policies and decisions that led to the debacle," George said sweeping his hands across wildly.

"But there must still be some general understanding of why did these things happen?" I probed further.

"People only knew that it was to do something with the way things were managed, but could not clearly figure out the root cause, as there were so many rumors floating around."

It meant that nobody was really attached to the organization.

"Oh! That is why the remedy sought wasn't an effective 'change management' but an immediate 'change in ownership'?" I guessed.

"For a significant number of owners of pharma companies, ownership is about investment. Gone are the days when most of the entrepreneurs in health care sector would create an organization to eliminate diseases and relieve people from pains. *These days, more and more businesses are done to exploit an opportunity than fulfill a necessity*." He was very critical.

"So what do we see here?" George asked me after a while.

"People are good; they really intend to improve the situation. Somehow organizations react to emerging situations using over simplistic approach rather than systematically identifying the root cause and evolving a robust solution," I said by connecting the dots quickly.

George slowly nodded thoughtfully and added, "You know, teams have a tendency to be blinded by outcome-based approach and they forget to calibrate their assumptions with the ever changing internal and external environment."

He continued, "An improvement in an organization is not about improvement of one team or one function. An improvement that is made anywhere in the organization must be linked to the overall improvement of the company, i.e., the improvement must take the company as a whole one step ahead towards the common goal."

"But things started well for Pharma One, when it had redesigned the stock levels!" I pointed out.

"Yes, but it was too big and too hard an initiative in one part of the organization without realizing its linkages to the rest of the company," he said emotionally as he slowly let the wine flow down his throat.

"Certainly, the sales team must have pressed the accelerator... They should have cooperated with the production team," I tried to find out if some way, the situation could have been improved.

"Some of the smartest people in any organization are from the sales. They view the organization from the customer side and have a very good idea when to act. When the plant had filled the stocks to a reasonable level, the sales team did start preparing for a sales drive. But before it could implement its extended sales plan, the odd behavior at the plant rapidly deteriorated its service levels. So the sales quickly pulled the plug off," George absolved the sales team of all responsibility.

And then he said, "May be a better coordination between the production and sales would have helped. Such coordination would have alerted the sales team much before the throughput peaked. Or, because the jump in throughput was too high for the sales to manage, the plant could have taken a lower target. Or, is it the trust deficit between the two teams?"

"In retrospect, there seems to be several possibilities that could have occurred to salvage the situation," I said.

"Perhaps a prescriptive strategy, as adopted by the management of Pharma One, needed mellowing down a bit," he said.

The operational psychology of the team at Pharma One seemed abnormal, and I said, "Macro factors of business environment do cause severe problems to unguarded companies. But internal events causing downfall of an organization is a bit too extreme."

"Let us get into the basics," said George as he leaned towards me on the table.

He looked far off into the coast and then, turning towards me, said, "*When people forecast on the positive side, they forecast too optimistically* and *go ballistic in their actions.* Then, they often lose track of the reasons and the assumptions behind their actions."

"There is a sort of psychology that plays when we forecast and then the numbers become too sacrosanct," I said.

"Indeed... By seeing a plant load of 1600 million pills, people went overboard for almost 2 years. They did not check the assumption behind the need to deal with the onetime spiked load, even though the initial conditions were no more valid within a few months of starting the improvement project."

"It does happen... In the thick of action, people do lose sight," I said.

George's chef and crew had laid flexi-tables in a row and started placing the dishes. The aroma of barbeque triggered my appetite. I got up and walked around to have a look at the delicacies; George followed me. It was a sumptuous spread of sea food, baked dishes, cheese, turkey like game bird, fresh fruits and wine...a gala dinner setup. I picked up a piece of bread.

We turned towards the band that had started playing the Zulu tunes. The band bowed to us and we reciprocated with a gentle bow. It was quite an animated band, and one guy performed an acrobatic dance.

George waved his hands upwards to the band, signaling them to raise the tempo. Coming closer to me, he spoke into my ears, "Often emotions rule business; perhaps, modern management is yet to provide a measurement system to observe, control and direct emotions to achieve the desired results..."

"...Unfortunately, the plant kept itself busy, working on other things, for the sake of being busy and defending self imposed targets," I replied the same way.

"Absolutely! There is no other reason why its performance deteriorated. This is one reality that must be recognized and it demands a major cultural change." I saw anger in his eyes; and then, surprisingly, he smiled as he stroked my shoulder.

Suddenly, the surroundings bloomed merrily and the band raised its tempo. The yacht was still, the crew, George's family and guests thronged around us, tapping their feet, as the song ...*Long Days and Lonely Nights*...filled the air.

I looked at the starry sky above and the deep dark still water around... found myself totally out of place in an ecstatic setup... and then... joined the party...*Long Days and Lonely Nights*...

Mt. Kilimanjaro - Tactics for Dealing with the Unknown

The cruise on George's yacht, *The Waves,* was quite engrossing and fulfilling. Complications at Reamedics topped with those at Pharma One made a heady concoction, giving me much to think about. Both organizations faced similar performance problems, took slightly different routes, but experienced similar backlashes.

In Reamedics, it was the top management's sledgehammer approach to bring about quick change; while in Pharma One, there was an added spice of the way people behaved. It became apparent to me that identifying a problem and finding a direction to solution alone are not enough to improve performance of organizations. Something must be missing in *the way a solution is implemented.*

In the morning, I rushed to Jo'burg, where the session ran quite late into the evening. I was totally exhausted by the time I returned to the Hotel.

The following day, I took an early morning flight to home. I fell asleep as soon as I boarded the plane.

My ears faintly caught the announcement of the cabin crew, "....please avoid crowding...."

I did not bother to open my eyes. The cabin crew's announcement continued and said in a husky voice, "We are taking two rounds of Mt Kilimanjaro. Guests on the left side of the plane are requested to be seated for their turn. We will fly back in the other direction in a couple of minutes."

It woke me up; a few minutes later, the airplane turned around, and we were treated to a sight of Mt. Kilimanjaro, a gigantic black chocolate colored mountain. I was seeing anything like this so close for the first time in my life. The conical black structure with a flat top had snowy patches scattered all over.

I still remember Krishna, my 6 year son, later on read out to me that Mt. Kilimanjaro is the highest freestanding mountain in the world, measuring close to 6000 meters. It was scary to see the dark structure and I felt if this would live up anytime, like a big Guerrilla or a mammoth African Elephant. I murmured aloud, "Awesome! This is not just amazing but also terrifying!"

"You got to go to the top; and you would know that it is really amazing... But the way to the top is extremely arduous," said the gentleman, who was seated next to me, and looking over my shoulder.

"Really!" I prompted him to speak more.

"I was here five years ago!!!" said the gentleman.

My fear evaporated in a jiffy. I looked at him and immediately shook hands. He was big and strong, sun-burnt with a crew cut.

"I am DJ, very glad to meet you, you must be a legend," I said.

"Hi, I am John, John Kaufmann," he introduced himself. "I am not really a legend. These days, we have a lot many guys climbing up Mt. Kilimanjaro."

"It must be very difficult to negotiate the climb and you must have prepared for a long time. Did you make it in the first go?" I could not resist my curiosity.

"The climb is tough as there are not only unknowns but also unknowables. Nevertheless, it is possible if you follow some simple rules... I served the army, so I had a little preparation though; and before retiring, I climbed Mt. Kilimanjaro," said John.

"I see," I said as Mt. Kilimanjaro glided past me.

Soon the airplane was back on its course, and we moved away from our seats to the free space near the cabin crew station.

"What do you do DJ?" he asked, while stretching his arms sideways.

"I am a business coach," I said.

"Great! I too am involved in coaching entrepreneurs, and I can tell you that climbing Mt. Kilimanjaro can give a few great lessons to any entrepreneur or manager in running a high octane business," he made a good connection.

"Wow! Running a business is like climbing Mt. Kilimanjaro!" I exclaimed.

"Yes, quite a bit, at least in today's business environment," he said and continued, "After retirement, I began handholding new business leaders in dealing with ever changing competitive environment. And, it has been working out well. I do not feel myself out of place." He smiled.

John continued, "Successfully climbing a mountain is like fulfilling once-in-a-lifetime-wish. It needs determination, you can't fail... just like in a war. Hence, you need strategies and tactics that help you win despite all odds, risks, unknowns and un-knowables. And, so is for serious entrepreneurs, who give up everything to pursue a new business, chasing a big and long distance objective."

The Path

"What's your broad strategy when you go into *unknown and unknowable situations*?" I queried.

John replied, "The broad strategy in such a scenario is to prepare well and know one's capability. Hence, before taking the first step towards climbing Mt. Kilimanjaro, you must be mentally and physically fit (need not be extraordinarily built). And, carry the essentials."

"Essentials… you mean run through a check list?" I asked.

"Yes, a short one is enough. There are several checklists and so many different stories about how people triumphed in their climb. However, it is practically impossible (and it does not make sense) to accommodate all suggestions before you take the first step. A majority of learning occurs on the way; and one must be committed to this sort of learning." He gave a perspective.

"You may still need some strategy… some plan…" I persisted.

He said, "Climbing a mountain, fighting a war and running a high octane business are about working in ever changing and threatening environments. In a stable environment, you normally plan well, set milestones and set targets. However, in an ever dynamic condition, it is very difficult to set a definite target and a date to achieve that target. In such a situation, tactics outweigh strategy; and hard coded planning is futile!"

I interrupted John and asked, "What is special about these tactics?"

He said, "The tactics start with the recognition that you are venturing into an ever-changing, unpredictable, risky, unknown and unknowable domain. Taking one measurable step at a time is the key to reliable tactics."

"But you still need to decide which step to take?" I expressed my doubt.

"Actually, every step you take is a step in the direction of your goal; and often, it must be taken to overcome the obstacle in front of you. When you take a step, you need to keep enough reserves, so that you can retrieve it if required," he explained.

"So, it is action-based learning!" I said to myself while internalizing the concept.

Rotating his fists, John said, "This is exactly how we do it in the armed forces. When you are in the enemy territory and want to move forward, you keep firing shots while taking a few quick steps forward. And then, you take a few steps back or side ways to take a shield. You then wait and watch for a while, see the reaction from the surroundings and then start the next cycle. Thus, you cover the field by taking small steps. This is fundamental."

"That is a tactic to achieve more ground by containing the real risk," I said.

"And, in mountaineering?" I asked.

John looked at me and said, "In mountaineering, you not only have to climb up but also ensure that you do not slide back and kill yourself."

He added, "Here, you do not have a direct enemy checkmating you, but the new found environment could throw up big enough obstacles and threats. You provide for a buffer in the tactics you adopt to ensure that you have a stable and safe fall back in case your upward movement is suddenly blocked."

"Does sometimes this fallback mechanism also paralyze the person from moving ahead?" I realized that sometimes people play too safe.

"Yes, sometimes, for the weak hearted... Before falling back, you would often try to dig through the obstacle or go around it. But, at the first instance, you do not take too long a leap; you move one step at a time and hence, you dramatically reduce the chances of sliding back. And remember, each obstacle you overcome is exhilarating and confidence boosting; and takes you significantly closer to the summit. Then, you start taking bigger steps."

It reminded me if Reamedics and Pharma One tried to take too long a leap without leaving enough room for building necessary capabilities.

Picking up a coke can from a passing by airhostess, he continued, "However, the biggest lesson which we pick up from the armed forces and mountaineering is that once you are in action, you do not fantasize about your step number two, three, four... before you complete step one. Actually, there is no way you can predict your future moves. *Only completion of step one lets you know with 'confidence', if you can take the next step or not. At every step you would face a new challenge and you need to 'figure out' or 'negotiate' the next step only then.*"

I said, "This is a remarkable approach to move ahead under ever-changing situations."

John said, "Actually, it is a profound approach which comes naturally to armed force personnel. We are commissioned to take up audacious and risky tasks, where the predictability is very low. In most of the cases, we would have only a rough or rather imperfect plan. When we go for a do-or-die mission in an enemy territory, the plan gets corrected as we get into action. And the approach, which we call '5 steps forward and 2 steps backward' helps us in taking care of the risks and unknowns on a regular basis, and builds up our competencies rapidly."

I asked him curiously, "How do you do this in business?"

John smiled and said, "It is exactly the same in a high octane business...which we call as the behavior of 'reflective actions'. In our Breakthrough Performance Workshops, we coach entrepreneurs who are in highly competitive and turbulent markets, and where the landscape of business is changing dramatically. Under such situations, the traditional strategy and planning need dramatic improvisation."

"Yes, I understand. They are forced to be on guard always, as new business models disrupt their businesses from unexpected directions. Hence, learning from execution is the way for them to constantly build their competitive edge," I said as I thought about the situations of some of my clients, for whom business has been a roller coaster.

John said, "They can neither afford to be indifferent to the change nor do they have sufficient time to get into an elaborate strategy session. They need a methodology to embrace change so that their organization has a stable growth year on year."

He continued, "We train even established businessmen in war games to run their organization like a start-up company or a troop in a war. This means that they must build most of their winning capabilities on the go, by keeping in touch with reality."

I said, "You are right, under such situations, a dynamic operational strategy will have significantly more weight than a static one."

John continued, "Since change can come from any direction, my clients are now moving away from tight jacketed strategy and hard coded number or dollar-based goals, since they have understood the futility of such approach. Rather, they are moving towards purpose-based organizations, where *the leadership teams steer respective organizations in the right direction by continuously evolving workable tactics, and thereby, constantly moving the organizations closer to the objective.*"

I couldn't avoid myself in briefing him about situations at Reamedics and Pharma One. I asked, "What do you think about them?"

John said, "Sometimes, I do work with such mature organizations. But even they have turbulent business environments that constantly disrupt their businesses... I have a feeling that they are working in the old paradigm of command and control, and they need to take a fresh look at the way businesses must be run under rapidly changing circumstances. Thinking that assets, number of people and huge money can help in maintaining your leadership is no more valid. *You need the agility of operational tactics to survive and navigate in today's battlefield of business.*" I was all ears listening to Colonel John Kauffman.

Overawed by meeting this Ex-Kilimanjaro climber and army officer, I captured him in digital camera for my kids.

Preparing for the Change

Re-reading the Situation

In March 2008, Ajay re-connected with me. He had moved over to Terra Pharma as the president for corporate HR.

Terra Pharma, based out of a suburb in the western plains, was the most respected pharma company in emerging markets. It had one of the best human resource pool and for Ajay, it was a dream place to make significant contribution.

Despite it being a well-managed company, Terra Pharma was not immune to the undesired effects of rapid changes in the Pharma Industry. The management of Terra Pharma was under an increasing pressure to match its past performance.

During the summer vacation, Ajay visited us with his family and we had a very good time. But as our earlier discussion of the flight revived, he revealed the main agenda of his visit saying, "DJ, could you guide us through the current situation?"

"Is there a direction your team has already identified to take?" I asked.

"There is a realization that we need to change the way we operate in the current business environment. Seth, therefore, wants to make operations central to our core strategy." Seth was the CEO of Terra Pharma.

"Yes, but what is the issue? Why do you think making operations central to your strategy will help? Is it merely to give operations its importance in the organization?" I asked.

"Actually, the board asked him to work on a new business model." So the approach was already finalized.

"Business Model!" I said expressing my surprise.

"Yes, Seth believes that the current business model is outdated. And that we need to change the way we operate," said Ajay. It was the same thing put in a different way.

"Do you guys know what a business model is and how to describe it?" I asked curiously.

"No, not really! To most of us it is like a new management jargon. But we have heard it enough times to know that it is rapidly becoming a dominant tool to innovate business. We need somebody to help us put it together. The requirement is to innovate and make it contemporary, so that we could deal with the ever changing business conditions." Ajay explained.

"Yes, it is one of the most talked about concepts. It helps in providing a common understanding of the business and in identifying areas for radical innovation. But the key to achieving success in the marketplace is in operationalizing the Business Model," I said.

"Yes indeed. Realizing the rapid changes around, we felt the need to have a closer look at our operations. For this, we need to give it a stronger position in our corporate strategy. Our operations must be designed to provide us the required responsiveness to deal with the ever-changing business environment. That is how we felt the need to first model our operations from a business perspective... and so we came across the phrase 'Business Model'," explained Ajay his new-found understanding.

"Now I understand... you want to develop an Operation Centric Business Model, so that it is possible to deal with the rapid and uncertain changes in your business environment," I paraphrased for him.

"Yes, that is what we think. It is important to have a more responsive operations in the existing business environment." We were on the same page.

'Business Model' has been a buzzword amongst management experts for more than a decade [2,3]. But it came to prominence only during the Y2K (year 2000), when the new economy driven by digital revolution disrupted businesses across industries.

If you ask anyone in the top management of a company what their specialty is, responses would be along the following lines: "Our Business Model is different... We have a unique Business Model"... "Our Business Model is customer centric", "It is the innovative Business Model," etc.

However, the key contributors who proposed Business Model as a framework to innovate business often wondered if organizations really innovate or use the term as a jargon, with little knowledge about what it means. Every member of the top management would have a different answer for the question regarding their Business Model. What people really needed was a consistent, unambiguous, intuitive and practical way of describing, analyzing and innovating the Business Model.

Realizing this, Adam Weisner, a researcher of business management, spent a lot of time to prepare a doctoral thesis that brought clarity regarding Business Model as a framework for innovation. I happened to find a link on him during my attempts to straighten businesses of my clients. I also got his help in working through a couple of new Business Models.

I pinged Adam regarding the requirement at Terra Pharma. Incidentally, he was scheduled to travel to our region in the following month. He readily agreed to spend a day with the top management of Terra Pharma.

I was excited to have him at Terra Pharma and to see him demonstrating the power of Business Model again. However, Adam said that he would conduct a short session to describe the current Business Model of Terra Pharma, and then, he would guide me in taking it forward from there.

Describing the Business

The following month, I flew down to Terra Pharma's office along with Adam. Ajay introduced us to Seth and key executives. To start with, we had brief meetings with individual executives.

Ajay had done a good groundwork about the intent of our visit. We found Seth and his team to be well-rounded professionals and good individuals. They seemed to have all necessary skills that would make a good pharma company. Our initial guess was that perhaps they were missing the big picture and it was necessary to align them along a common objective. Perhaps Business Model was a good concept to begin the discussion with.

We were taken through a presentation on Terra Pharma by the Vice President, Corporate Communication. It included a description of Terra Pharma's legacy, products, markets, financial trends, facilities, CSR initiatives etc.

Most of the presented details were available on their website, which I had gone through before boarding the flight. The presentation did not give me any new understanding of their business, although it gave a little better articulated description of the company.

I already had some insights into the way of making drugs and the pressure points of the industry due to my exposure to Reamedics and Pharma One. But I still had difficulty in understanding the logic of the business. I raised my ignorance about the industry to Adam. He asked me not to worry too much and persuaded me to follow the proceedings.

Before the team could start spilling the problems it was facing, Adam wanted to make sure that we understood the current Business Model - the very logic of conducting Terra Pharma's business.

Adam asked Seth, "What is your Business Model?"

"You mean how do we make money?"

"Yes, something like that but in layman's terms." I wanted a simplified articulation without any management jargon.

"We sell a large variety of drugs," replied Seth.

"And who are your key customers... that is, who pays you most of the money?" asked Adam.

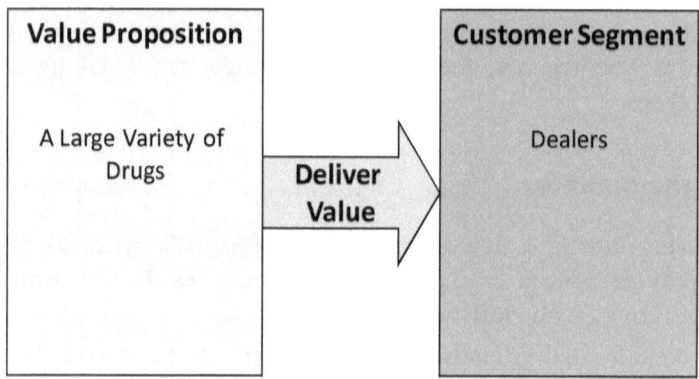

Figure 3.1 A Value Proposition is offered to a key Customer Segment

"Our dealers... they give over 90% of business," Seth was precise.

"So, Terra Pharma sells a large variety of drugs to dealers, who are its key customers," said Adam.

"You offer a large variety of drugs... i.e., products. And how do you get these products?"

"We have a whole lot of infrastructure, including plants, where we make drugs," said Seth.

"So, you manufacture a large variety of drugs in your plants and sell it to dealers who pay you money," Adam constructed the logic.

"And finally, what are your key expenses?" He asked.

"We use the money we get from dealers to pool back into the organization for buying materials and services to make drugs," Tony, the Head of Supply Chain, said.

"Good, at a very basic level, your Business Model is visualized like this."

Adam walked up to the white board, drew a set of 4 blocks and connected them with arrows [4]. The block diagram showed that the business manufactures drugs for dealers and gets money to feed back into its cost elements. It connected value creation, value delivery, value capturing and value investing logic of the business.

The Path

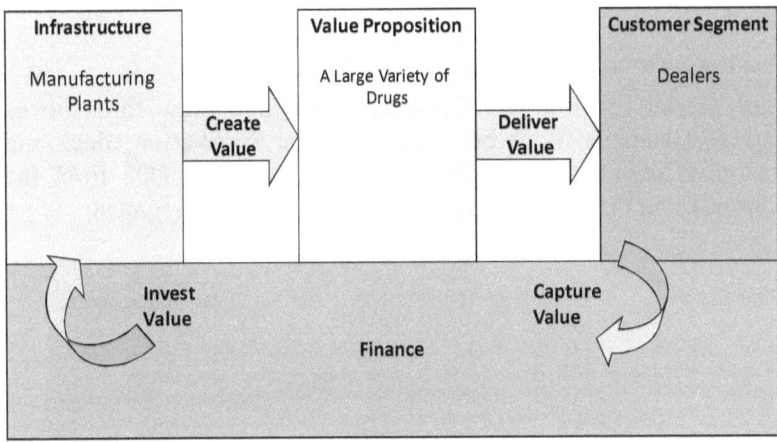

Figure 3.2 The Four-Block Business Model

"The arrows show the interaction between the building blocks," Adam said pointing to the interfacing arrows.

"This is a very high level logic of the business for most of the generics pharma companies around here," said Tony.

"Yes, this is too simple but all of us agree that this is the highest level of visualizing how the organization delivers value and makes money." I said.

"True," said Seth.

"Now we need to get into the next level, where we can do some thinking," Adam said.

While pointing at the arrows, Adam said, "Let us look into the interface between the Value Proposition and the Customer Segment."

He gave a brief background, "To convert a Value Proposition into Sales, we need *channels* for communication, sales and distribution to reach the customers, make sales and deliver the value proposition. We need a block called Channels, and it has an interface to the Value Proposition block and the target Customer Segments block; the value delivery arrow, therefore, flows from the Value Proposition block through the Channels block to the Customer Segment block."

And then he asked, "What are your channels for communication, sales and distribution?"

Ranbir, the Head of Sales, said, "We have sales reps who interact with doctors to effect prescription of drugs and work with dealers to fulfill their quarterly demand."

"And, how do you deliver drugs to dealers?"

"Ah! We have warehouses in various places," said Ranbir.

"I see!"

Thus, the customer side model became a little clearer.

Adam moved towards the flip chart stand and drew three boxes showing the Channels Block between the Value Proposition Block and the Customer Segment Block. It showed the flow of value from the Value Proposition through the Channels to the Customer Segment.

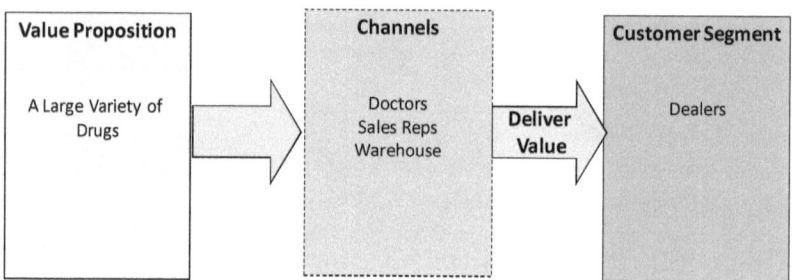

Figure 3.3 A Value Proposition is delivered through Channels to the Customer Segment

"And I believe we get paid based on individual price of the drugs," he stated the obvious.

"Yes... This is straightforward... number of pills multiplied by price and a discounted factor," said Seth.

"Let's look into the interface between the Infrastructure and the Value Proposition," Adam said as he pointed towards the arrow between the Infrastructure block and Value Proposition block, Figure 3.2.

"What are the key activities we do other than manufacturing?"

"We buy and stock materials, we do quality assurance and quality checks, we have a drug development process, and of course, we manage sales and delivery over a wide geography," said Seth.

"And what do we need for these activities?"

"As I said, we have plants, QC labs, warehouses... we have an IT system for capturing information... and most importantly, people," Ali, the Head of Operations, who was quiet so far, said.

"So you buy materials from suppliers. Are there other services or goods that you have partners for?"

"Yes, in addition to material suppliers, we have transporters who have been working with us for a long time," said Ali.

"Excellent, so on the infrastructure side, you have your own resources and those from your trusted partners to help in conducting activities in a way that you produce a large variety of drugs," said Adam and took a long breath.

By then, I had walked up to the flip chart board and redrawn the infrastructure side of the Business Model.

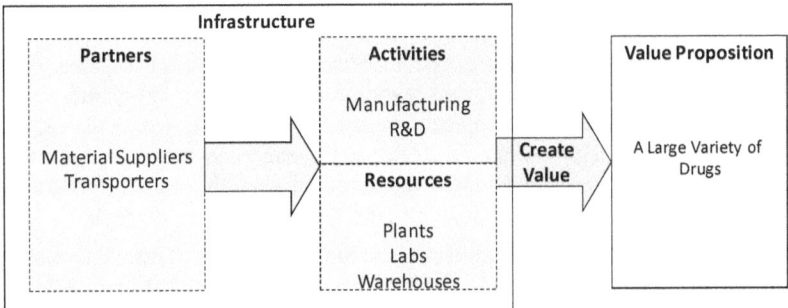

Figure 3.4 Partners and the Organization provide Resources to perform desired Activities to create the Value Proposition.

"One more thing!" he said.

"What are the cost elements? Only the major ones..."

"Raw materials, people, utility, transportation..." Ali counted on his fingers.

"That is, in order to support the infrastructure to make and deliver the drugs, you incur these costs," Adam said. "And, to meet these cost elements, you get money from your revenues. Let's put all these details into the Four-Block Business Model," he said as he pointed towards the basic framework of the Business Model.

"Can somebody read attributes of each block aloud?" he asked after a while.

Seth raised his right hand, while others were still connecting the dots.

"Okay, let me help out... it should not take long," I said.

Then I helped Seth in reading the boxes, connecting them to each other and explaining in greater detail. Tony helped Adam in capturing the description of the Business Model on the white board. Adam asked me to type the description of the Business Model in my laptop computer.

Visualizing the Logic of Business

The description of the extended Business Model became quite interesting.

> Value Proposition: Terra Pharma offers a range of therapeutic drugs of different dosages in the form of tablets, capsules, injectables, lotions and creams to the mass market.

Customer Segment: Its key customers are dealers/distributors who stock drugs for subsequent sales through sub-stockiest and retail outlets (Pharmacies).

Channels: In order to promote drugs, Terra Pharma has built a huge team of marketing, sales representatives and detailers, who meet doctors in various geographies. In turn, doctors write prescription to patients, who buy medicines from retail stores. Its marketing team also participates and liberally sponsors leading pharmaceutical conferences to showcase efficacies of its drugs. Quarterly and annual dealership conferences organized around the region provide an opportunity for the company to share information about its product launches and push its sales and distribution strategies.

Key Activities: In order to deliver the value proposition, Terra Pharma is involved in development, manufacturing, delivering and selling activities.

Key Resources: In order to carry out its key activities, Terra Pharma has cGMP (Current Good Manufacturing Practice) compliant formulation plants and processes. Its plants have world class machineries and qualified pharma graduates to turn raw materials into finished dosages.

Terra Pharma has a talented team of researchers and scientists who are continuously engaged in developing new formulations. Para IV filing is a strategic component of its business that allows it a lead of 180 days market exclusivity for the generic version of patented drugs.

The finished dosages are stored in its own warehouses before they are shipped to distributors on a pre-agreed monthly and quarterly plan.

Key Partners: Terra Pharma sources APIs and other materials from reliable suppliers. It has long term contract with transporters who deliver its supplies.

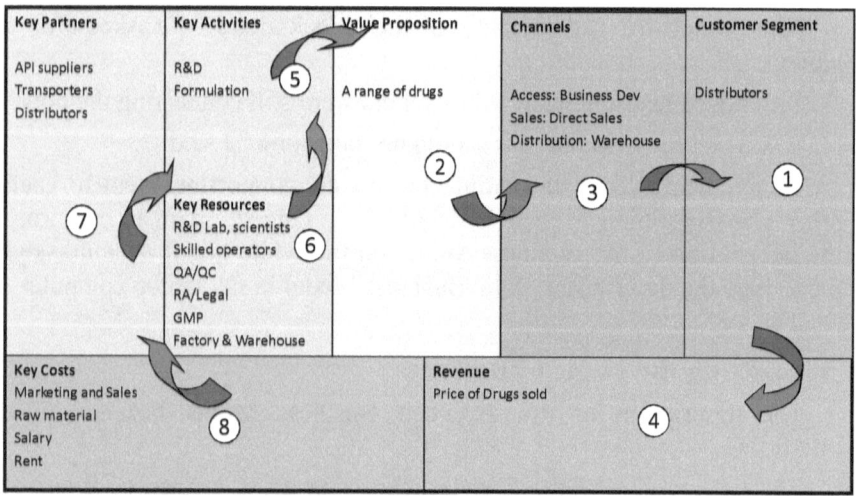

Figure 3.5 Visualization of the Business Model under construction

Key Costs: Like other pharma companies, Terra Pharma has huge margins on its products. Its raw materials are barely 10% of its sales, while employee cost is just 7% of sales. Marketing and Sales (including promotion) are its main cost elements that accounted for a whopping 40% of sales.

It took just a few minutes to read out and capture the blocks of the Business Model. Tony did a brilliant work and made the Integrated Business Model look like a Canvas of Art.

"How does it look, Seth!" I asked.

"Excellent! Actually, the process of describing the Business Model is like self evaluation. It helped me in integrating my visualization of the business. *I did feel uncomfortable in describing some of the interfaces*, but could not figure out the reason. Good thing is that we are able to describe the complete logic of the business."

"Indeed, when we try to connect the various building blocks of the business, it reveals many things and the interfaces force us to rethink the logic of the business. Inconsistencies will surface as we move ahead. So, do not worry about them right now... we will have an occasion to talk about them," said Adam.

"Sure!" said Seth.

"The Business Model is not yet complete!" Adam said after a while.

"What's missing?" two or three voices rose together.

It was the most difficult block to understand. Adam needed to provide some background.

"First the fundamentals: A business like that of Terra Pharma is an ongoing entity and must be built to last. This will happen if and only if significant needs of customers are fulfilled the way no other significant competitor can, NOW as well as in the FUTURE. We therefore must provide an element in the Business Model that establishes *long term viability* of the business, the foundation for which is Customer Relationship. The organization, therefore, needs to build a Customer Relationship block that constantly upgrades its Value Proposition based on the feedback derived from the strong relationship with the customer segments."

"I see where it is coming from," said Seth as he leaned back on his seat.

"So what type of Customer Relationship do you have?" was Adam's question.

"Through our huge sales team we maintain a close relationship with dealers and doctors. Keeping stakeholders on the client side engaged through meetings, conferences and outreach programs is essential. But nothing represents our relationship with the end consumers more than the community of doctors," said Ranbir.

"Very good, the long term value creation arrow flows in opposite direction of the normal value delivery flow, i.e. from the Customer Segment block to the Value Proposition block; and then merges and strengthens the cycle of value flow," Adam said, while he inserted block number 9 as the Customer Relationship block between the Customer Segment block and the Value Proposition block.

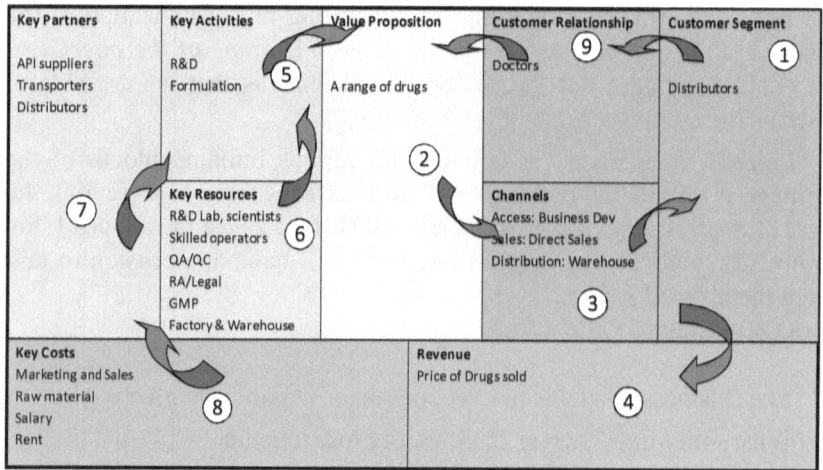

Figure 3.6 The Canvas for the Current Business Model of Terra Pharma

Thus, together we built a Nine Block Business Model Canvas [4] of Terra Pharma, which we realized, was applicable to a vast majority of pharma companies, and in a general sense, to several manufacturing organizations.

"What about our end customers, i.e. consumers? Why are they not seen here?" Tony threw the critical question.

Adam said, "Your current logic of business is such that consumers of drugs are hidden behind 'Distributors' and 'Doctors'. I do not think that on day to day basis, you are directly involved with consumers in creating and delivering value. Let's park this issue for the time being."

Discussions continued over the Canvas, and people started building their own logic as different issues surfaced out. They were also talking about the interfaces that were not so seamless and about the blocks where they had pressure points.

"I think that this is a good enough description of the Business Model. Let's have this captured in a Power Point™ slide, and have it printed on a large enough sheet of paper as a Canvas. We will work on it in the afternoon," Adam said, concluding the pre-lunch proceedings.

The Secret to Sustainable Operations

After completing a working lunch, we returned to the Board Room, while Adam got busy talking to someone on his mobile phone. To my amazement, the Business Model Canvas of Terra Pharma was printed on an A0 size sheet of paper and was pasted on the wall. I saw a couple of new attributes already scribbled on the Canvas and people gathered around discussing the flow rather vocally. The simplicity of the Canvas as a strong visualization tool in understanding the working of an organization perhaps grabbed the attention of Terra Pharma's management.

"The Canvas is a powerful tool to connect vital attributes of the organization. We can use it as a sounding board during cross functional discussions," said Seth as he took a seat next to me.

"Indeed," I acknowledged.

We were aware of the power of the Canvas and its multiple usages, but did not wish the team getting into more details than was required. Adam needed to bring back the focus on the next step.

He returned soon, and as everybody settled down, he said, "In the last session, we visualized the current Business Model. We might have missed some attributes here, but it is ok to start with the ones we have captured."

"So what is a Business Model?" Adam asked casually.

"I think it can be defined as the rationale of creating, delivering and capturing value of a business," said Tony [4].

"Excellent!" Adam's eyes brightened to see how well Tony had grasped the insight.

"As we saw in the morning, we start with a four block model of value creation (infrastructure side), value proposition (the value), value delivery (customer side) and value capture (financial side)," explained Adam.

"Also the Value Investment, i.e. the Key Cost block," said Ali.

"Yes, of course. And, the Business Model is further broken down into 9 blocks, which significantly improves its comprehension and visualization."

He said, "This is how Business Model can be described fairly through 9 basic building blocks that provide the logic of how a company intends to fulfill the necessary conditions of making money faster in a sustained way. In fact, it represents the blueprint of a company's logic of doing business that is then implemented through organizational structures, processes and systems [4]."

"A point to note here is that the visual part (Canvas) of the Business Model identifies 'KEY' attributes of each Block, and the list of attributes is not deemed to be comprehensive." He wanted to avoid any further scribbling on the Canvas.

"Nine blocks are more than enough to capture the Business Model," said Seth in an assertive tone.

"Yes, the arrows show how 'value flow' can be modeled. But the most important thing is something else," said Adam, looking around.

I saw everybody looking at him with rapt attention.

"What does the set of arrows that pass through different building blocks indicate? ... They tell us that for the success of the business, the value flow between the blocks along these arrows must be seamless."

He drew a clock-wise circle connecting the blocks, and while tracing it, said, "It is the prime responsibility of the Operating System of an organization to make flow of value *as fast as possible*. For this flow to be faster, it is important that the key disruptions and blockers to flow, where ever they occur along the circle of flow, are dealt with effectively."

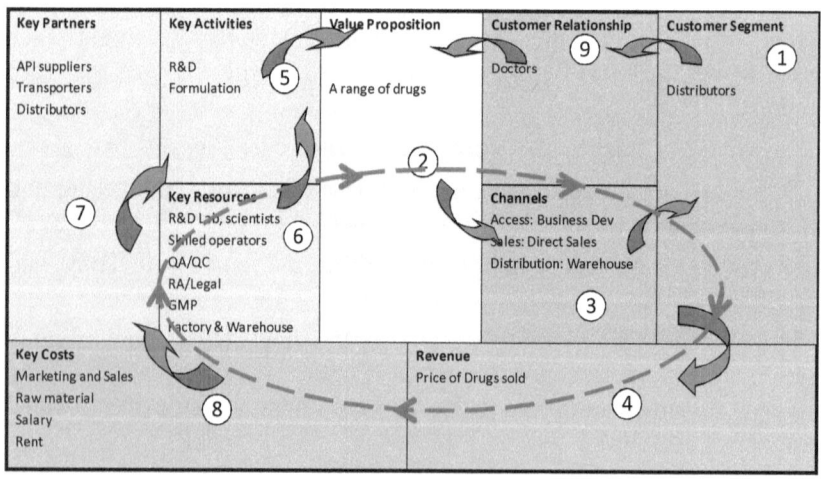

Figure 3.7 Ever improving the flow of value is the prime role of the organization.

"And that is what Operations means, *to make the flow of value faster and faster; and thicker and thicker*." He emphasized this by repeatedly and briskly running the marker on the circle.

And then, he said, "This flow of value is nothing but flow of money. Anything that disrupts the flow of value disrupts the flow of money. And this can happen anywhere along the circle in any block due to inability of any attribute to deal with disruption."

"So it is about rotation of money, material, process, information, decision and orders. It means revenue, profit and ... cash flow. I see the logic, our job is to rotate this circle as fast as possible," quipped Ali.

"And as thick as possible..." said Ranbir.

I realized that people had started relating themselves with the Business Model Canvas.

"Yeah, from time to time external forces and internal limitations constrain the Business Model. They disrupt and block the flow of value creation...flow of money. It is important to recognize this and build an operating system that smoothens and reinforces the flow of value. In an ever changing business environment, in order to have sustainable growth, the Business Model needs to be reviewed and innovated more regularly," was Adam's direction on the importance and use of Business Model.

"We have too many disruptions and worries," said Ali.

"We will get into those," Adam said as he paced along the room.

After a while, he said, "Let's do it now... What we are going to do now is... start capturing the disturbances in the business environment and supcrimposing them on the Canvas, and get a sense of how these are disrupting the current Business Model."

"Ok, it should be interesting," said Seth, as he straightened himself and sat attentively by resting his hands on the table.

Gazing the Environment

"Seth, would you like to start with the major changes taking place in the environment?" he asked the top most guy in the team.

Seth was ready, "The landscape of our industry in undergoing major shift. There is now an increasing pricing pressure and our margins are falling. At the same time, our managers are struggling to deal with unpredictability in the market as well as inconsistent internal operations."

"Let's capture, Pricing Pressure, Volatile Demand and Unstable Internal Operations, as factors adversely affecting flow of the business." He picked a bundle of Post-it® pads and scribbled on them. Then he pasted the sticky pads on the print of the Business Model Canvas.

"It may mean that our offer to the market isn't strong enough to fetch good price. In other words our value proposition mayn't be significant enough to the customer segment to command high enough price. It may also mean that our cost factors aren't efficient enough." Adam provoked them to think as he kept pointing at the arrows between the blocks.

Ranbir added, "In fact, world over, governments are restructuring their buying process. And we do see a lot of volatility in demand."

Then Adam said, "Volatility in demand is a reality. It may affect stability of the internal system, if our order handling process is not robust enough. In order to come out of such instability, we may have to innovate scheduling and stock management process." He rolled the marker around Activity, Resource and Channel blocks. Thus he explained how the Business Model Canvas could be analyzed along with problems faced by the business and the likely direction to the solution.

"Very good!" said Seth.

"Now this is the way you would use your Business Model Canvas to question the existing way of doing things with respect to the type of pressure points you have in the business," I said.

"It means that we pick each factor affecting our business and see its effect on each or relevant block on the Canvas. This will help us in knowing if our current processes are good enough or not. That is, how contemporary is our Business Model," said Tony as he assimilated the importance of the business model concept.

"Exactly!" said Adam and looked around at the team.

Seth nodded and said, "Excellent tool for decision making process."

"Let's move ahead and complete this exercise to visualize how stressed is our Business Model... Anything happened on the consumer side?" Adam asked as he looked at Ranbir.

"Yes, new regulations are shifting buying decisions from doctors to intermediaries and consequently, effectiveness of sales representatives is reducing. Local markets are also seeing seismic shift in demography and spending pattern. Therapeutically, demand is shifting towards chronic to life style drugs." It was an honest and well thought out feedback.

Adam noted down, Shift in Buying Decision, Growing Role of Intermediaries, Demography Shift and Therapeutic Changes, and pasted them on the Canvas. In the meanwhile, Tony got up and took Adam's place to manage the Canvas.

"A decade back, we had a clear advantage on new therapeutic drugs and skills, but now it is difficult to have such differentiation." said Seth.

"You mean that the product feature or newness is no more an advantage?" Adam sought clarification.

"It is still, but not so much that you could make it a decisive competitive edge easily," Seth clarified.

"What is the biggest visible damage seen so far? That is also scary..." Adam asked.

Seth replied, "There are increasing litigations on Para IV filings that have been our prime route to seek significant upside in revenues. ... And regulatory audits are stricter than ever. A year back, a majority of top 20 generic pharma companies suffered blockade of their dominant drugs owing to ban from regulators..."

Ranbir said, "Moreover, innovator companies are entering into generics space, making the competition stiff and beyond price factor."

Seth had more to add, "There is an increasing level of consolidation in the market and innovator companies are increasingly gobbling up regional companies to garner market share and increase reach."

"As if these are not enough, increasing number of medicines are being included in the list of 'price controlled drugs' by the government, putting a lid on the margins," said Ranbir. That was the real worry.

Tony had almost fully covered the Canvas with Post-it® pads.

"We have collected enough factors... may be a final one from Seth," Adam realized that Seth wanted to say something.

Seth waited for a while, as if to consolidate his thoughts, and said, "While the current market has already shifted from product features to low price regime, it would get further commoditized and will have a higher level of unpredictability [5]."

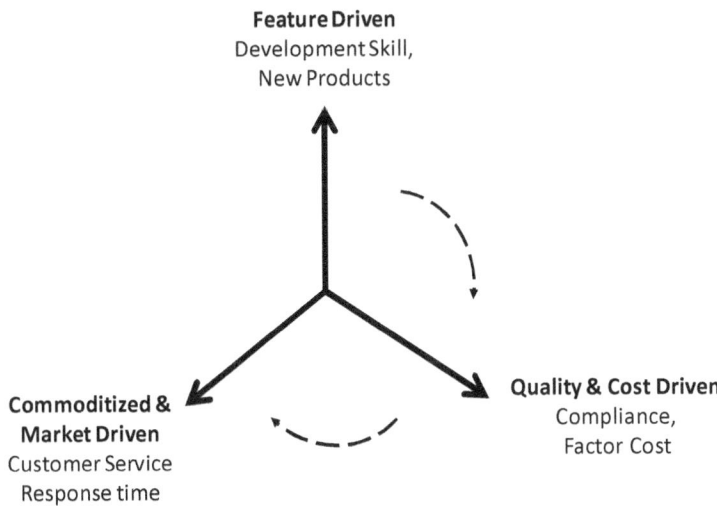

Figure 3.8 The shifting axis of the Pharma Industry

He continued, "I think that for a company that doesn't have deep innovation and execution excellence background, it won't be too long before it would succumb to market pressure." He not only blew out the big secret, he actually revealed his biggest worry in dealing with disruptions to his current Business Model.

Tony added a few more Post-it® stickers to the Canvas.

As Tony stepped back from the Canvas, it had morphed into a riot of colors, flooded with factors that were potential disruptions to the Business Model of Terra Pharma.

The Canvas looked like a collage (Figure 3.9), with annotations of various trends, issues and impacts superimposed on its existing Business Model.

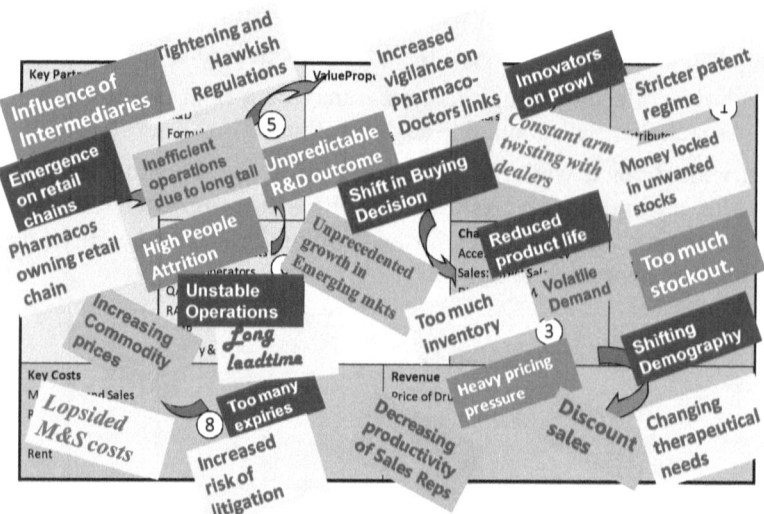

Figure 3.9 Capturing the megatrends in the Pharma Industry

"Oh my God! Our Business Model is too stressed," exclaimed Seth.

"Now what do we do?" asked Ali.

"A traditional way to clear up the things is to start looking at each block of the Canvas and find a strategy to deal with each of the likely disruptions and the likely opportunities." I said.

"It will be too exhaustive and time consuming exercise. After all, we also need to do day to day activities," Ali voiced his hesitation.

Seth said, "For us, the reality is not just the number of disruptions in the environment, but the rate at which these disturbances are coming in."

"Yes, seeing the rate at which the things are changing and the level of unpredictability around us, we need a different approach." said Tony.

"Ultimately, we must be able to make the flow of value creation faster and thicker with time," said Seth, as he tried to focus on the objective.

"I agree. So we are talking about something that is *operational*," said Adam.

"I think that you also need to look into the type of problems you have internally. Then pick up a problem that disrupts functioning of one of the blocks. *And since the blocks are interrelated, trying to solve the problem in one block will any way take you around the value flow cycle.* This approach would be better than trying to attack all the blocks simultaneously."

"That's a good one," said Ali.

"But we still need to make a choice - which block do we start with?" asked Tony.

I suggested, "Let's start from the Customer Segment block. It means that we try to improve business of our customers and do everything required internally to align with that block. The key will be the interfaces between different functions and departments... Though dealing with these interfaces will not be easy."

"I like this... after all, we make money when our customers make money... so we can trace back the flow of money and value," Seth said.

"Yes, this is the most preferred way," Adam approved.

Adam was already running late for his flight. He grasped his laptop bag and said, "It's time for me to leave. Why does not this team sit down together and figure out at least one significant problem faced by the customers? And therefore, one significant need of the customers which is worth fulfilling by an order of magnitude. We will then trace it back along the value flow cycle and get into actions that would drive improvement across the value curve and simultaneously innovate the Business Model." He spoke so quickly that I wondered if people understood him properly.

Adam looked at me and then said, "DJ will handhold you from here onwards. He has been through the concept several times. When it comes to operationalizing the Business Model, I would rely on him."

"Good, we will have an internal discussion and figure out what is it that our customers are more worried about," assured Seth. He walked up to Adam and shook hands while thanking him for the session.

Adam lifted his bag and bid good bye; Ajay and I escorted him out. I stayed back to ensure that Terra Pharma's team was clear about the next steps involved in innovating the Business Model.

Grasping the Problem

Seth felt that his team needed to objectively and critically look into Terra Pharma's Business Model. He wished for a Business Model that by design would allow his organization to adapt to the rapidly changing business conditions. Although, it might mean dramatically changing the way Terra Pharma operated, he was willing to take the chance.

Seth had already held a few brief sessions with his senior management team. But he was frustrated with attitude and resistance of the team in effecting the desired changes in the working of Terra Pharma. His team still wanted to run the organization in the traditional way of taking lopsided sales centric approach and relying on the inherent low cost structure. Since no concrete actions were surfacing from the conversations, he needed to do something different.

Knowing well what happened in Reamedics, Ajay called me to get into a deeper engagement with the top management of Terra Pharma for a complete organizational transformation.

Terra Pharma was quite big and complex. I also realized that the pressure to transform its business was becoming too much for the team to bear. I needed to be a little cautious in taking the complete organization in one go.

When I checked up with Adam, he advised to adopt a process that would allow the team to find its own way to innovate the Business Model. He suggested an iterative way of improving operations one step at a time, thereby strengthening each block of the Business Model on the go. And, instead of managing the complete top tier of Terra Pharma, he asked me to drive transformation through Seth.

I would meet Seth once a month and work with him in deciding the next step he would need to take forward. After meeting Seth one on one, I would often be a silent presence in the management and staff meetings, observing the underlying culture. I could not think of any other mode of engagement. Ajay had agreed to such an arrangement, since ultimately the transformation would have to be driven by Terra Pharma's management. In the initial days, Seth used my shoulder to shoot hard messages, but I realized its limited impact. Before our engagement could run into the danger of becoming a routine affair, I had to get into the background and force Seth to take the plunge.

Taking Initiative

One day, Seth called Ali, the Operations Head, and Ranbir, the Sales Head, for a closed door meeting. He was aware of the traditional rivalry between the two functions and wanted to take it head on. He allowed the gentlemen to speak about the problems faced by their teams, and gently let them open up their wounds.

Ranbir gave his version, "For every sales order, we are required to chase Production; and it consumes a lot of our time. My people spend more time with Production than with customers; and there is no other reason why we miss customer insights. Whenever we walk into the production office, its team seldom gives firm delivery dates, and we keep following up with them. Every one of them seems to be always busy with one thing or the other. Finally, by the time we get the committed dates, the customer would have already gone to our competitor..."

"Yeah! We know that the Pharma Industry is no more the same. There are now plenty of alternatives for customers," said Seth.

Seth's statement encouraged Ranbir further, and he said, "Even for ongoing customer orders, we continue to follow up with Production, and at the last moment, something goes wrong and our orders are never delivered on time. And then, we face great difficulties in managing complaints of our customers."

Seth gave a cursory glance at Ali and kept mum.

Ranbir paused and then said, "Actually, every quarter, representatives of both the teams meet, do a two day planning exercise and agree on things in detail; but at the end of the quarter, we meet less than 50% of our commitment."

Ali, who had listened patiently till then, burst out, "The reality is that production is increasingly becoming complex. We have over 1000 SKUs to produce on a limited set of resources, and the resources are not readily configurable for all products. We have a few SKUs that give good volume per batch, while a majority of SKUs give awfully low volume. Our portfolio is pathetic with longer than the Long Tail characteristics [6]. Almost 50% of our SKUs run a demand of only a few thousand pills at any time."

He continued, "Further, there are products for which, we are asked to produce very small quantities on *highly urgent* basis. This takes a lot of our attention in preparing, cleaning and changing our manufacturing lines, which invariably delays other promised orders. And with a higher level of regulatory and compliance requirements, it has become very difficult to have high level of availability of our machines. While that is the case, we find our priorities being changed every day. The product mix and volatility in sales orders have absolutely no predictability."

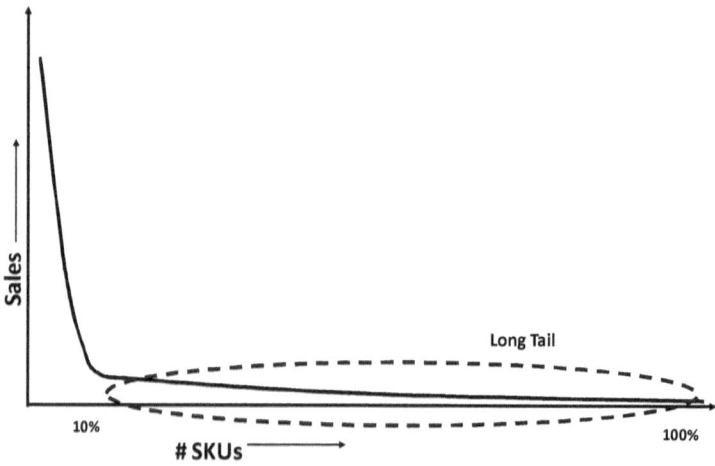

Figure 3.10 The Long Tail effect

Ali looked at Ranbir from the corner of his eyes and then, turning back to Seth, said, "The priorities we agree to in the quarterly forecast meetings hardly remain valid for long. My people have terrible confusion, as they are chased day in and day out by the sales staff to change the priority of products. You ask for volumes, we will deliver for those that move fast in the plant. For others, we need more volumes, and then we need more machines and more people."

Ali paused for a while and then continued in a rather animated way, "And, our processes are not so robust. Once we release batches into the shop floor, we have a good number of them stuck on the way. And then, to meet the deadlines, we start additional batches and thus fall into the loop of working on too many orders for too few pills. Added to all these, frequent breakdowns in our aged machines do not help either."

Seth opened his mouth to say something but kept quiet.

Ali got up from his chair, bent forward and said in a lower pitch, "Of course, we have a high WIP in the plant and huge inventory stacked up everywhere, but that is how complex production is. Something or the other gets stuck, because of people, material, machine, priority, and sometimes external factors like holidays, traffic jams, absenteeism, strikes and flood. And above all, we have too much of documentation to do. Every batch needs over 300 pages of documents to be hand filled correctly by my staff. So we are not just manufacturing; we are also required to provide documentation diligently."

Ali was trying to control his helplessness, but it was showing on his face. He took out his spectacles, picked up a bottle of mineral water and emptied it down his throat.

After a while, Ranbir blurted out, "But that is what production all about. Your people must know how to deliver. Everybody does it in other organizations."

Picking a Direction of the Problem

Before Ali could fume out again, Seth took charge and said, "OK guys, looks like we are talking too many things in the same breath. I understand from you that there are a lot of issues within our system that are making it difficult to *get the best out of our best efforts*. I get the impression that almost everything that you guys talked about has the power to prevent us from performing well."

Ali said, "Everybody is working hard."

"Yes, fire fighting … But why do we not get proportionate results?"

And then, he said thoughtfully, "We have seen the connections in the Business Model Canvas. Unless we find the effort made in one function, by design, passing through others seamlessly and in full, we will mess up the system. People are working hard only means that they are working in different directions and as a result, the organization isn't moving anywhere. We are playing a zero sum game. Let's try to understand it in the business context."

Seth continued, "We have always been striving to be customer centric. Adam and DJ too suggested that we look at the business from customer side. If that is so, let's start with customers."

"What is the story on customer front?" he asked.

Ranbir gave the details, "We lost four vital customers within a span of two months. Key reason: we are not able to deliver drugs when they were needed, even though the demanded lead times were reasonable."

Seth waved his hands and said, "Actually, a large part of these drugs are supplied through our warehouses, but consistently, we have failed to fulfill our commitment to these customers. For the past one year, we never had enough inventories of these products in the warehouses and we have been forcing ourselves to arbitrarily ration the little that the poor customers could receive."

Till then keeping mum, I said looking at the two gentlemen, "Do you think it is a sales or production related problem?" I wanted the gentlemen to stop the blame game.

Instead, Seth said in a softer tone, "I still do not know where the problem is. But I do not think that Sales or Production can solve this problem alone. This looks like a bigger problem."

Understanding the Bigger Problem

Seth paused and then continued. "We have a good product development team and we have one of the best marketing teams in the industry. Our marketing initiatives are pulling customers to buy our products but we are not able to supply and satisfy them."

"Do we need additional infrastructure?" I asked.

Seth said, "During the past few years we extended facilities in the plants with new machinery and infrastructure, but we continue to have the same problem of non-availability and low reliability, while our sales volumes have not gone up much. I also do not think that there is anything wrong with people. They are good and I see them striving more than ever."

"Is the problem only ours? How are other players in the industry doing?" I asked.

His hand swept in an arc, and he said a little loudly, "If you look around, you would see that the problem is not unique to us. Almost everybody in the Pharma Industry is facing this situation. You know, some of our new customers had similar experience with our competitors, and *some of them turned to us for the same reason that others turned to our competitors.*

"Customers are running in circles and looks like we are taking advantage of their vulnerability," I commented.

Then I suggested in a low voice, "Let's see the current situation of the company as an opportunity to solve a problem that is ours as well as of our competitors. At present, everybody is equally ignorant in defining the problem correctly. And this is the *industry's age old problem*. If we could solve it, we will be way ahead in the perception of our clients, and especially when the margins are shrinking, retaining customer by solving the problem of inconsistent delivery will be a big achievement for us."

Direction to the Solution

Seth waited for a while and allowed the larger problem to sink in, and then looking at Ali, said, "You are right about the Long Tail characteristics of our business. But it may not be very easy, and in some cases, it may not be possible to cut the tail." Looked like, he wanted to start from somewhere.

"Yes, I know Seth, but we can't ignore its impact on productivity," said Ali quickly.

Seth said thoughtfully, "The solution to the problem must be in improving supply reliability of products in demand, without compromising on our commitment to the Long Tail."

All of a sudden, as if something strange occurred to him, he said effervescently, "If in-demand products tend to stock out in the warehouses or reach late to the customers, *then the only thing we need to focus on is to ensure that these drugs do not stock out and they reach our clients in time.* And, since this is a big enough problem, it makes sense for all of us to give this issue a high priority."

Ali said, "Unfortunately, Seth, several of these products move rather slowly in production."

"You would not be wrong Ali. From business point of view, on day to day basis, first we need to pay attention to these in-demand products and improve our capability to produce them faster. The point is that we already have customers who come to us but return empty handed. As managers, it is our responsibility to spend our time more on these things. *If for the lines which manufacture these products, you could improve efficiency even by 10%, our bottom line will improve by much more than 10%.* Is there any other issue that you spoke of that guarantees such high returns? Do you get me?" asked Seth.

Ali said, "Seth, I agree. I understand. We have the best margins on some of these products and these products are in demand, we only have to make them available somehow. And nothing takes us closer to our organizational goal faster than this."

Ali was bang on target and Seth knew he had his buy-in.

Ali had a strong operational career. After receiving his engineering degree, he had been over two decades in Chemical and Pharma Industries. Last quarter, he completed 12 years in Terra Pharma. He had handled his responsibility of managing Terra Pharma's multi-site operations very well. Being a very down to earth and hands on professional, Ali was extremely comfortable with machines and people. He was an archetype Head of Operations; full of intuition, emotion and action. Making Terra Pharma's workforce skilled in best practices by remaining constantly engaged with his team, earned him good respect across the organization. Although he would, at times, burst out shop floor emotions in management forums, people liked him for his native truthfulness.

Seth said, "Exactly, we now need to find a way out and that is our job."

Ranbir jumped in, "If we can achieve this, then I have 50% additional market for these products. But we must be careful not to antagonize our clients by adding any more delays to the long tail products. They are important."

Seth saw Ali staring at Ranbir, and then said in acknowledgement, "Of course, we must take care of the Long Tail."

Ali said, "Seth, we need to be reasonable in our expectations and must recognize that the Long Tail will eventually impact high margin products. It is very difficult to control deviations on the shop floor unless we have a system in place." This was his way of seeking help.

Seth did not wish to argue out everything right away, and said, "Ali, lets walk into prioritizing the high margin products and see how big the problem is. We may find that our people already have some solution." He was ready to test the waters.

Ali said, "Yes, of course!"

Common Understanding

The top three executives of Terra Pharma were able to see a common point. Seth was satisfied a bit, since it would reduce the blame-game at the top management level. He did not have answers for all the questions and apprehensions raised by Ali, but he was not worried, since their direction to solution was logical. He was also very clear that there should not be any compromise between fast moving and long tail products.

After a couple of days, the team met again and Seth asked, "So what shall we do, if we need better availability of products?"

"Let's get a list of these products and their stock out situation. The products that are receiving constant complaint of shortages and delays must be given higher priority across the supply chain," suggested Ranbir.

Seth said, "I think this is a good way to start with."

Ali asked, "What does this mean?"

Seth explained, "This means that, say, if you want to release a batch into the shop floor and if you have input materials for several products, then you release process order for the batch that is higher on priority list first (i.e., a product that has higher demand and has higher margin). Similarly, if QC (Quality Control function) has a list of samples to be analyzed, it gives priority to these products. If engineering is short of people and there are breakdowns to attend, it deploys the available people, first on those machines that carry these priority products."

"So, we need a mechanism to tell us on a regular basis which products are moving faster in the market...and therefore, about the need to replenish them in time," said Ranbir.

Ali said, "It sounds simple. How about consulting Tony, since his team manages the stocks? For Production, he is the immediate customer."

"Yes, we need to," said Seth and buzzed his secretary to get Tony in.

Better Understanding

Tony was the man behind the management of Terra Pharma's mammoth supply chain. He peeped through the glass window of Seth's room, pushed the door and walked in.

After he got a quick briefing, Tony said, "For a vast majority of our portfolio, *by knowing frequently how products move in the market will certainly help.* We could have more realistic priorities for the plant and the delivery team. On a daily basis, Ali's people would know which products are in the danger of stock-out in the market, i.e., fast moving in the market. This will help them in aligning the plants with operational priority and move these products ahead of others."

Ali asked, "But how do we get the signal to replenish consumption from the stock?"

Ranbir realized that this would also mean changes in the way his team behaved and sensed the hassle in making his team adapt to the new way of disciplined working. He said, "That will be too much work..."

Tony cut Ranbir short and said, "It may not be so difficult Ranbir, with the power of today's communication technology."

Ranbir asked, "What do you mean?"

Tony replied, "We are already connected across our distribution chain on intranet and we do get data on real time from our distribution centers. The priorities will be set automatically. In fact, it will be a big relief to your people who spend hours in setting the right priorities."

"I see!" said Ranbir.

"Great! Let's talk to Mickey, if we have any obstacle there," said Seth. He buzzed his secretary to get Mickey online. Mickey was Terra Pharma's IT infrastructure manager.

Mickey came online. Without getting into details, Seth asked, "Mickey! We have a business problem related to availability of our products. And the problem could be solved quickly if we could know which products are being sold how much, say every 2-3 days, at an aggregate level. Is it possible?"

Mickey replied, "Of course! Our complete distribution network is connected to the ERP system; and distributors can upload dispatch data. We can get dispatch data almost daily, if our guys in the distribution centers co-operate."

Tony enquired, "What do you need for distribution centers to 'co-operate' with?"

Mickey said, "We update our ERP data daily, and if distribution centers could diligently key in daily dispatches by the close of business hours, we will have the consumption data as well as stocks position every morning at 7:00 AM."

Seth said, "What do you think Tony? We have a big opportunity. Do you see any problem?"

Tony, the ever committed guy, said, "I do not see any problem, we will talk to our folks in distribution centers and have workflow of 'stock taking and reconciliation' revisited. Actually, our boxes are bar coded, so probably, we can automate the dispatch data. Even if we do not do that, I see no reason why some body can't key-in dispatch data daily. We need to come out with a modified rule of stock closing across the organization, and this is small work compared to the possible level of improvement in fulfilling our promise to customers."

"Very good!" said Seth, recognizing Tony's forthrightness.

Consolidated Understanding

That night, Seth called me over the phone and said, "I took the plunge. My key managers have come out with a direction to the solution."

"Excellent! What does it look like?"

"They agreed to produce drugs based on actual demand."

"Actual demand?"

"Yes, as per consumption of stocks," said Seth.

"This means that the IT system of Terra Pharma would provide the plant with daily consumption and position of stocks. Thus, the plant will not only know which products to work on, it will also know which one to give higher priority," he explained.

"Good! Could your team visualize the benefits?" I asked.

"We feel that such a system of replenishment based on consumption from stock will soon increase availability of products and reduce stock-outs," Seth said enthusiastically.

"What else?"

"Further, I expect that by producing only as per consumption, the noise in the system will reduce and the working environment will improve significantly."

"I see! What's the next step in your plan?"

"We need to work on classification of products and capture their daily consumption from the stocks."

"But how is the current situation of stocks? And to what level you want to fill them?" I asked.

"It is quite crazy! We have too much of those, the market does not need now and too less of those, the market needs now. I think we must first rationalize stocks and set a reference for 'desired' stock levels. I know that Tony's team is good at it."

"Yes, do that first! By the way, how are you planning to roll out the initiative?"

"We thought of picking up our main plant, where we have the biggest chaos. So if we succeed there, it will have an immediate ripple effect elsewhere."

"Mmmm! Let's start there. But remember to take one step at a time and get an early win," I said, and we closed the call.

Leadership at Work

Seth realized that if data about consumption of stocks in the warehouses were available over a short interval, say, at a frequency of 2-3 days, then his plants would have more reliable data to replenish the right products. Given this, the schedule of the plants would follow closely the immediate demand in the market; and it would significantly reduce mismatches and therefore, stock outs and delays.

A reduction in stock-outs of drugs would mean a possible improvement in sales.

And if the benefit was so apparent, then his team and he must give a disproportionate level of attention to this initiative; and rapidly deal with anything that prevented the plants from reducing mismatches and delays.

By doing this, it also seemed logical that products with less demand would also be automatically produced just to demand and not in excess.

"Aha!" a realization came to him. "If we do not produce too much in advance, especially those moving slower in the market, we will have fewer expiries and added savings there from. *Improving sales by reducing stock-outs and reducing cost by not producing slow movers ahead of time will be a double edged advantage.*"

He was visualizing over 10% improvement in the top line and over 20% in the bottom line, just by making the right products available in right quantity, at right time in right place. It was an amazing revelation for him, since for the envisaged benefits he would not need to start any new initiative in R&D or marketing, but only leverage upon the past work done by them.

Seth knew one thing, that an improvement of 10% in the top line along with 20% in the bottom line, *without exhausting resources and without taking real risk*, would not be a small achievement. And if this were true, his intuition told him that the actual challenge must be in some other form. He realized that the real challenge would be in the 'transformation' of his people in making the new system work.

By the measure of possible improvement, his team was probably committing itself to the biggest transformation initiative. The initiative was highly customer centric; and although *the solution seemed simple, it would not be easy,* since there would be surprises on the way.

He thought that the efforts needed for the change management - what Adam called as Operationlizing the New Business Model - should not be underestimated. And he understood that the complete value chain must be aligned, with a directionally same *priority for everybody*. He realized what Adam had meant by 'seamless flow of value'. He knew that if the top management was to focus anywhere, then it was on this particular initiative. This thought placed him at the top of the accountability curve [7].

Common View

The following week, Seth called a meeting of functional heads. He rolled out his broad Operational Strategy for building an aligned organization that would deliver high performance year on year, with minimum risk and without exhausting critical resources.

He presented the immediate agenda based on the discussion he had with the leaders of Operations, Distribution, Sales and IT. And he spelt out the new priority mechanism.

He also showcased instances of people taking decisions to honor the new priority system, function by function. He showed the model of supply chain and how the goods, information and decisions would move across the value chain seamlessly. He took a slide from Mickey to show the infrastructural integration issues. He also allocated a separate IT team for this effort.

He made it very clear, "It is now time to make use of data. We must base our decisions on facts and dovetail it into our experience and logic."

But he warned, "'Data integrity' of our ERP system has been awful, and it needs to be straightened within 10 days, otherwise this project will not fly. It means that all the master databases, including product codes, BOM, recipes, vendor data etc., are up to date and relevant reports are in place."

He also declared, "The project team will be an empowered team and for the coming 3 months, I myself along with the senior management team will drive it, by when the needed systems will be in place."

He then clearly spelt out the plan for the project on which he had worked in great detail with his colleagues during the past few weeks. The plan also showed the immediate preparatory and execution steps. He ensured that the project milestones, priorities and metrics were aligned with those of the organization, and that there was no major conflict between the ongoing business and the project.

Aligned View

Much before Seth met with functional heads, he had discussed with each one of them individually to assess their views and reservations. He had also sought unconditional support from them on this project.

Tony, on the other hand, was thinking a lot since his meeting with Seth and the team. Being the owner of the entire supply chain, he was aware of his forthcoming responsibilities and the critical role his team would play in implementing the new system.

He realized that by adopting the logic of 'production based on consumption', they would be challenging, a deep rooted practice of the industry, which was 'production based on forecasting'.

For decades, the Pharma Industry has been operating based on quarterly forecasting. All planning across the supply chain and scheduling within the plants were based on 'forecasted' sales orders. And perhaps 'millions of pills' as the key performance metric of plants was also as old a concept. The 'forecasted' orders (which would become inaccurate the moment they were published) were felt necessary to provide the plants benefit of aggregation and better utilization numbers.

The tendency to produce "millions of pills" had become so dominant that the plants tended to produce a large number of batches of some products continuously, before other products would be taken into the shop floor.

This dominant behavior often ignored undesired effects that came naturally in running a process based on forecasted orders, while the market was ever dynamic and Terra Pharma had a wide portfolio of products. Across the supply chain, pills were produced and delivered in bulk quantities creating huge mismatches at different nodes of supply chain. And as a result, too much stock waited in too many places for some products, while too less stock was available for several other products.

It therefore dawned on Tony and his team to implement a system that would replenish pills as close as to actual consumption from stocks. They were, actually foreseeing a possibility of not only a dramatic rationalization of inventories across the chain but also improvement in response time and flexibility of supply that Tony used to call as 'velocity' in supply chain.

Tony did a back of the envelop calculation to estimate the effect of production based on 2-3 days consumption data while forgoing the habit of producing based on forecasting. He felt that inventories would be down by at least $1/3^{rd}$, very soon. He wanted to put all his might in challenging the assumption of 'forecasting on quarterly basis' by 'supplying on 2-3 days consumption basis'.

Ali too realized the benefit of closely matching his production priorities to that of the market. He was sure of seeing a dramatic impact on the Work In Progress (WIP) and the Plant Lead Time (response time).

A big relief for his team would be due to a uniform priority system that would significantly reduce chaos and fire fighting in the shop floor. It would also give them peace of mind to work more efficiently.

He knew that when the new scheme would be implemented, his machines would possibly see an increased number of product changeovers (the setup time is substantial in the Pharma Industry, for some products it was longer than 24 hours).

Earlier, he had spent substantial time in understanding the changeover process and had some experience in Lean Management. He had referred his notes and built a small team to deal with long setup times. He felt that the time had arrived for his team to employ their specialized skills.

He, however, knew that it would not be easy to follow the natural market flow, as they were challenging some old assumptions and decades of established culture in pharma manufacturing. But, given the focus on the initiative, he was confident of reducing the Plant Lead Time that would improve his responsiveness to market changes.

Committing to Fundamentals

With everybody on board, Seth rolled out the program and installed a Project Management war room.

Most of his colleagues realized that if they ever had to do something big in a smart way, then its time had come, and they eagerly volunteered participation.

Seth went a step ahead and organized colloquium with the staff of one of the largest consumer goods manufacturers to make his people see how other industries were dealing with similar problems. It widened their perspective and also clarified some of the implementation issues. It confirmed his next level of assumption that the phenomenon of supply-demand mismatch and poor supply reliability existed across industries, although a bit too much in pharma.

The team in the war room started sequencing activities of the project. They roughly scheduled the activities; and took care to leave space for learning and correction on the way.

I made it known to Seth that his team had a single goal, although alternatives to reach that goal could be several. The path that they were taking would be revised on the go, since they were charting into unknown transformational journey. As they moved ahead, and as and when they would face a problem, they needed to have faith in their experience, intuition and analytical power to invent their steps.

In fact, I warned his team to be aware of the dynamics of change management, as they were dealing with a live system. "There will be several unknown hurdles on the way, but the secret of change management is in constantly inventing new rules to resolve the problems and coming out victorious over them quickly," he had started saying this to his colleagues.

For implementing the initiative successfully, he also foresaw the need for a dramatic change in attitude and culture of Terra Pharma that would be less dependent on contemplation and forecasting but on experimentation, fact finding and execution rigor. Knowing the existing culture of Terra Pharma very well, he was actually seeking to change the DNA of his organization.

After taking commitments from the team, Seth moved over to implementation which traditionally had been the sore spot of such initiatives in Terra Pharma. He also ensured that necessary infrastructure was in place to facilitate commitment of the team.

Seth got onto his work. Talking to people, detailing and understanding the way not only production but individual blocks in the plant work, and the rules that govern Terra Pharma.

Every day, his team faced challenges and obstacles; young and old alike joined together determined to find a solution, debating issues, generating ideas, writing down new rules, forming policies, working through cross functional teams, hand holding the operational teams to redefine their practices, metrics, roles and responsibilities... and all the time, Seth was listening, thinking and doing with his team.

Before he took over as the CEO of Terra Pharma, Seth had participated in several improvement projects. But this one was altogether of different size and impact.

His guesstimate did show him a huge scope for performance improvement. However, he was wary of giving his people a large numerical target and a hard coded timeline. From past experience, Seth knew about the negative impact of being paranoid about the numerical goals and time lines of such projects. Rather, he felt that it was good to be directionally clear. He made his team to be meticulous and diligent in achieving smaller weekly milestones; and placed a rigorous review mechanism to make them realistic about the ground realities and the gaps in their capabilities.

He did not give any indication that he was the boss and that it was not his job to know details. He visited plants, distributors and customers, to convince them on piloting the new concept. He stood by them to see that the first few pilots were successful and institutionalized.

The company was due to change several business rules, probably many more than it did in the entire 25 year history. With the air charged; people had begun seeing eye-to-eye and were all ears to new ideas.

Of course, during this period, some people who could not bear the heightening transparency, crumbling hierarchy, evaporating bureaucracy and focused accountability, left mid way. But like a rolling stone, his team had gathered huge momentum.

Installing the New Paradigm

Building on Intuition and Coming out of Chaos

Terra Pharma's team started the new initiative at its largest setup, the Sanovi Plant. Its immediate goal was to prevent stock outs. Hence Tony's team redesigned the desired level of stocks based on the recent consumption pattern and the lead time of SKUs.

Due to the new estimates, the desired levels (targets) of the stocks for quite a few SKUs zoomed up significantly, compared to the existing desired levels.

An increase in desired level of stocks across several SKUs meant an addition of 60 percent batches into the production pipeline (Figure 4.1). It seemed that the plant could achieve a high availability of its products only by processing these batches.

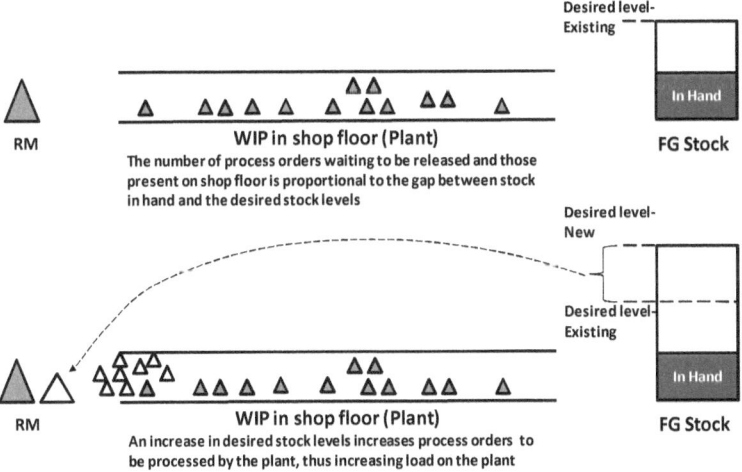

Figure 4.1 Products for which desired stock levels increased as per the new design, needed additional process orders to match the increased stock requirement

When the team began scheduling of batches, it found that some SKUs had too much work in progress (WIP) compared to what was required to fill their respective stocks to the desired levels. On the other hand, several other SKUs had too less WIP compared to what was required to fill their respective stocks to the desired levels.

Thus, there was a gross mismatch between what was needed in the market (as indicated by low stock levels) and what was being worked upon in the shop floor.

Visualizing Likely Chaos in the Plant

Ali realized the danger of taking additional 60% of load. He thought, "My staff is already overworked. If we allow this additional load, all of its time will be wasted only in administrating process orders than processing them. The process orders would flood the plant with unwanted activities and run it into chaos; and our lead time will go for a toss."

Then, he approached his colleagues to explain his thought process. He said, "You know, the presence of process orders in our plant, for that matter those in the rest of the supply chain, represents a situation similar to that of the traffic on the road. When you drive from home to our office, say on Queen's Road, in the morning at 7:30AM, you reach here in 20 minutes. But when you leave home at around 8:00AM, you take more than 60 minutes. Actually, sometime, for every minute's delay past 8 AM, for the next half an hour, you get late by 2 minutes. Why?"

Everybody looked at him with rapt attention. "Between 8-9 AM, you have far more number of vehicles on the road, and so when you get onto the road, you are behind several more vehicles than when you leave home at 7:30AM. This is the theory of Queuing. When there are more vehicles on the road, the traffic pace slows down, the average speed reduces dramatically and every small deviation, e.g. stoppage, turning, breakdown, overtaking, accident etc, magnifies into elongated delays. It causes you to take more than double the time to reach office than you would otherwise take in a streamlined and light traffic situation."

He continued, "That's exactly what happens in the plant. It has a capacity to deliver batches at a certain speed. A batch, say in our case, takes 60 days from entry to exit. Now, if we have too many batches inside, then a particular batch will have to wait behind a queue of other batches that wait for the same operation. Thus, the lead time of the new batch extends by a minimum of the longest queue in front of different operations, although the situation would be worse in reality."

Ali's vast experience enabled him to put the undesired effect of the new design in perspective and demand a careful consideration.

Tony pitched in and said, "Ali, your analogy is correct. If we add 60% more orders to the already busy shop floor, the queue in front of various operations will increase; and for sure, our lead time will go for a toss. Of course, you may choose to activate some of the machines that are currently off, and put a few more resources to move things faster. But given the quantum of additional orders that our new design of stock releases, we can expect the process orders to be far too late by the time they are completed."

Seth looked at Ali and asked, "Ali, How much productivity and capacity you can increase immediately? 10, 15 percent!"

Ali looked at his people and said, "We already have a portfolio of improvement projects under Lean and Six Sigma initiative. They do promise substantial benefits, but will take quite some time to see light of the day. Frankly speaking, as a team we are still learning these techniques."

"Oh! I was thinking if a bit of improvement in productivity would reduce the load..." said Seth.

Tony interrupted Seth and said, "Seth! It is not necessary that reducing the load a little would reduce lead time to the desired degree. We would need substantial improvement in productivity, which is not possible in a short time and without heavy trade-offs and burn-outs."

"Why do you say so?" asked Seth.

"Because, lead time is not a linear function of load."

He walked up to the white board, drew a curve (Figure 4.2) and said, "Based on the Chaos Theory, for a load beyond say 80% of the normal capacity of the plant, *the Lead Time would deteriorate exponentially [8]*, jeopardizing availability. And, we are certainly talking about much more than 80 percent load when the 60 percent additional load is considered on the existing one."

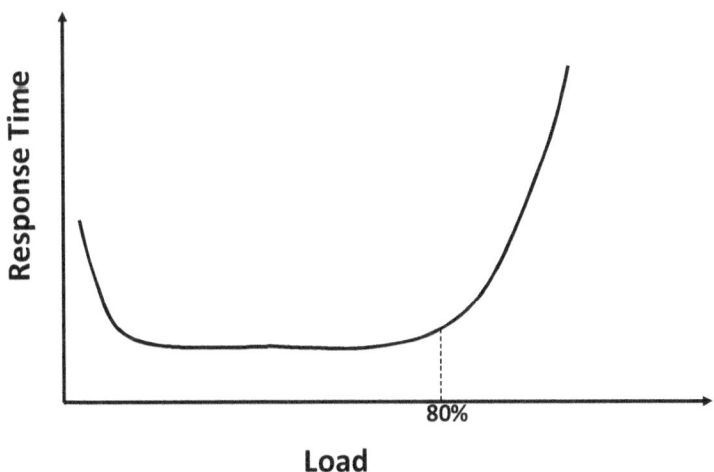

Figure 4.2 If the plant is loaded beyond 80% of its capacity, the lead time grows exponentially with the load, and operating at such high levels of load may force it to compromise on reliability of supply

"My goodness!" said Seth, understanding the danger they were getting into.

"And so, if we have an overload of 60%, we are on the right side of the curve. That is why you said that by tinkering just a bit on the capacity or load will not help. We are way off into chaos."

Seth always appreciated Tony's insights on things that were intriguing for people who were occupied in their day-to-day activities. Tony came from a family of statistical experts. His dad worked for the National Statistical Authority, his mom was a prominent economist and his siblings were deeply engaged in complex statistical phenomena related to meteorological predictions, population growth and global warming. Tony had a way of getting into details and building insights that often provided significant organizational benefits. He was one of the most valued members of Terra Pharma's leadership team.

Seth was confident that the new design of the supply chain was in the right direction. He needed to keep the design intact. Perhaps the analysis following resizing of stock levels revealed the gap between the current and the desired way of working. To take care of that, perhaps something else was required in implementation, about which he did not have any idea at this stage.

He knew that the existing productivity levels in the Pharma Industry were very low. Utilization of most of the equipments was just around 30%. And, every time he questioned his people, he would hear, "This is how the Pharma Industry works and 30 percent utilization is the norm."

Figures were readily available to validate utilization numbers. For example, in several of their blister packaging machines, it was normal for machines to be interrupted more than 100 times a day, for some reason or the other. This would make the stop time of machines to shave off over 30 percent of the scheduled time, while the product changeover and cleaning of these machines would consume another 30 percent of the time.

"We have so many SKUs and there are so many changeovers. We have so much online documentation and quality checks, we can't go beyond this level. Going beyond 30% utilization will only mean compromising on quality and regulatory standards. We do not want to have any problem with regulatory agencies," he had heard this quite often.

He had full faith in Ali's team that had identified projects to improve productivity by using Lean and Six Sigma techniques. And there was always a temptation to latch onto these techniques. Over lunch, he had another discussion with Ali about productivity improvement possibilities. But seeking quick improvements that would absorb the impulse of 60 percent overload was too big a risk to take up. *It would sap too much energy of the organization, and perhaps might call for taking unwanted risks.* He did not want to push Ali's team too much.

Making a Strategic Choice

Later on, Seth met his strategy team. He had already shared the Business Model Canvas with them, and set them up to work on innovating the model. He briefed them about the difficulties faced by the operational team. The strategy team concurred with the likely risk of creating chaos in the plant, but urged him to stick with the new design of the stocks. The meeting led to him making an interim decision of applying the new system first on a part of the product portfolio (high margins or fast movers).

The team also suggested that he move towards the target of availability in a graded way and start at an absolute 80 percent levels instead of 100 percent, which was still significantly higher than the then 55 percent level of availability. Thus, the strategy team helped him in setting the near-term achievable goal for his project.

> **Definition**
>
> % Availability = 100% - % Stocked out SKUs

Given this situation, they were looking at 80 percent as the first milestone for availability.

Now, based on the agreed logic of improving availability of drugs, it was important for the team to give higher priority to the products that had dangerously low 'stocks in hand'. This would also align the priority definition from both customer and organization perspective.

It took quite a while to segregate the list of high margin and low margin products. Each team, i.e. from Sales, Marketing, Strategy, Manufacturing and Delivery, had its own definition of high margin products. Several lists floated around. Seth looked into everyone's argument and then led them to a consensus.

Two lists were formed, each defined with respect to the money made (margins) during the past four quarters. The first group consisted of the fast movers, while the second group was made up of the rest (the majority) of the product portfolio.

It became clear to the team that since the first group of products had higher potential to increase margins of the plant, it might be good to first stabilize this group of products based on the new design of stocks.

They re-looked at the design of the stocks with a bias towards the fast movers. This they did by designing the desired stock levels of the first group optimistically, while those of the second group a bit pessimistically.

They also found that several of the second group of products were often not required in a hurry and customers were willing to wait a bit longer. In any case, performance of these products would not be affected more adversely than it was already.

This consideration reduced the net overload on the plant to 30 percent. Based on Tony's explanation of Chaos Theory, even this overload was dangerous.

Seth was not very comfortable with the overload. Although, the team worked out in detail how to deal with the SKUs by dividing them into two separate groups, he felt that it would be too difficult to isolate attention of people on day-to-day basis, since the two groups of products shared quite a bit of common resources and policies. He was worried if this over simplification would create dependent complexities.

He said to himself, "If possible, we should avoid grouping of SKUs and must apply a single rule to all SKUs in one go. And, I would not mind reversing my decision of looking at the portfolio as consisting of two groups."

Later, he sat with Tony to get a handle on the chaos phenomenon caused due to the exponential characteristics between load and response time (Lead Time). He also opened up a discussion on his dilemma of implementing the new stock design across the SKUs or limiting it to fast movers. He wanted to find a solution without compromising on the scope of products.

Tony took him inside the Chaos Curve, which opened up the concepts of 'Vicious Cycle' and 'Virtuous Cycle'.

The Vicious Cycle

Tony used the Chaos Curve he had drawn earlier and explained, "We have a situation where the number of work units increase within a short time. In such a short time, it is difficult to quickly reconfigure resources. Also, a significant effort (people's time) will be required in only dealing with logistics of process orders than doing the actual work on them. This includes activities such as arranging, moving, listing, counting, prioritizing, tracking, storing, retrieving, discussing, retesting and analyzing process orders."

He paused a while, raised his thumb and continued, "The point I am making is that if there are too many process orders open in production floor, every order cries for the attention of the staff. Despite the use of best management system, it becomes impossible for people not to pay attention to a work that is waiting, without disturbing the work that is in progress. Further, when a process order invites attention, there would often be enough reasons to pick and choose work on inconsistent priority and individual choice. In turn, it leads to breaking the rhythm of the plant and distracting people. It thus leads to *bad multitasking* and swells the work in progress (WIP)."

"But it is well known that multi-skilling or multitasking is good, it adds to significant flexibility in the staff," said Seth.

Running his fingers through his shoulder-length hair, Tony said, "Yes, multi-skilling is good for an individual as well as for the company. But switching between tasks midway leads to *bad multitasking* and tremendous delays in response time."

He took a white sheet of paper, started sketching and said, "Let's suppose a team has three tasks each taking up 15 days to perform, (Figure 4.3). Often the team receives preferences from several directions and often it itself has certain priorities and likings. So, let's think that it is working on task-1, and it finds a good reason (often difficult to validate) to switch over to task-2. After 5 days, it stops task-1 midway, and starts working on task-2. However, very soon, it finds another reason to switch over to task-3 by stopping task-2 midway. This phenomenon of changing priorities takes place several times, before all tasks are somehow delivered. Now look at the completion day of these tasks. Although each task was of 15 days, they were delivered on 35th, 40th and 45th days. In reality, none of the tasks would be finished by even 45th day, since there are delays associated with switching between tasks. In terms of delivery performance, it means poor lead times and poor due date performance. However, if the team does not break tasks in between, it could have completed tasks on 15th, 30th and 45th day. This is the effect of *bad multitasking* on the lead time [9]."

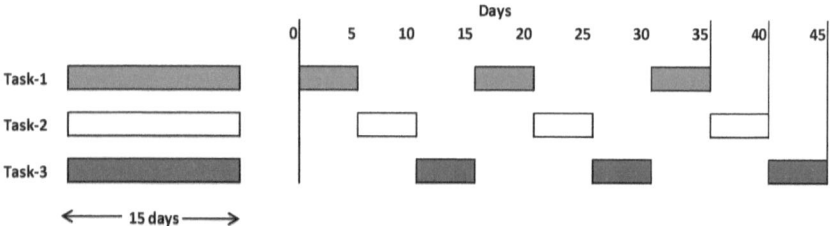

Figure 4.3 Bad multitasking is a key reason for poor lead time

He looked into Seth's eyes and said, "This is exactly what happens when there are too many batches or process orders opened in front of the staff to process. Because of the multiple options and the unchallenged changing priorities, too many local and short term decisions are forced and chaos builds up. As a result most of the orders are delivered late. Actually, in this example, the tasks would be delivered much later than it seems to take."

Seth said, "I see. Bad multitasking must be a key reason for poor lead time."

"Indeed!" said Tony. He got back to the Chaos Curve and circled the right knee of the curve (Figure 4.4).

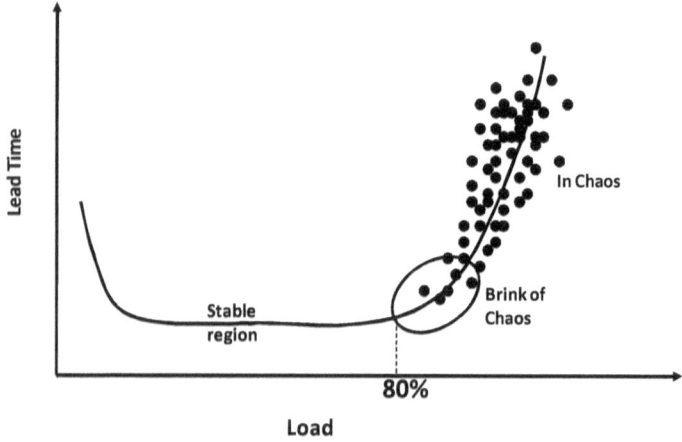

Figure 4.4 Most of the traditionally managed organizations are at the brink of chaos, if not in chaos

Then he said, "It is a very profound theory that just around this knee, the increase of chaos is dramatic and the complete process becomes unmanageable and complicated. I guess that with a lead time of 60 days, we are already into the chaotic zone, and are somehow able to deliver process orders."

Seth said, "Now, if we add more load, and even if we think ourselves to be at the brink of chaos, the system will bump into full chaos and the lead time will shoot up. If the lead time shoots up, process orders will become further late. This will place more pressure on people. More pressure on people will only create more chaos and our problems will never end."

"Yes, this is a typical Vicious Cycle [10]; where the system is trapped into a chaotic loop and the situation increasingly deteriorates, irrespective of the amount of good work put in. Under such a situation, *use of even the most sophisticated tool of productivity improvement will not enhance the performance quickly*," said Tony as he returned to his seat.

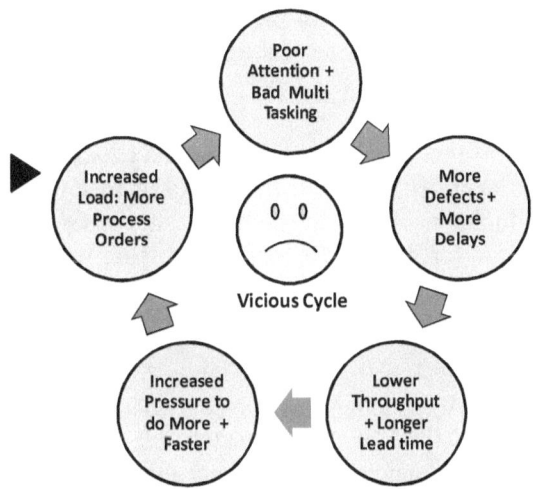

Figure 4.5 Increasing the load beyond a level leads the plant into a Vicious Cycle.

"So, once we fall into the chaotic trap, any amount of productivity improvement will actually not help. So, we can't expect much from the standalone productivity improvement projects of Ali's team," Seth inferred.

Intervention to Create a Virtuous Cycle

That evening, Seth and Tony called me over a teleconference. They briefed about the likely chaotic situation if they went ahead with the new stock design.

And then, Seth said, "We resized our stocks based on reality of the market and the plant. However, it would push our plant into chaos... We are struggling to marry the information from the new design of stocks with the load versus lead time characteristics. That is... we are not able to come out of the Vicious Cycle?"

I said, "There is a general belief that a Vicious Cycle carries the clue for its Virtuous Cycle. And, the way to come out of a Vicious Cycle is to identify a corresponding Virtuous Cycle and provide a policy *intervention* accordingly. In fact this is the only way to come out of the Vicious Cycle."

"I see!" exclaimed Seth while absorbing the new knowledge.

"But where do we begin?" asked Tony.

"Trace the Chaos Curve in reverse direction." I said without giving a deep thought.

"Reverse direction!" Tony sought clarification.

"Yes, start from the highpoint of the curve and go down. And closely observe as you move past the knee of the curve." I said.

"OK. Let's give it a try," said Tony.

They got back to the white board, redrew the Chaos Curve and then, while tracing the exponential curve from bottom to top, Tony said, "If chaos is likely to be accentuated such that it causes an exponential increase in lead time for just a little increase in load, we need to think in the reverse direction."

"Yes, as DJ said...," murmured Seth.

Tony marked a point on the curve (Figure 4.6) and said, "Yes. Say that we are at point A, which is 100 percent load, and for example, it corresponds to a lead time of approximately 60 days. When we trace back the asymptote, we reach point B, where the lead time reduces by about 70percent (more than $2/3^{rd}$) for a mere reduction in load by 30 percent (less than $1/3^{rd}$)."

"Yes...," said Seth.

Tony continued, "Following what DJ said, if around the knee, the lead time *increases dramatically due to a small increase in the load, the reverse of this process must* also be true, i.e. the lead time can be *decreased dramatically* by reducing the load by a much lower proportion. This means that if we find the logic to reduce the load by 1/3rd, we can reduce the lead time by around 40 days."

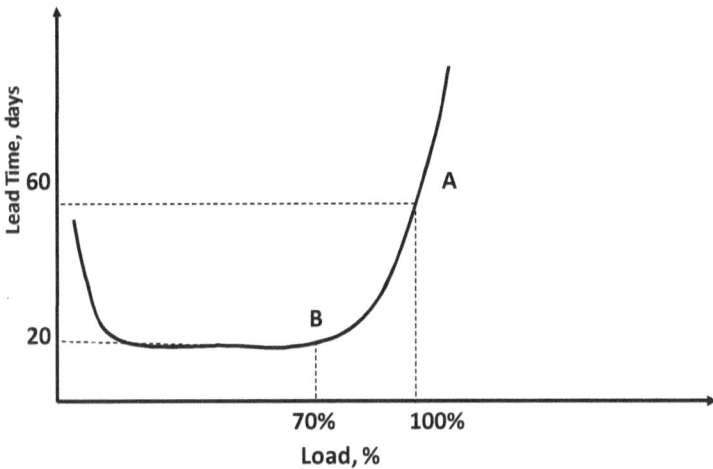

Figure 4.6 If a plant is in chaos, then a significant reduction in performance can be obtained by reducing load by a comparatively smaller proportion

"Looks like, the knee holds the inflection point..." said Seth, in an unknown excitement.

Then, Tony scribbled the following.

> **Lead Time of the First 70% load = 20 days**
> **Lead Time with the remaining 30% load = 60 days**

Tony asked Seth, "What does this mean?"

While Seth was still grasping the meaning, Tony answered it himself, "It means that today, the additional 30 percent load causes a 40 day impact on the lead time. Now if we just delay introduction of this 30 percent of load into the shop floor, we could produce the first 70 percent load at 20 day lead time AND the next 30 percent load in a similar shorter time. All in all, we could process the 100 percent load in much less than 60 days."

"Aha!" Seth was overwhelmed.

He said, "So, it means that instead of releasing the entire load at once, we must limit the load, through a policy, first to 70 percent, and then release the rest of 30 percent."

"Absolutely!" Tony exclaimed.

"Now it looks as if, if we could somehow limit the load on the shop floor by 30 percent, it is reasonable to expect reduction in the lead time by much more than 30 percent. The improved lead time will further reduce the load that in turn will trigger the Virtuous Cycle. Our job is to see that we continue to be in a stable situation without getting into chaos," said Tony and threw himself on the chair.

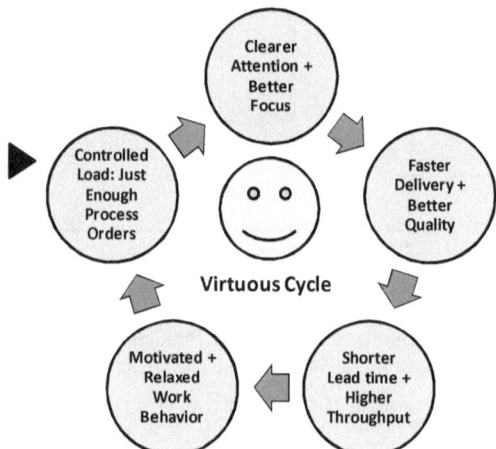

Figure 4.7 In order to improve performance significantly, the Vicious Cycle must give way to the Virtuous Cycle

"So, we limit the release of our process orders to just enough numbers, so that there is a clearer attention and better focus on them. This will lead to faster deliveries and less quality problems. As a result, our lead times will be shorter, while throughput would be higher. By experiencing such positive effects, the staff will be better motivated and relaxed to give its best," saying so, Seth completed the description of the desired Virtuous Cycle, Figure 4.7.

"Now I understand, why they say that *for an organization to be on a sustainable growth curve, its Business Model must have at least one Virtuous Cycle*," said Seth in a relaxed tone, as the 'Circle of Value Flow' drawn on the Business Model Canvas by Adam kept appearing in front of his eyes.

Then he asked, "Now, how do we accomplish this 'sudden or instantaneous' reduction in the lead time?"

"I think that now we can marry the new knowledge (Virtuous Cycle), with the exercise we did for stock redesign. It must trim the negative effects of the new design," said Tony.

"Incidentally, we had redesigned our stock levels with an *anticipation* that it would take an average lead time of 60 days, and therefore, the suggestion was to size the stock levels to approximately two months of consumption," Tony explained.

"Yes," said Seth.

Tony got up again and wrote the word '*Anticipation*' on the white board, and drew a big circle around it.

Before Seth could say something, Tony asserted, "Since we are talking about *anticipated* lead time; based on our discussion so far on the chaos phenomenon, it is fair to *anticipate* reducing the lead time significantly, if we reduce the load by 30 percent."

"Yes! Yes!" said Seth, while expecting another jolt of insight from Tony, and then asked, "By what amount can we bring the lead time down?" asked Seth.

"There is no straightforward way to get an accurate number in chaos phenomenon. And it is good to be approximately correct than wasting time in achieving too much accuracy. It is certain that the improvement will be substantial," said Tony.

Tony said excitedly, "If it is so, we must design our stock levels for around 30% of current lead time, i.e., 20 days and not 60 days, and that in effect will reduce the load substantially."

"WOW!!! We intervene to design the stock levels for 20 days (i.e., 2/3rd of the current lead time), which will bring the load down substantially and therefore the lead time," Seth got up as he internalized the concept.

With a glimmer in his eyes, he said, "It is quite an amazing argument, but is a simple way of looking at things."

"Yes, but remember that the phenomenon is quite nonlinear and for most of our folks who are used to linear thinking, it is not as straightforward," said Tony.

Agreement on Stock Design

Next day, based on the new knowledge, the manufacturing and delivery teams reworked the desired levels of stocks.

Being paranoid about the availability of SKUs, the team could muster strength to size the stocks for no less than 40 days, expecting to bring the system to just around the brink of chaos. The projected load on the plant was thus reduced to almost its AS WAS level; i.e., no additional load.

When the revised design of the desired stock levels came out, Ali's intuition told him that the then performance of the plant was poor also because there were too many process orders in the WIP. Of these WIP orders, there were batches of certain products in the shop floor that were not needed to be there at that time, as per the new design of stock levels.

They were, in fact, released into the shop floor earlier than they were due.

The team went into the outcome of the new design exercise. It fished out the products with adequate stocks. It found that *approximately 10 percent of the load on the plant was 'phantom' load that was unwanted WIP*. Practically, it meant that this 10 percent of phantom load could be frozen without any negative effect on performance in near term. The team decided to *quarantine* these batches till their demand would kick in.

It then occurred to the team that the net load after carrying out redesign of the stocks was actually 10 percent less than the then existing load. This was a remarkable revelation to Ali, and he rushed into Seth's cabin to brief him about the new reality.

Seth said, "Somehow, I was not willing to compromise on the design and wanted to have it tested. It is good that the solution has surfaced out on its own."

Ali said, "This means that performance (Availability and Lead Time) of the plant can now improve significantly, since the load is less; and we can soon have a very healthy stock situation."

Seth looked at his laptop and said, "Tony is ready for the roll out and is asking to kick off on Monday; is it ok for you? Is your team ready?"

Ali said, "Yeah! We are mentally ready, but need to roll out instructions specifically for scheduling, warehouse, QC and QA teams in the plant."

He continued, "The key message is about giving priority to the first group of products, especially those that are in danger; we have around significant conflict with the second group of products on certain resources."

Raising his eyebrows, Seth said, "Not a surprise, Ali!" He then shared his dilemma on dealing with all products together or in two separate groups.

He said, "Just check how far the two groups interfere. Do we need to swap products between the groups such that *the flow of both groups are independent*. May be only by doing so, our improvement methodology would be replicable."

Ali said, "We have already worked that out a bit though. Nevertheless, we will have this classification completed by tomorrow. Then, we will revalidate some products on alternative machines."

Seth said, "I see."

The War Room

Within a few days, Seth assembled a dedicated project management team and nominated his Executive Assistant Rita to manage the roll out of Life2.0. Immediately, Rita and her associates moved out of the corporate office and relocated into the admin block of the plant. She set two days and the weekends to kick start the new system.

Her team began discussions with the staff and the managers to understand the way work was actually being done. They reviewed the First Group of SKUs and the exact status of process orders. A majority of the SKUs showed quite a regular consumption pattern. However, frequent occasions of stock-outs were also clearly visible.

By Monday morning, the team needed to be ready with a mechanism to identify batches to be produced in accordance with the new design of stocks. This would help the staff in the plant to start following the new priority system.

By Friday evening, Susan, Rita's software development associate, had created a small Java App. It picked up real time data from the ERP system and displayed stock levels, WIP and status of process orders. She filtered the data set and segregated the SKUs in the order of 'the danger of being stocked out'. These SKUs had far less stocks in hand compared to the desired levels.

Rita suggested, "Let us flag these endangered SKUs. They must get higher priority across the supply chain." Susan marked these SKUs in red, and made a note there to indicate the urgency of the 'Endangered' SKUs'.

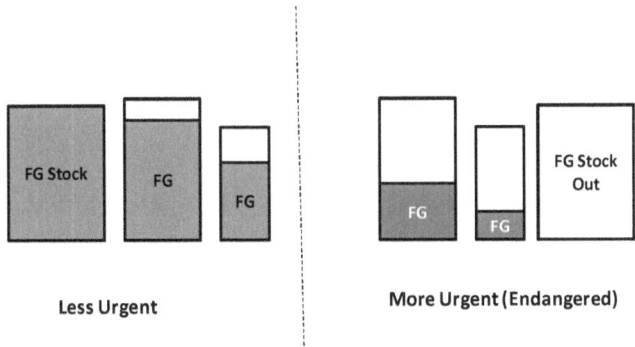

Figure 4.8 Urgency based upon level of unavailable stocks

Ali felt that it was a smart move.

The team found that for some of the products, too many batches were to be produced (as many as 30) and they barely had any stock in hand.

Siban, the planning guy from Rita's team, said, "If we try to produce so many batches of one endangered SKU, it will take a long time to fill. And by then, other healthy SKUs flowing through the same route might become *endangered*."

Susan understood the implication. "This means that we are dealing with shared resources. So, we can't give the same priority to all the orders within an endangered SKU."

"The resources must be time shared between different sets of orders of different endangered SKUs based on some rule. We therefore need to define within each 'endangered' SKU, how many orders should be considered high priority," said Siban.

Susan continued pointing at the list of orders, "For example, the orders which fill bottom 30% of desired stock levels could be the 'real' endangered orders - Figure 4.9. Then, for an SKU, it may be a good idea to give higher priority to these 30% of the orders filling the bottom of the desired stock level over orders filling the rest of the 70%. Thus, if we have two endangered SKUs, say A and B, once the first 30% orders of SKU-A is completed, we must then switch over to the 'endangered orders' of SKU-B."

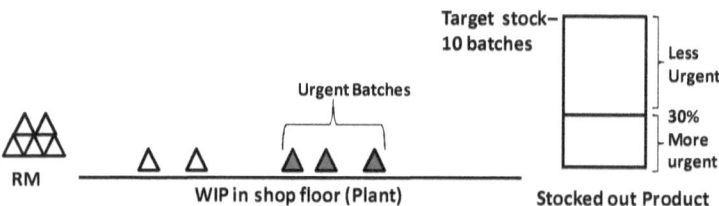

Figure 4.9 When multiple products flow through the same resource, it is important to define urgency at 'Order/ Batch level'

To illustrate the concept, Susan walked up to the whiteboard and quickly sketched an example (Figure 4.10).

She said, "Two products, Glimepiride and Cetrizine, pass through a common set of coating machines CMY-10-12. Both the products are in the danger of being stocked out. If the plant chooses to give priority to Glimepiride and plans to produce the required 23 batches, then considering per batch coating time of approximately 24 hrs, it would take around 23 days. But by then, Cetrizine would stock out."

"Twenty three days is too long a time!" said Rita.

Then she said, "Yes. Instead, the plant can take a local decision to give higher priority to, say, 10 batches of Glimepiride and then to, say, 6 batches of Cetrizine. Once high priority batches of Cetrizine are done, it can revert to Glimepiride; thus ensuring better availability of both products."

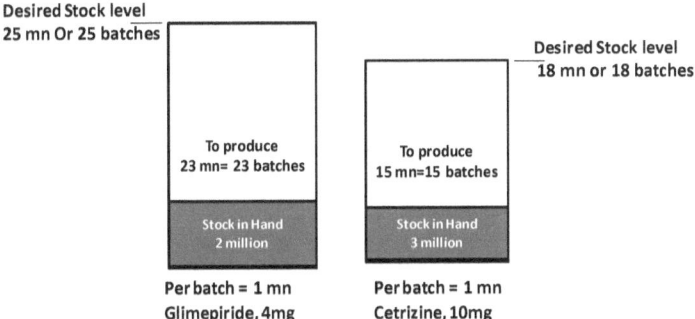

Figure 4.10 Prioritizing process orders (batches) is based on relative position of stocks

Siban was excited with the logic, and said, "This aspect is crucial, since there are multiple products that are in the danger of being stocked out. Regularly, a number of them would be competing to get into the same machines. *It is therefore important that 'urgency' be defined at process order level too.*"

Subsequently, scheduling and the delivery teams came to an agreement on the logic of prioritizing at process order levels. They looked at the time required to process the orders by critical resources. Then they compared the order backlogs of 'endangered' products. Subsequently, guidelines were created to estimate clubbing of batches for an endangered SKU before a switch could be made to take the process orders of the next endangered SKU. It ensured that just because of working on one SKU, several other SKUs did not become 'endangered'.

Figure 4.11 shows how the urgency of a set of process orders looked on Susan's computer screen.

Process Order #	Urgency	Product
N002543	Endangered	Cetrizine 10mg
N002570	Endangered	Cetrizine 10mg
N002556	Endangered	Omeprazole 20mg
N002577	Endangered	Omeprazole 20mg
N002523	Endangered	Glimepiride 4mg
N002554	Endangered	Glimepiride 4mg
N002588	Endangered	Glimepride 4mg
N002511	Endangered	Simvastatin 80mg
N002545		Cetrizine 10mg
N002590		Cetrizine 5mg
N002623		Omeprazole 20mg
N002643		Omeprazole 20mg
N002594		Glimepiride 4mg

Figure 4.11 Prioritization by process orders

By Saturday, the operational deck on Susan's computer screen looked magnificent. It could show the level of inventory across the supply chain. It could figure out not only the 'endangered products' but also the level of danger these products faced in terms of availability.

She could show Ali's team, at one go, all the endangered SKUs and process orders. She printed out the list; and the job was now simple for the scheduling team to identify SKUs to be taken on higher priority per machine.

Rita realized that the plant was widely spread out and the number of people who touched process orders flowing in the plant was large. She asked, "Susan, can we have this deck available to people across the plant *in real time?*"

Susan said, "Yes, we can do it, but need a couple of days to make it web enabled and have it validated by Mickey's team."

"Fine," replied Rita. She called Mickey to brief him about the new App and the help her team needed in making it available in real time across the plant.

In the meanwhile, Siban agreed to sit with Ramesh (the plant scheduler) to have a list of priority orders circulated to relevant staff over the e-mail first thing every morning. It was necessary that everybody clearly knew the batches that were expected at various nodes of the supply chain, and do enough preparation to move them faster.

In the meanwhile, Rita's team prepared a clear and bold communication about the new priority system. They highlighted how it impacted each function, right from the warehouse to the last operation in the shop floor. These functions also included quality assurance, quality control, engineering and housekeeping staff. It described the ways to deal with conflicts and mentioned whom to contact in case of doubt. The instructions were very clear on priority at process order level and about switching between SKUs.

Her associates along with Ali's production staff conducted face to face sessions with the plant staff, the whole 1500 of them. They took the staff through mock exercises before the system would go live on Monday morning. They prepared presentations, posters, work instructions, help notes, displays and banners; and had them placed across the plant. She knew that in the western plains, people were not used to ask for help, but rather try to solve the problems themselves. Hence, she did not want to risk overstepping; and placed management trainees across the plant with a clear communication to remain engaged with the staff in the shop floor.

What was looking like a simple concept of priority management was widening in its scope the moment it was interfaced with people and processes. Rita remembered Seth's warning, 'It is simple but not easy,' especially when she had 1500 people on this transformational exercise. The team was going for a big change from 'produce as much as you can' to 'produce as per single priority system'.

She realized what Tony used to say, 'Speed is OK, but we need velocity'. And the *single priority system provided the direction to the speed and turned it into velocity.*

Before she left for the day, she called Seth, Tony, Ali and Ranbir and updated them on the status. Everybody was pepped up and excited, and wanted to see action on Monday.

Scheduling @ the Speed of Light

Monday morning, Siban came early to office. Susan had left a note on his desk about a small software client she had loaded on Ramesh's desktop. Siban joined Ramesh, and in a moment, they saw the operational deck spread across 26" flat screen of Ramesh's industrial PC. It looked colorful and appealing.

Several process orders colored red (urgent) were screaming for immediate attention. Siban helped Ramesh filter them out and run the routing algorithm. Several of the orders got allocated to machines, while others were shown in their respective queues. This was a superb snapshot of the plant. It showed where an order stood and also where the most urgent orders stacked up. The snapshot closely resembled the screen of the SCADA system that the engineering department used in managing the plant facility.

Ramesh downloaded the list of allocated orders into an XL™ sheet, and organized them. Then, he shot a mail across the plant, informing everybody about the launch of the new way of working and attached a brief on the priority system. He was excited since the priority of the batches to be processed was unambiguous.

After sending the mail, they got up and moved towards the canteen to build on their morning energy. While sipping his favorite green tea, Ramesh thought how different life had been for him till last week. He would come to the office in the morning and would have mails from all over: Marketing, Sales, Delivery, Warehouse, Quality, Production, Planning and Dispatch guys. Everybody would have a request to change priority of one or more batches. He would then spend 4 hours till noon talking to the people one by one, understanding the urgency and scheduling batches for production. Every morning he would work under terrific pressure. And, people in the plant knew that his time was precious, any delay from his side would delay the plan for the day and everybody would suffer.

But that day had had a rather cool start, thanks to the 'single priority system' and the speed with which Rita's team handheld him.

As they saw more people entering the canteen, they moved out wishing them a good day. On the way, they took a glance at colorful posters that were depicting messages about the simplified way of prioritizing process orders. It looked like a celebration, and they felt good.

The War Room had now shifted into the shop floor. And, the 'Sanovi Plant', as it was called after the village that had transformed into a buzzing town, became the most focused location for Terra Pharma. By Monday morning, even the sales staff, distributors and clients knew that there was something new at 'Sanovi'.

The message from Rita's team to the outside world was well tempered: "The folks in the plant are working on improving flow of orders, and it would definitely be not worse than the current situation."

She did not want to make any tall claims; rather, as Seth said, "Just give the direction and let people align. We will then move one step at a time and let the journey continue to bring out the results."

She wanted to take measureable small steps that would have significant impact.

When she returned to the War Room on Monday morning, she was very happy to see that Ramesh was pretty comfortable doing the prioritization on his own. After dumping her bag in the War Room, she ran into the plant, where the real action was. As she walked by, she found the management trainees spread across the plant.

Near the entry door of each operation, she saw SKU name, batch number and priority of the batch. Several of these displays were in red, and she understood that the staff therein was working on high priority batches. The walls of the corridors were prominently speaking of the priority system and the white boards were announcing induction program for the staff. At the far end of the corridor, a 42" LCD screen was relaying information on the new priority system.

She walked towards Production Office in the South Wing.

It was the first time she had entered the Sanovi Plant on an assignment. She had been with Terra Pharma for over nine years, working with the C-Team on business strategy. This project was altogether in a different domain, amongst different people and with different rules she was least familiar with. Seth had a big role in convincing her to take up this challenging initiative that he called as 'Operationalizing the new Business Model'.

On Friday, Seth's office had communicated her elevation to anchor this high impact project called Life2.0. The project was aimed to change the way work was being done not only at 'Sanovi' but across Terra Pharma. He had written in his message that Terra Pharma had recognized the need to leverage operational excellence to drive its competitive strategy.

Seth had told her, "This is not too different from what you have been doing; rather, it is a logical step forward. This project has the potential to add sharpness and realism into your work on strategy. This is unique, since very few people understand the connection between Corporate Strategy and Operations."

In fact, she was surprised when Seth made the offer to her. But knowing Seth and the impact that she could make through this project, she grabbed it with both hands.

Fortunately, all functional heads were in full support of her nomination. Each one of them had already counseled her and helped in making her understanding of the operational issues better.

As she entered the Production Office, Raman, the Production Manager, walked forward and welcomed her. She exchanged greetings, looked around the room and wished all with a smile. On the wall a colorful grid was displayed. It was flashing the resources being loaded with red orders.

Raman gave her some statistics and said, "We have around 300 red orders in the pipeline, and considering the queues, we have allocated 50 onto different machines. All the red orders have been pushed in front of the queues, where ever they are."

She learnt that the material dispensing team was giving first priority to red orders, which meant that the priority is controlled at the point where the batches entered the plant. At each machine within the plant, red batches were being accorded the first priority. Post packing, red orders were being accorded preference in loading and dispatching by trucks.

Raman informed her, "Now, the QC staff will sample and analyze those batches first that are in red and in front of the queue for manufacturing; while QA staff will allocate its resources on priority to those areas that have red orders to be processed. Engineering staff is adding one more layer to their SCADA system. It will pick up data from Susan's deck and overlay upon the plant infrastructure model. This will then allow them to know those equipments and facilities that are being fed by the 'endangered' orders. Then, they will be able to give closer attention to such equipments which, if stopped, would jeopardize the flow of orders in the shop floor."

"Excellent!" she could not stop expressing her amazement.

Almost every function was represented there, and one by one, everybody was introduced to her by Raman. Of course, Siban and Susan were also present. To her, Terra Pharma was looking bigger and far more powerful inside the plant, with so many experts together accounting for 1000s of years of experience. The reality of people power inside the plant dwarfed her earlier impression of Terra Pharma seen from the ivory tower of the Corporate Office.

Raman told her, "Normally, we meet in this room every day for around 60 minutes to take stock of the situation and prepare for the day. Today is a special day and I wanted everybody in the plant to get acquainted with the new priority system and also meet your team. The new system gives everybody the same view of the priorities and resolves conflicts quickly."

That day, the plant team felt that things looked simpler, and with priority being very clear, they had enough time to focus on real issues of production.

Aligning Upstream

Every day, Ramesh would download the list of process orders, sort them as per the priority system, and send it across to respective functions. Then, he would attend the morning priority meeting, where Rita's team often joined him. The process orders were being released, produced and dispatched as per the new priority system. The stocks in the warehouses were gradually building up for some of the endangered products. The plant staff was talking, pushing and working on red orders across functions. Everywhere, the talk centered on 'red' orders.

It was now 27 days since the Sanovi Plant launched Life2.0. The stocks were building up gradually, the work-centers were running red orders; but the number of red orders in the plant was not falling significantly.

On 28th day, Rita's team studied the trend of red orders. It found that while the total number of red orders in the system did not drop that significantly, not many red orders were being worked upon the machines. She learnt that sometimes, it was not possible to load a machine with a red order not just because it waited behind another red order to be completed, but for other reasons.

Her team figured out that while there was focus on pushing red orders faster, the raw materials (APIs and Exepients) as well as packing materials, were frequently stocking out. And hence, several of red orders were waiting for materials to be available. In fact, its WIP had started swelling up.

It became obvious that since the flow of some products had increased, the raw material stocks did not keep up the pace.

She realized the omission, "When we had redesigned the stock levels of finished goods, the desired stock levels for several products were revised upward. By logic, it was necessary to increase the desired stock levels of respective raw materials and packing materials as well."

Although Terra Pharma had a tendency of maintaining high raw material stocks, it did not take much time to reveal the *logical* hole there. Rita convened the SCM team and immediately put them to work on the redesign of input material stock based on lead time of suppliers and consumption pattern.

Tony had clarified, "We have materials with lead times as short as 1 day and as long as 6 months. We need to have some rationality in raw material stocks for long lead time items and those which are as costly as gold. We can't apply one rule for all."

His team came out with a scheme to rationalize stocks of input materials. For almost 70% of the materials, it decided that the stock levels would be in line with consumption and the supplier lead time. It adopted JIT method for items where suppliers could replenish daily. However, for long lead time items, especially those which came from abroad, had uncertainty in logistics and were too expensive, they used the traditional risk management techniques to plan their inventory.

With the new design of input material supply in place, the supply chain was aligned from end to end to follow the concept of supply based on consumption. However, one thing was still needed to plug the shortages of materials.

Data analysis carried out by Rita's team revealed that in addition to inadequate stock levels of input materials, the unreliability of suppliers was a key culprit. She also knew about this issue from her engagement with global supply chain forum, where Terra Pharma's entire supply chain performance was reviewed once a quarter.

"Unreliable supply of input materials is preventing us from following the priority system in the plant. We need to take immediate action to debottleneck and act on supplier end," said Tony.

"Who can help us out?" asked Rita

Tony replied, "We have a team of forty specialists from quality, process and logistics. They work with our suppliers and are responsible for qualifying their processes and approving partnerships. We immediately need to review supplier metrics to improve the flow of orders in the shop floor. Perhaps, it is time that we install some sort of SPC (Statistical Process Control) tools to improve process quality of suppliers. We will make supply reliability as the theme of this quarter's Suppliers Meet. In the interim, we will have suppliers sensitized and have a checklist in place to increase reliability of our buying process."

"Very good!"

"In the meanwhile, please brief Satyam, who heads supplier development group, about the new system. I would not mind him working closely with you till we come out winners," he said to Rita.

"Thank you. Let's get going," Rita acknowledged the good gesture from Tony. She moved quickly to co-ordinate with the SCM team and they started working feverishly on the new design of material supply system.

Rita's associates led the supply side process very well, and with Susan's help, they linked the data flow of batches into the plant with the purchase orders being placed on the suppliers. Susan also developed an interface for the suppliers to see real time status of stocks at the incoming warehouse of the Sanovi Plant, which gave them enough time for preparation. Tony's buyers too got a 'Buyer Deck' to view status of stocks, customized to their needs and embedded with their key metrics.

Satyam's team members were excited when they saw material requirements in direct alignment with the market demand. Now, it became so simple to prioritize their work. They were very happy since this got rid of the hassles of handling expediting calls from Sales, Delivery and Manufacturing teams. Now given the strong alignment across the supply chain, it was very clear where to expedite and where to negotiate for faster deliveries.

When Tony saw the Buyer's Deck on his laptop, he was delighted, and said, "I think that this is an awesome dashboard for buyers. It clearly tells the priority and, most importantly, the priority that you guys see is the priority of the plant and also of the sales. Perfect alignment - now no two teams have different priorities. Good bye to daily conflicts!"

The forty odd experts of Tony's team went around meeting their suppliers, educating them on the new process of replenishment and introducing the key supplier reliability metrics. They emphasized how it would align both sides and thus minimize conflicts. To their surprise, some of their suppliers, who were dealing with the FMCG sector, were already following similar methodology. Most of the suppliers readily accepted the offer, while the rest were handheld further to comply with the new priority system.

It took over a month for Rita to have the supply side design and methodology communicated within the organization. By the third month, they could see impact of the alignment on production.

During this time, a number of policies on supplier approval, manufacturing process, order handling, pricing, transportation, incoming acceptance and returns were significantly simplified [11]. It was a revelation for Satyam's team on how much inefficiency their system had inherited and the level of bottleneck it had created for the flow.

As soon as the flow of orders was established across the supply chain, the team also introduced the Second Group of products into the new system. This relieved the team from the conflicts involved in handling the portfolio of products in two separate groups. While doing this, they ensured that the WIP did not run into chaos. Thus, the Sanovi Plant was working on replenishment based on actual consumption across its portfolio of products. In the 1st quarterly review meeting of Life2.0, Rita unveiled the supply chain topology, as shown in Figure 4.12.

The Path   111

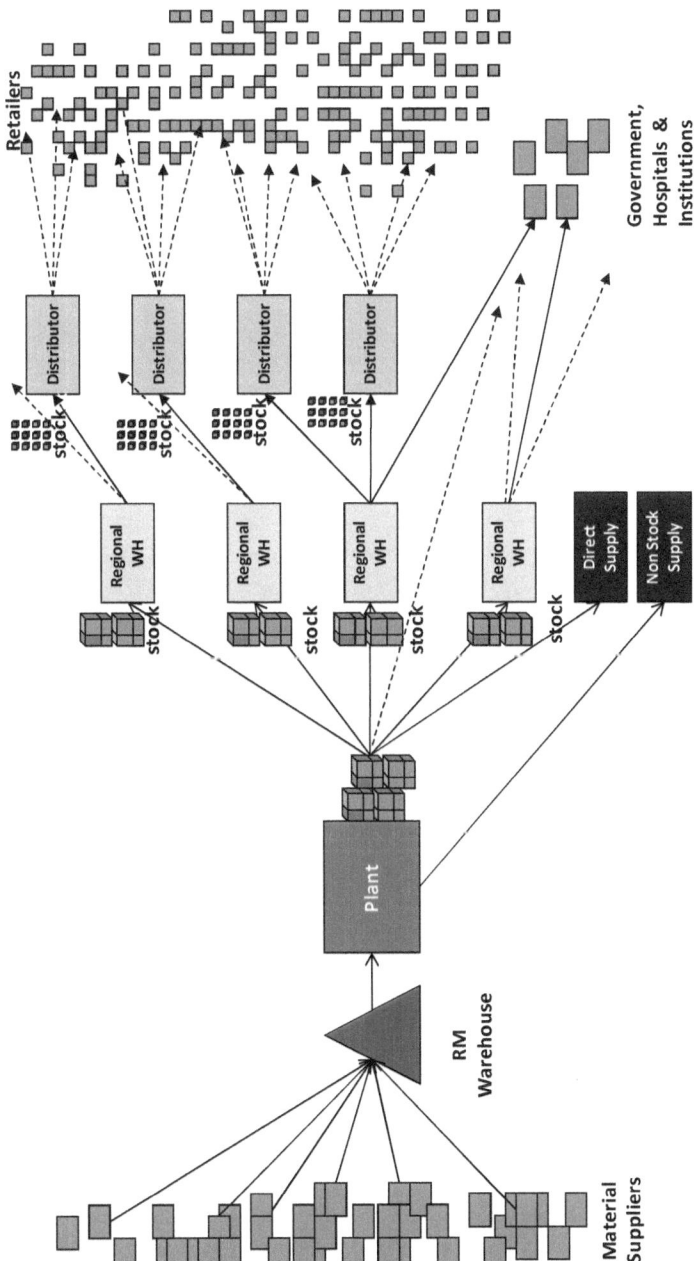

Figure 4.12 The supply chain of Terra Pharma

Nurturing the Right Behavior

Evidence of the Need for Behavior Change

After aligning supply of input materials to the consumption pattern of the finished goods, availability of raw materials improved significantly. Consequently, availability of finished goods stocks also improved by about 10%, though not as much as Seth had expected.

Seth, along with Rita's team reviewed the trends of operational metrics. The metrics included number of red orders, stock-out situation, lead time and inventory. He also called Ali and Tony to join them in understanding the reality.

While they acknowledged the improvement in raw material supply, they found that the percentage of red process orders in the plant was still large enough and was creating too many urgencies. Often, Ali and Tony found themselves spending a significant part of their time in fire fighting and unable to focus on strategic issues. It was important that the number of red process orders decreased significantly and the plant was brought to a more stable environment.

Problems a Plenty

Rita's team was involved in tracking movement of red orders. It seemed that every day, there were more than 30 different reasons to explain, why some red orders were not being worked upon. These reasons included:

1. Machine break down	8. Delay in document release
2. Unstable process	9. Renewal of license
3. Unavailability of raw materials	10. Delay in sample analysis
4. Input material quality problem	11. Batch out of Trend
5. People unavailability	12. Missing Spare parts
6. Batch out of specification	13. Delay of dispatch truck
7. Unavailability of packaging labels	14. And more than 20 other reasons

During the discussion, Raman said, "We have too many issues in the plant. Despite our best effort, we are not able to reduce disruptions to the flow of batches. Various issues prop up at different places, at different times and in different form. We have a tough time managing so many problems."

Seth said, "While things will often go wrong, correcting all of them together may not be in our hands. We must find a way to respond faster and resume normal operations. Perhaps there is too much instability in the system and it is leading to too much fire fighting."

Tony pitched in, "Seth, it is quite possible that too many varieties of disruptions are overwhelming the current capability of the team. We probably need a way to give a breather to people, so that they can build a capability to respond faster to these disruptions."

Seth said, "Do you suggest that we send people for training?"

Tony said, "No, probably we need to filter out these problems and focus on essential ones. During their day to day work, the staff could be trying to attend too many problems and as a result, is not able to address any of them. In reality, all problems may not be equally important at a given time."

Seth said, "But, we already have a policy decision on this."

Seth saw the team numbed by his statement.

Ali said, "Isn't it the red color of process orders …"

"Yes, indeed. I agree that there is a possibility of too many disruptions diluting attention of the staff. But not all disruptions would be equally important and urgent, even though all of them need to be resolved. But the disruptions to red orders, are the most important to handle and resolve. Isn't this logical?" asked Seth out of desperation.

"It is obvious…did we miss something here?" Ali looked at Raman.

He was wondering why his people could not figure this out themselves and why they needed Seth to explicitly specify the rule for prioritization.

Tony said, "Possibly, we need to draft a policy on dealing with urgency." He knew that formalization of the new prioritization system was important.

Seth looked across his team and said, "May be, yes…We are committed to improve availability of our products. If so, for example, a machine with significant queue of red orders breaks down and we do not have a spare part, then we have two things to do. First, *Expedite*: do whatever is needed to get the spare part faster. Do speed processing of purchase orders, get the part by flight. If there is further delay, send somebody by flight to the supplier and get the part personally."

Then he looked at the assembled team and asked, "What is the second action we need to take?"

Ali said, "*Innovate and Institutionalize*: immediately review spare parts management policy to ensure that we have better availability of spare parts. We must ensure that critical machines are not left in a similar emergency situation again. In fact, figure out what prevented us from having this spare part in our inventory, despite of an advanced preventive maintenance practice in the plant. And, it would most likely point to a policy that is waiting to be changed. We need to involve the engineering maintenance team on this. Tony is right, we may ultimately need to get into details of the respective policies."

To ensure that people understood the behavior of urgency very well, Seth gave another example, "Similarly, there could be a delay in the input material to execute process orders of a stocked out product. Then, the approach should be to raise alarm, run up to the supplier and get the material. If required, fly it down to the plant, even if the cost of one time transportation is high. This is the way to deal with urgency. *Under emergency, normal speed of work (lead time), is not sufficient.* For us, a stock out situation demands the highest level of urgency. Subsequently, start working on the root cause of non availability of the input material. It could also be possible that there are some issues at the vendor site, and we may need to involve Tony's team in improving the things there."

Tony took the clue, "So, it means that we need a policy to allow us to *expedite* the red orders."

"Yes, precisely; the cost of delay of endangered orders and the subsequent stock out is too huge and so avoidable delays are not acceptable to us. We must make the necessary modification in our policies to help us in achieving higher availability," said Seth.

Ali summarized, "Now that we have a clear priority system, we must ensure that our ability to adhere to the system is enhanced. I propose drafting a mechanism of escalation right from the operators till my office. Whenever the flow of a red order is disrupted, I expect that the issues are escalated faster."

It wasn't that Terra Pharma had no expediting or escalation mechanism; just that expediting merely equated to fire-fighting.

Seth said, "Priority by urgency of the process order is the single priority system, not only for processing but also for dealing with disruptions."

Thus, the team came out with a policy:

<u>Policy for deciding priority of work</u>: Disruptions to red orders must be dealt with on high priority and if required, work must be expedited.

"Will this help Raman?" asked Tony.

"Yes, indeed. It will improve our focus on important things. We will build a deliberate practice to limit the number of problems individuals and teams are exposed to. It will also improve our effectiveness," said Raman.

"But this does not solve systemic issues. We must also have a process in place to log systemic issues and effectively deal with them through corrective and preventive actions," warned Seth.

"We need to build this capability of quickly dealing with disruptions. We will come out with a system to reduce the occurrence of such disruptions and their impact on the flow," Ali assured.

Violation of the Prime Rule

The team looked deeper into the status of process orders in the shop floor and the way orders were being processed. It got some more clues on why improvements were not taking place at sufficient pace.

It was found that process orders with low priority had made way into production. In fact, several of them were already dispatched, while red orders were still waiting for their turn for a long time.

Ali asked Raman, "What's the issue here?"

Raman said, "Although there is a high alert on red batches, often machines are found to be waiting for these batches to come from previous stages."

"How long could the wait be?" asked Ali.

Raman replied, "Sometimes, this wait could be as long as eight hours. The waiting for red batches often leads to idling of machines and people. Hence, in order to avoid idling of machines, operators pull a batch that is not high on priority and process it through."

"But did we realize what happened to the already delayed red orders?" asked Ali.

Raman looked around for help, and then said, "We would have *ultimately* produced them."

In a flash, data came from Susan's laptop. It showed that while low priority batches were already worked upon, red batches were made to wait in queue for 30 to 600 hours.

Rita said, "A significant delay in red batches is attributed to bypassing the priority system. Once a batch of lower priority product is taken out of turn, work on the 'red' batch could only be commenced upon completion of 'the out of turn batch' and full changeover of the equipment." The full changeover involved equipment disassembly and reassembly, parts cleaning, machine cleansing, room cleaning, startups and QA approval.

Then, Seth said, "Moreover, when an operator processing a red batch knows that the downstream machine is processing a non-red batch, one would lose the enthusiasm to work on priority. This will develop excessive slackness in our process. Perhaps, the undesirable effect of this phenomenon is not very intuitive."

"Yes, indeed!" said Ali.

Initially, people thought that taking one batch out of turn would average out over a period of time. They thought that if some high priority batches would be late to reach their workstations, running an idling machine with low priority batches would offer an opportunity to do some extra throughput. However, in reality it was causing severe undesired effects. The truth was that *"producing low priority batches out of turn, resulted in far more delays of endangered batches. In the meanwhile, stocks of low priority products were hitting the roof in warehouses for want of demand in the market."*

There was more to it! Susan flashed another set of data on the big wall of the war room. It seemed that more deep rooted behavior dominated across the plant.

Some of the machines which were recently commissioned based on previous year's capacity planning, were sitting idle. And, people who had bought these equipments were becoming nervous, as their justification of 'Return on Asset' was taking a beating. Together with the finance staff, they were placing enormous pressure on the production staff to activate these equipments. This led production releasing 'special' batches into the shop floor to utilize them, although these batches had no immediate demand. This was a major default and violation of the basic principles agreed by Seth's team.

The plant was actually manufacturing products that did not have high priority ahead of ones that were endangered. It was thus jeopardizing the commitment of 'Reliable Supply' to its clients. Seth realized that such behavior was due to the pressure for achieving higher utilization of machines and people. *He was convinced that it was good to have resources a bit idle than produce batches out of priority.*

The team also realized that the key reason for the high occurrence of red orders and their delays was not just the lack of expediting behavior but the very first level of non-adherence to the desired policy of process order generation. Thus, came in another policy.

<u>Policy for process order creation:</u> The process orders for products must be triggered only by the actual consumption of the stocks.

This was a policy that production was bound by, when releasing any material into the shop floor. Seth felt that it was obvious, but could not figure out, why a policy is required to tell people such simple things.

The Right Behavior

Seth was trying to understand the difficulties faced by the staff in the plant.

The staff needed a lot of forbearance to accept that situation in market would change unpredictably and from time to time, some equipments would stay idle. Making these equipments occupied without honoring market driven demand and priority would however, be futile. Thus, the reality of dynamics imposed by the market required a change in behavior of his people.

In Terra Pharma and for that matter across industries, staff members were hired for work and they were expected to work every moment of their presence in the plant, barring prescribed breaks. This has been the rule for centuries. Seth realized that this rule came into existence a long back, when people were paid for their labor 'on per piece' basis. By nature, people got the idea of working as much as possible 'in order to earn more'. The idea that one must work all the time during one's stay in the workplace got engrained into the habit, behavior and belief of the people. Gradually, it became a rule and management policy that people and machines must always work without being seen sitting idle.

Now, for past several decades, cost of employees has become mostly a fixed cost. Employees are largely paid on monthly basis and not on per piece basis. Yet, nobody seems to revisit the initial assumption or change the psychology of the industry. Hence, today, when a resource or staff is seen idle, managers run up to them to ask, why they are not working. In fact, managers will find some work to make the staff busy and justify their own resource management skills.

That's exactly the situation that had led the staff in the Sanovi Plant to work on out of priority orders as well as undesired batches. This behavior in turn prevented higher priority orders from being processed on time, and for a while, led to stock-outs.

When the team met a couple of days later, Susan had some more data points to show. She had classified the 'delays in red orders' based on reason, and had found a common thread, Figure 5.1.

When the team analyzed the reasons for the delays in red orders in the light of the prevailing behavior, a possible organizational inertia emerged as a major reason. Seth's team realized that while the basic rule of priority had been agreed on, something was making people bypass the rule and violate the priority system. It realized that these violations were actually not looked on thus but as exceptions (legitimization of non-adherence), e.g., release of 'unneeded' batches into the shop floor to improve productivity of machines.

It was apparently a vicious behavior.

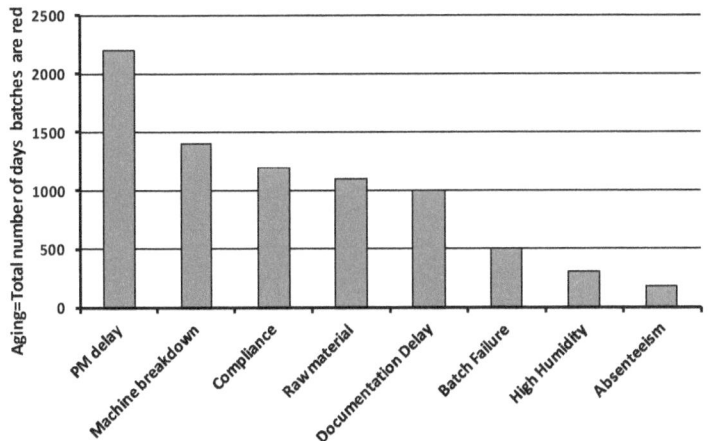

Figure 5.1 Reasons for delay of Red batches

Seth got up and said, "We need to dramatically improve reliability of our deliveries. We must therefore, improve availability of our drugs from around 55 percent to first around 80 percent and then, close to 100 percent. I think that we must understand the transformation in performance better."

He walked up to the white board, drew an arrow with the two ends marked A and B, respectively, Figure 5.2 (i) and said, "So, let us say that we need to improve our performance from level A to level B."

He continued, "Now in order to move from level A to level B, based upon our intuition and logic, and supported to certain extent by data; we agreed to follow certain rules. We designed our system around these rules. These rules should take us towards B."

"What are these basic rules?" he asked looking at Raman.

Raman said, "In our case, producing as per the consumption of stocks and the single priority system across the supply chain are the two basic rules."

"Correct!"

"But, the movement from A to B is not a step jump. We definitely have a number of uncertainties and unknowns, on the way," said Raman.

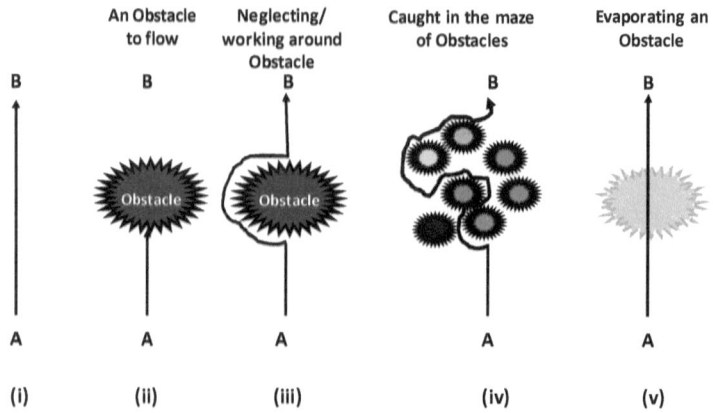

Figure 5.2 The behavior pattern in dealing with disruption to flow

"Of course," said Seth and then, he drew an obstacle on the way from A to B, Figure 5.2(ii), "So, when we started following these seemingly simple rules, obstacles began to emerge, since the system is new and we have been thus far operating a different system."

"Thus, the red batches despite being given high priority, were getting stuck somewhere for some reason or the other," inferred Ali.

"This is natural," accepted Seth, "There are some disruptions that we can't prevent but there are those that are in our control."

Raman said, "Wherever possible, we do try to solve them quickly, but we struggle on several of those that take time to resolve. However, people are good and they come to work in the plant, and for them, idling without running their machines is not an acceptable behavior. So they start working on something that is available." He was indicating the difficulty in changing the behavior.

Ali said, "Raman, in the end, 'endangered products' are not available and 'endangered orders' are not being served reliably. This is because when a red batch is ready, the machine would be busy working on some low priority batch."

Tony added, "The point is that first we must be fully committed to the new system. And then, we must adhere to the rules that govern the system. *The obstacles that we see are actually indicators about the inadequacy of our actions the system is trying to tell us. These are not 'exceptions', rather they are the obstacles that are preventing us from reaching our goal, i.e., point B.*"

Seth waited for a while, and then, walking towards the white board, said, "Now that there are over 30 such issues that prevent us from reaching B, what are we doing about them today?" He drew Figure 5.2(iii), by marking a path bypassing the obstacle.

He pointed to the figure and continued, "When faced with obstacles, we are trying to 'work around'. What we call 'actions taken against exceptions' are actually procrastinations and *poor improvisations.* We are trying to shy away from recognizing and challenging the obstacles. This is what I call limitation of our capability to deal with real problems."

"For example, when a batch is stuck mid way, we keep it on the side, without bothering to address the root cause of its delay. This we do, even when we know that if the batch does not move soon, we would not be able to deliver it on time. Instead, we take another batch and move ahead. While we do so, we continue to store all the problems in different forms at different places as long aging batches. These problems could be a recurring machine break down, sticking of tablets on punching tools, humidity creep due to unstable HVAC system or for that matter, occasional delays in input materials."

"Possibly, before we build the capability to resolve a specific problem, we need to learn how to approach the phenomenon or pattern of disruptions correctly," said Tony.

"Yes. So, what is our current approach?" asked Seth as he looked at Ali.

"Our current approach towards dealing with obstacles is primarily, a trading or ostrich mentality. We tend to hide ourselves behind the claim of being busy with new or out of priority batches, while we accumulate so much bad WIP in the system. But in the end, it does not help. And hence, we create a very ineffective and inefficient system, that is flooded with WIP and characterized by long lead times," Tony inferred and picked up a marker as he walked up to the whiteboard. He added several obstacles and a workaround path to draw Figure 5.2(iv). It gave a powerful visualization of inefficiency caused by the compromising nature of the team.

"You are absolutely right. The good thing is that, today, we have the advantage of the new system that tells us very systematically, the major problems in our current way of doing things. Of course, *these problems were there earlier also, but we had no systematic way of convincingly identifying and prioritizing them.* The new system of prioritization tells us, which problem is the gravest based on Susan's Pareto chart for the red SKUs. It gives us the most important problems that we need to attack first and attack NOW," said Seth.

As Tony walked back towards his seat, he said "It now demands that all of us pick up problems from our respective domain and apply our skills to solve them, *one by one.* I think that each one of these problems, is like the regular turbulence on the way to a flowing stream and we need to deal with them effectively, in order to increase the flow significantly."

Seth said, "Looks like the secret of improving flow of process orders across the supply chain lies here. We need to overcome these disruptions one by one and improve flow. We must realize that quite a few of these disruptions may not emanate from smaller problems, and must avoid trivializing or ignoring them. Actually, they would need substantial effort and logistical support, since many of these would have an underlying big root cause. But if these are the ones that are preventing us from reaching our goal, we better spend our time, effort and money on them and address the core problem in order to improve the flow." He drew Figure 5.2(v) by drawing the arrow from A to B through an evaporated obstacle.

Ali took the cue from Seth and said, "Seth, you are right. We have got so used to working in the traditional way that we thought the new system will solve our problems on its own. We forgot that the system can take us closer to the problem, but we must solve it ourselves. Actually, our behavior has a big role in making this simple system work for us. Our people have excellent skill sets for this."

Turning towards his colleagues, he said, "Until Life2.0 started, we have been trying to improve everything everywhere in the organization. For example, when we wanted to implement something like, Lean practices, we had started a mega initiative. We had tried to implement Lean principles across the organization and run some 100 projects in various places, simultaneously. And, we know that none of these saw the light of the day, for the very reason that soon we ran too thin on resources as well as capabilities."

Then he advised, "Susan's Pareto gives us the exact reasons for the delay in red batches. I think that operationally it is a very good way to prioritize problems and identify exact resource, policy and process that needs improvement. We can now apply our skills of TQM, Six Sigma and Lean with proper focus."

The discussion was an eye opener for everybody in the forum, as it deeply touched upon behavior of the team. The team realized that Susan's Pareto was showing the most important operational problems that the organization was facing in meeting the commitment made to the market. Since, all these reasons were linked to the delays in red orders, if they were able to tackle them one by one, the flow and availability would definitely improve significantly.

After he moved out of the meeting, Seth realized that it would not be an easy task to change the age old *psychology of procrastination and poor improvisation.* Perhaps, he needed a specialist's advice. He called Ajay, to seek his guidance on this matter.

Ajay said, "The agenda of our transformation is really big and we must accept its detailed complexity. The new system may look simple from the conceptual point of view, but it is not easy to implement in a deep hierarchical organization. In fact, it challenges several of our long and deeply held fundamental assumptions. Under such a situation, we must tread carefully, one step at a time and go through tremendous learning while implementing the changes."

"Yes, we realize," said Seth.

Ajay said, "When we make a rule or a policy to implement change that has a big impact; it is very important to see if sufficient conditions are fulfilled for the success of the new rule."

"What are these sufficient conditions?"

"For example, the basic rule of 'Produce as per Consumption needs a sufficiency check. This means that while it is necessary to tell people 'What to Do'; it is also important to clearly communicate, 'What Not to Do'," said Ajay looking into Seth's eyes.

He continued, "I think that rule #1 for this project is – *"Do not work on a batch that is not required to produce NOW"*.

He warned, "It is not trivial to establish this rule, because people believe that they come to the plant to work and they will work on anything that is there unless they are specifically told not to."

"I see."

"In a system with interdependent resources, if you try to do what is not required NOW, you would soon tend to dramatically delay what is required NOW," Ajay gave the insight on delays. His emphasis on the logic of failure in meeting the promise made to customers was evident.

"I agree. Also, the assumption that all resources must always work even if the market does not dictate so, is not right," said Seth.

"Absolutely correct!" said Ajay.

Seth got a crucial insight from Ajay, who had majored in Industrial Psychology and had done the much acclaimed thesis on 'Necessary and Sufficient Conditions for Paradigm Shifts among Industrial Staff'.

Subsequently, Seth and Ali extended their discussion with Ajay on making the methodology more fool proof. At the end of the day, Ajay promised that his team would support Rita in creating behavior-based transformation in the shop floor. They realized that as Life2.0 moved closer to action levels (shop floor), policies, procedures and instructions must be explicit and standardized without any ambiguity.

Codifying the Desired Behavior

Scripting the Operating Rules

At eight that morning, Rita was consolidating the previous day's discussion when Nidhi from Ajay's team entered the War Room. Rita knew Nidhi as the 'policy simplifier' for the organization. Five years back, she was recruited from a premier MBA school during campus interview. She had taken several high end policies by the neck, brought them down in rather simplified versions and added significant speed to their compliance.

Nidhi had already got heads up from Ajay, and she was excited to have her hands onto something that was closely linked to the goal of the organization. She came prepared. Rita listened to her attentively. They were also joined by Ali's team.

Nidhi first clarified her understanding of the situation and the behavioral issues faced by the team. She said, "This sort of behavior is expected, when people are given a new system."

She went through various communication materials used by Rita's team and discussed them thread bare. She found that the existing communication package was overwhelming; and it needed to be simplified and be made more actionable. As an immediate step, they agreed to bring out guidelines on the new behavior required for the success of Life2.0. After 3 hours of brain storming session, following guidelines were framed.

Objective of Operations: Ever improving flow of process orders is the prime objective of Operations [12].

Promise to Customers: High Availability of Drugs

Guidelines: In order to fulfill its responsibilities, the working rules for the team are as given below.

1. Do not work on a process order that is not triggered by the consumption of stocks.
2. Work on process orders triggered by consumption of stocks.
3. If multiple process orders compete for a resource, then an order that is in the danger of being stocked-out must be given preference.
4. While work is being done only on orders that are triggered by consumption and 'endangered orders' are given priority, orders will often get stuck and will be delayed for various reasons.
    a. Since, time is the key constraint, trying to improve everything will dilute attention and exhaust the scarce human resources.

Hence, a focused approach must be adopted, to systematically address the cause of delays.
   b. When there is a delay (disruption) in processing an order due to an assignable cause, pause for a while, use local ingenuity to solve the problem, otherwise summon seniors or domain experts to seek quick solution.
      a. All improvement programs related to operations must be those popped up while following the priority system across the flow of process orders.
      b. Problems within the scope of operational team must be promptly dealt with.
      c. In order to rapidly come out of disruptions, an effective escalation and expediting procedure must be followed.
      d. For each disruption, the reasons of delays are collected, and analyzed on a periodic basis. Improvement teams are created to solve the core problems, one by one starting with the most prominent ones first.
5. The Plant Management must monitor, review and manage the portfolio of improvement projects.

For Rita and team, it was a perfect summary of the rules, they were trying to implement. The list now provided a very crisp description of key responsibilities for the operations team. It was also short enough to memorize. Subsequently, they sat with Nidhi and Ali's team to detail out the Standard Operating Procedures, (SOPs).

Improving System Design on the Run

The rhythm of reviews by Seth, served to renew and reinforce improvement activities in the organization. The principles of flow seemed to be seeping into the bones of the organization and tremendous sense of focus developed in dealing with disruptions to flow across the supply chain.

People became conscious of the rule that if there was no consumption from the stock of a product, there should not be any process order for that product. To a great extent, the quantum of red process orders reduced. Identification of disruptions across the supply chain created projects for ongoing improvement of flow. Teams got together and the review of improvement projects started gradually reducing hidden waste in the system. It gave significant confidence to people that improvement in right place allowed even a small team to make significant contribution to the growth of the organization. The operational team led by Ali, then moved from reviewing compliance of the priority system to reviewing flow improvement projects and facilitating the staff in dealing with disruptions.

Within six months since the launch of Life2.0, several things changed one by one, and people remained engaged, monitoring, tracking and speeding up process orders. The number of red orders came down by 50 percent, availability of orders improved to beyond 80 percent. WIP was down by 25 percent.

As the team moved ahead reinforcing the rules of improved operations, in the following 3 months, the improvements stood stagnant and measurements started fluctuating a bit. The 13 week average performance was actually showing a slight downward trend. This was a clear indication that the flow was still not under control.

The team traced the trend of 'endangered products' for 6 months and the demand thereof. It found that there was significant change in the consumption pattern of the products during that period.

There was a seasonality behavior and some of the products were losing their pace. It actually meant that the desired level of stocks for some of the products needed re-calibration. A quick analysis by the SCM analytics team showed a seasonality effect of four months on more than 50 percent of the products. However, there were products, which were not affected by seasonality but showed irrational level of stocks in hand. The team found that the demand of some products had reduced significantly but their stock levels remained full for months. At the same time, stocks of some other products were regularly hitting low levels.

In fact, Tony had revealed a secret of the industry when he said, "You know, the demand in our industry is quite unpredictable. Seasonality and competitive opportunities swing the demand of products too wildly. The fast movers in winters are different from the fast movers in the summers."

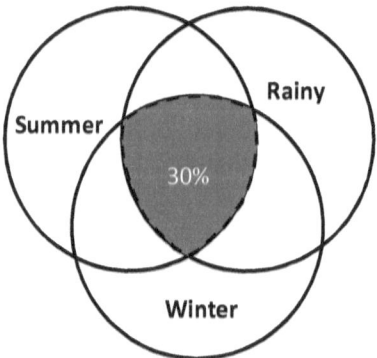

Figure 5.3 Seasonality effect in the portfolio of drugs

"And since, our products are supplied widely and each geographical location has its own regulated environment, it may be difficult to have a fixed definition or list of fast movers, barring a few. Further, there are spikes and transients in demand, due to the launch of new products and the rapidly changing procurement schedule of our big clients".

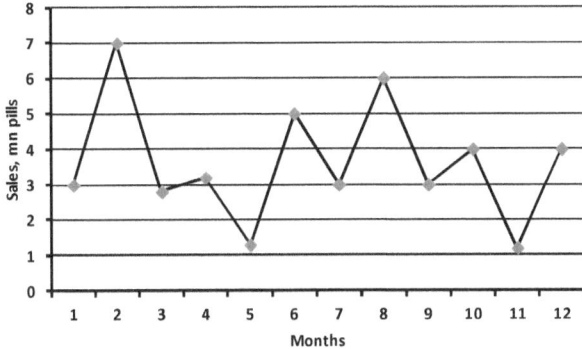

Figure 5.4 Wild fluctuations of Sales for an anti-inflammatory drug

One reason was also that for a large number of products, the lead time had reduced by over 30 percent.

Considering these factors, Tony expressed that despite aggregation, the demand on the plant was uncertain and a bit too fluctuating. Probably, they needed a mechanism to periodically adjust the desired stock levels with the reality of the market.

Satyam had earlier worked in hedging mechanisms and had a good idea of uncertainty in the commodity markets. He used the lead time and demand parameters to come out with a definite periodicity to do sanity check of desired stock levels and environmental factors.

In fact, his analysis provided two levels of periodicity for reviewing stock levels. First one was at 30 days period, for which Susan helped in automating a trigger, whenever stock level adjustment was required. The suggested adjustments in stocks would be above or below the prevailing mark of desired levels. Second one was need based for 20 percent of products, where Satyam worked out a process to re-estimate the target inventory levels. By picking historic data, Susan ran the simulation and they hit the accuracy of prediction by an acceptable margin.

The team recognized that variability and uncertainty in demand were unavoidable. Hence in order to improve flow and promise high availability, it defined a specific SCM role to ensure that desired stock levels reflected the reality of market and the capability of production. A new autonomous role 'Stock Controller' was created to take responsibility of dynamically managing the inventory. This role was similar to that of a traffic control officer.

Upon initiating the inventory correction process called the Dynamic Inventory Management, the net load on the plant adjusted a bit. This was an innovation in flow management, and it added the next level of agility to the system in responding to the dynamics of the market. As the days went by, the response of the system was further tuned and 'Dynamic Inventory Management' became one of the most talked about feature of stabilizing operations in Terra Pharma. It did though improve availability by another notch.

There still remained one more irritating issue to be resolved. Frequent incidents of sudden spikes in clients orders would often empty the stocks at one go and release huge load on the production system. This caused chaos across purchasing, manufacturing, dispatch, and delivery chain. Since, the response time of the plant had improved significantly, the disturbance due to sudden spikes of client orders was less than it was before the initiation of Life2.0. But it was still significant to create instability in the system and cause bullwhip effect. The team worked out a deal to initiate a modified offer to clients who had a need to place large sudden orders.

Some clients of Terra Pharma did understand the problem caused by their ordering pattern and agreed to co-operate. Collaborative discussions with matured clients led to the implementation of levelized loading of the plant. The clients agreed that larger orders would be broken into smaller orders and delivered over a period of time, thus preventing the bullwhip effect along the system. However, this was possible only because increasingly, *clients realized the benefit of improved reliability and faster response of supplies* from Terra Pharma. Such an arrangement avoided huge stock of inventory, otherwise maintained by both Terra Pharma and its clients.

Moderating the Message

The senior management of Terra Pharma was superbly aligned and the departmental heads were seeing benefits of the new priority system. However, the staff in middle management and below was still struggling to manage its work and was in an ever grinding mode. It was following the instructions built by the project team, but was still somehow a bit aloof from what Seth often called the 'relay runner behavior'.

Often, the staff in the shop floor and in other functions would do adequate preparation and work at peaked urgency to deal with endangered orders. However, it was found that during other times, there was a tendency to take it easy and accumulate delays (like, student syndrome of postponing preparation for exams to the last moment). These were two opposite behavioral situations.

It was also found that 'urgency' was equated to 'emergency' and people over exerted themselves to deliver 'red' orders faster. And since, there were significant number of urgent orders, after exerting to push them through for a while, people relaxed or rather, 'over relaxed'. Given the size of the load, while 'over exertion' led to 'burn outs' and 'exhaustion', the 'over relaxation' led to leniency (i.e. the normal behavior was below par).

In fact, the cycle of 'exertion' and 'leniency' led to a sort of self created 'Bull Whip' effect that started 'endangering' availability of healthy process orders also. It was very important to arrest this lumpy behavior of extremes.

Rita called a meeting with Ali's and Tony's team. They needed to be on the same page and evolve a common understanding of the desired behavior to drive the flow.

The objective for the team was to ensure that moderate and extreme situations of stocks were unambiguously defined. Life2.0 was intended to reduce urgencies and give a balanced life to the staff of Terra Pharma. It was therefore, important that urgencies were not created as a result of 'over relaxed behavior' and at the same time, people avoided overexertion when not needed. The team knew that occasionally there could be 'real emergencies'.

When they looked into the logic of the priority system; the word 'urgency' needed a redefinition.

Till then, people worked on high urgency for a product, if its stocks in hand were below 30 percent of the desired levels. However, there was a high probability that stocks would be replenished before they are emptied, if the respective process orders were given right priority as soon as they were assigned red color ('endangered' status). In order to further strengthen such a possibility, the team decided to reinforce the strength of 30 percent stock by using a factor of safety in the target inventory level.

It realized that high urgency was actually needed if there was a stock-out. It was likely that if for a significantly duration, the stock would not be available, sales would be lost. Hence, a situation of stock-out needed *expediting*. The team decided to indicate stock-out situation by a new color, 'Black'.

The team found out that very few instances of stock-outs occurred when red orders were accorded the right priority. It concluded that it would not need to *over exert* itself, when batches were in red. The behavior of placing red batches *in front of the queues was the only necessity* (unless an SKU was becoming *chronically* red). The team also realized that sometimes, a red SKU would become black (stock out) due to statistical fluctuation or unguarded large spike, and it made no sense to target an availability of 100 percent.

Thus, the team narrowed and mellowed down the definition of high urgency. However, it was important that the operations team organized itself to be sensitive to the reasons for the delays of process orders, and systematically weeded the root causes out.

Thus, a refined set of rules for urgency was drafted.

1. When a product is stocked out, it is an *emergency* and the highest level of *expediting* must be applied to pull the batches through the system.
2. When the stocks in hand for a product is in red, the batches must either be worked upon or stand in front of the queue. Thus, they are given *the priority to jump the queue*. There is no need to expedite.

Coming to the second point of 'over relaxation (student syndrome)', the team understood that it needed an emphasis on standard performance metrics. It redefined the prime responsibility of the staff, 'to move batches as fast as possible'. 'As fast as possible' did not mean 'Urgent'.

'As fast as possible' is the characteristic speed of an operating system which corresponds to the baseline speed of doing work. It means that when a staff member has a batch or work in hand, the work is done in the most efficient and productive way, without delay. Most importantly, the work must be started as soon as it comes into ones hands.

Across the plant, a batch moves sequentially one step at a time and thus, it actually moves like a baton in a relay race between workstations. And therefore, a runner (operator on a machine) needs to be ready to receive the baton, and once it is in ones hand, moves it as fast as possible. This is a prime behavior for the staff in the supply chain. Thus, the 'relay race' behavior drives the base speed of the organization. Amongst different organizations, this behavior of *'relay race' creates the very fundamental competitive edge* that is seldom discernible to the external world.

Of course, the priority rule gave a degree of urgency in Terra Pharma, but in no case it said that process orders with lower priority needed to start late or slow down. And hence, to clarify this point, the team came out with a corollary to the existing rules for managing the flow of process orders:

The Relay Race Rule: When there is a batch in hand, start it as soon as possible. If it is being processed, be as fast as possible (baseline speed). The team must show a Relay Race behavior.

The new rules provided a vital correction in the communication about priority system, by explicitly providing guidelines on the intensity of urgency.

It thus, brought down stress levels amongst the staff considerably. At the same time, the 'Relay Race' behavior ensured that the flow was stable without any bull whip effect. It lifted the baseline productivity of Terra Pharma significantly.

Reclaiming the Core

Dealing with High Attrition of Talent

Despite significant improvement in the operating behavior of the staff, at one moment, the trend charts of Life2.0 showed a significant short term dip in the performance. Susan's Pareto revealed, 'People not available', as the dominant reason for delays in the flow of process orders. It intrigued Rita though. Her enquiry surfaced a dangerous trend that at first seemed outside the scope of the operational team.

A discussion with Raman revealed that during the past three months, the Sanovi Plant had been losing 8-12 trained staff every week. The capacity expansion of the major pharma companies and opening up of manufacturing facilities by Innovator Companies in the region had resulted in a huge demand for trained manpower in the locality. This led to unabashed poaching of human resources.

Till then, people attrition rate at Terra Pharma had been well below industry average. In fact, during the past 6 years, the organization was consistently ranked #1 best employer by the independent employee satisfaction survey of the regional business council.

The impact of attrition was accentuated by the fact that an Innovator Company had opened a new plant just adjacent to the Sanovi Plant. And, it was offering Terra Pharma's employees a jump of 60-100 percent in their salaries to switch over.

The attrition rate was startling. Ajay's team was clueless on how to retain good people. Obviously, Terra Pharma was running into a dangerous situation. All the steps taken by Seth's team for Life2.0 would to be futile, if the attrition could not be arrested quickly.

Ajay's team had two things to achieve:
1. Immediately, arrest the attrition
2. Attract new talent to fill the gap and meet business growth.

It was very important that Terra Pharma continued to recruit staff and trained them quickly, so that the adverse effect on performance due to uncontrollable exit of people could be arrested. In order to do so, Terra Pharma opened up recruitment drive in a big way.

But where were the pharma graduates? The market was almost deserted. It forced an executive intervention to deal with the impending crisis.

Fearless questioning of the existing recruitment policies revealed that the Pharma Industry had been suffering from *misplacement of talent* in its operations, which was quite different from the scarcity of pharma graduates. It was found that although, the production work required pure manufacturing and logistical skills, most of the manufacturing activities in pharma companies were actually carried out by pharma graduates. In no case, manufacturing in pharma plants required, more than a basic knowledge of pharmaceutical processes. The revelation was appalling. It was analogous to the situation that you place a computer science graduates to assemble a computer in a PC manufacturing plant.

The team realized that the main domain of a formulation plant is manufacturing and not pharmaceutical.

Similarly, the key positions of managing flow of process orders were given to fresh pharma graduates, who had little insight of supply chain and logistical issues. The general notion of planning and control in production was that it needed a coordinator, who knew how to use ERP system, spread sheet and e-mail. The work definition included data crunching (read 'cut and paste'), preparation of reports and sending emails. The scheduling managers were too young to co-ordinate, control and engage in useful conversation with senior management in the plant. In contrast to the widely prevalent role of Production, Planning and Control Managers (PPC) in other industries, hardly any formulation plant in the region had anybody in such a role. This clearly showed how pharma companies gave low priority to operations. With the supply chain becoming ever more complex, using a non specialist to manage flow of batches only created chaos and firefighting in the supply chain.

The use of pharma graduates across the hierarchy, from Plant Manager, to Production Manager to Operator, for a facility that made over 1000 SKUs on over 500 machines using over 1500 full time employees, was a gross trivialization of specialization needed to run a modern production system.

Given this insight, Ajay's team went around the region and built a significant buffer of employees, who were good in manufacturing. The approach was a trend breaker. Of course, the new recruits needed a basic level of training in formulation process, safety and quality.

Within two months, Terra Pharma had built enough people capacity to weather the attrition. It maintained a buffer of staff such that there was no dip in production, even if people left at the existing rate. The attrition slowed down as Terra Pharma took a few more steps to retain employees in line with market reality.

By increasing the proportion of manufacturing specialists in its plant, the production began to run in a new format. Compared to the discussions that used to center around only pharma related issues, the change brought shop floor discussions around manufacturing system and flow of process orders. Earlier, the improvement areas were related to difficult to implement chemical or technical process improvements. Indeed, discussions in the plant shifted to innovation based conversations on what could prevent the staff from achieving better flow. The action points became more focused on manufacturing systems, flow, layouts, runtime, stop time, changeovers, preventive maintenance etc. In three months, the hue of manufacturing system in the Sanovi Plant changed significantly, thanks to their new recruits.

Manufacturing is a Core Competency

Bringing in, core manufacturing aptitude in the role of Operators, Supervisors and Production Managers provided the Sanovi Plant with significant benefits in an area that was long lingering for improvement.

In some of the packaging machines, more than 25 percent of uptime was lost only because of stoppages of the machines. These stoppages were both due to breakdowns as well as due to over hundred times unrecorded small duration stoppages that occurred daily relating to misalignments and poor setups. While breakdowns were not just a few, people knew that the large number of small duration stoppages aggregated to significant time loss. However, they had no way to isolate and deal with them. As a matter of fact, these stoppages were accepted as natural.

It was not that there was no maintenance strategy or system in the plant. Like any good organization, Terra Pharma had a maintenance management system. At a given time, it could provide maintenance status of the complete plant, costing of repairs, spare parts inventory and details of cost saving due to maintenance improvement projects. The maintenance engineering team had a full SCADA system for visualizing and controlling the complete facility at the click of the mouse. But, it was not adequate, as the downtime and the cost of maintenance were still high.

Earlier, there was constant dilemma and infighting between Operators and Maintenance Engineers. In fact, availability of machines almost always looked like the responsibility of Maintenance Staff than that of Operators and Supervisors.

One of the key contentions between operations and maintenance staff was about the misalignment between the production schedule and the preventive maintenance schedule. Sometimes, manufacturing staff would not release machines for the committed preventive maintenance jeopardizing future uptime. While during other times, when the manufacturing team would like to schedule preventive maintenance with off period or changeovers, maintenance staff would be busy on some urgent tasks. The day to day compromises in maintenance would often place intermittent huge load and overtime on maintenance staff on one hand, while resulting in lower productivity of the manufacturing staff on the other hand.

The new manufacturing inductees and the trained staff had a different outlook to the way of working. Primarily, they were naturally inclined to work with machines, tools, infrastructure and materials. They were not only good at operating machines but also at maintaining them.

They realized that the plant schedule was not realistic for it did not take maintenance schedule into account. It meant that at the planning stage itself, the expectations were set erroneously. The team first brought attention of the management to scheduling practice and embedded the maintenance schedule into the production schedule. This brought discipline into preventive maintenance culture.

In the Pharma Industry, the type of skills required in operating machines was not a simple industrial trade practice of job work, like welding, drilling, machining, shaping etc. It needed a significant training of managing multi trade skills, like mechanical, electrical, electronics, instrumentation, hydraulics and pneumatics.

In essence, the manufacturing staff was to be skilled not in just operating a machine but managing an equipment. Earlier, it was too daunting for the pharma graduates to get a grip on what was happening. As a result maintenance engineers were involved not only during breakdowns, but also during changeovers, setups and minor deviation or stoppages. The need of maintenance engineers in operations was such that you would find them running in the process areas from one machine to another. This, of course meant a swelling team of maintenance engineers that was in any case not cheaper than operators or supervisors.

The new inductees were better placed to understand the demand of such multidisciplinary activity. It meant that a lot of load was taken back from the maintenance staff by supervisors and operators. This practice dramatically reduced the wastage due to excessive stop time and gave immediate benefits of 1-2 hours per shift on certain machines. The benefit on packaging machines was the most surprising.

There was subsequently a realization that individual skills and average competency of operators made a lot of difference to the uptime of machines. In some cases, the team realized that in quite a few machines, the down time was cut down to 1/3rd. This was possible only because operators or supervisors were better adept at, understanding the equipment, setting up parts, aligning guide rails, handling tools, avoiding mistakes and keeping their machines well maintained. This led to standardization of tooling and setup practices. Also, SOPs and checklists were enforced to quickly bring back equipments from stoppages.

It was also realized that past poor maintenance of machines in compression, capsule filling and packaging resulted in significant variation in the overall process. The new skills, outlook and attitude brought in by the new inductees significantly improved stability in operations.

Within a quarter, availability of critical machines improved by more than 10 percent.

Knowing the effectiveness of the new teams, the management came out with a revised TPM framework (Total Productive Maintenance framework) that promoted good maintenance practices in the plant. Under the new framework, the maintenance team was then measured on an unambiguous set of metrics and was given the goals to reduce MTBF, PRM, MTTR etc.

The metric MTBF (Mean Time Between Failures) was measured on critical machines. Longer MTBF meant less breakdowns and longer uptime. This also meant that repair costs were lower.

For some of the packaging machines, sensors were placed on their motor drives to capture each moment of Cartonator's stoppage, whether it was 1 minute or 5 minute stoppage. This automated the accounting of machine run time.

The second metric was the Percentage Reactive Maintenance (PRM). Actually, there must be a balance between the amount of reactive and preventive maintenance. The team set itself to less than 20 percent reactive and about 80 percent preventive, improvement, or scheduled maintenance. This also meant that repairs that were previously outsourced could be done in-house due to fewer reactive activities. The time spent on improving skills of operators also added positively to do much of maintenance activities in house. Indirect benefits included using the same maintenance hours to speed up machines or improve quality.

The third metric was Mean Time to Repair (MTTR), the time taken to bring back the machine from stoppage. This of course often required collaboration between operators, supervisors and the maintenance engineers. As the things progressed, repairs were less serious and quicker.

Tracking repair hours, reducing response time to repair and lower downtime meant significant improvement in the maintenance practice at Terra Pharma. This also led to revision of policies on inventory management and procurement of spare parts, to a more realistic state of machines and operating practice in the plant.

Big Opportunity but People Hesitate to Commit

The significant work done in building the new system, setting up guidelines, upgrading skills and changing beliefs of the staff created a healthy working culture. But, Life2.0 presented its own challenges to Seth and his team.

Despite his firm belief that people are ambitious by nature, his project team faced severe resistance from the staff in implementing internally generated improvement ideas.

During Life2.0, it was a routine, for the staff to identify exact opportunities for improvement. At the same time problems themselves popped up as opportunities for improvement.

Rita's team used to conduct iterative brain storming sessions to institutionalize systematic methods to resolve these problems and derive long term benefits. Per problem, the team would provide around four days of analytical and managerial support work. It would hand-hold the plant teams in clearly defining the problem, sizing the opportunity and finding the solution. It would guide in coming up with precise implementation steps and preparing Power Point™ presentation to seek buy-in from the management.

The recommended actions for improvement would, in deed, be suggested by the plant teams themselves (who were in charge of machines, resources, processes or workflows). And, the promise of these benefits often did not require taking any real risk or exhausting costly resources.

Most of the opportunities were much bigger than the team had ever thought of or implemented. And they had the prospects of quick implementation.

Here is an example:

Improvement Project : 3-03-09/ Pan/03

Background: The demand of Pantoprazole is much higher than the supply. Its SKUs are chronically stocking out. The team found out clear action points to improve throughput of the drug.

Objective: To improve the productivity of Pantoprazole line.

Table 6.1 Summary of Improvement Proposal

Observation	20% Idle Time Changeovers	10% Idle Time Voluntary breaks
Solution	Better Tool Management	Staggering during breaks
% Run Time Increase	20%	13%
Bottom line Benefits	USD 1 million	USD 0.6 million
Expenses	USD 10k	USD 2k
Time to Results	2 Weeks	Immediate

The project offered a sizeable benefit to the bottom line of the plant. Surprisingly, when the moment for presenting the proposal to the management came, the team hesitated from committing to an aspiration of the real big benefit (~30 percent improvement in utilization) and proposed rather a scaled down scope of improvement with an overall benefits of around 3 percent. Why?

The Hesitation List

Seth took Ajay's help in analyzing different instances during Life2.0, when people hesitated to lap up opportunities of big improvements. The key reasons included the following:

1. People were generally used to small improvements.
2. People did not believe (even by their own insight) that the likely improvement could be of a higher order of magnitude.
3. People wanted to take time to check, if they had made any mistake in the analysis because they did not believe in their own capabilities.
4. People felt that if so much improvement was possible, so quickly, then they would be questioned about their past inactions, (what have they been doing so far?). Others would question their abilities, their involvement in real work and their attitude.
5. People also felt that if they were able to make big improvements, hardly anything would be left for them to improve in future. In a way, they felt that by making an unprecedented large improvement quickly, they would be advancing all future improvements substantially and then they would struggle to make any subsequent improvements.
6. People felt that once they achieved big improvements, the bar will be set higher and their future will be threatened.
7. People felt that whoever would be presented with the case would not believe in the possible big improvement and would question, put

The Path

hurdles, seek unnecessary justification and ask for too much paper work to convince the higher ups.
8. People were scared of making big changes and their implications, just in case something went wrong! What if they did not get the expected results, would the management spare them?
9. People were not sure of adequate support and reward from the management. They probably had a history, where a good work was not rewarded or recognized, or was perhaps discouraged.
10. People felt that new improvement ideas would unsettle ongoing initiatives and already set targets.
11. People felt that somebody else would get credit for their contribution.
12. People felt that once they committed to some improvement work, they would be taken away from their main function and team.
13. People felt that the new activities would hurt somebody else's work and it would spoil their relationships.
14. People felt that there would be too much of pressure to deliver. They would be micro-managed; and too many people would get involved.
15. People believed that any improvement promising substantial growth could be achieved only with substantial investment.
16. People had doubts that simple steps could deliver big results.
17. People felt that they were too busy and they did not have time beyond their daily chores.
18. People felt that ongoing daily work and making improvements were different functions and needed different skills.
19. People were happy with status quo.

Seth was pretty much aware of the hesitation psychology, which was a significant obstruction to the progress of Life2.0 in getting big results. He knew that this issue could not be solved by logic, rhetoric or charisma of line management. He involved Ajay's team in creating an operating system that would create a seamless process of initiating new and big ideas.

The direction to speed up the improvement work was to build a framework that would build trust, bring people closer to each other across the hierarchy, develop ownership and foster team spirit.

Setting up the Operating System

Ajay saw the organization as a pyramid made of layers of hierarchy, Figure 6.1. Each layer was responsible for taking certain actions. It was also responsible for supporting the actions of layers just above and below.

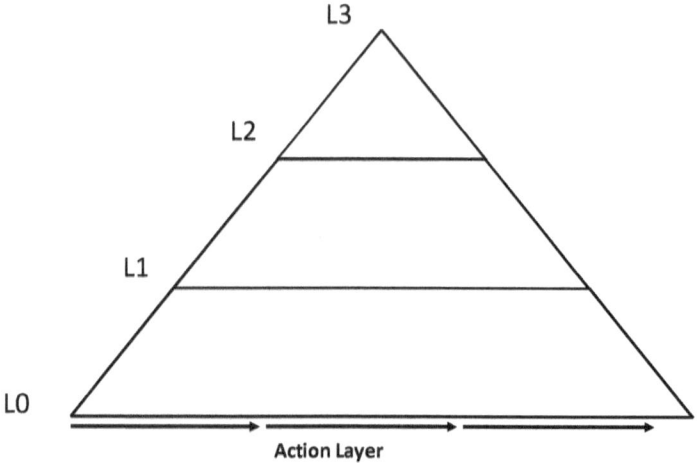

Figure 6.1 Organization as a multi layered hierarchical system

He said that following things must happen in order for the layers to work seamlessly towards the common objective:

1. Layer-0: This is the 'action' layer and it adds the most important value to the business, on a day to day basis. When the flow is faster in the 'action' layer, the company moves forward, as the value is immediately delivered and captured physically.

   This is the layer where people with specific skills take actions. For example, in the shop floor, people run machines on a day to day basis. Hence, once process orders are released into the plant, it is their responsibility to run machines as much as possible and as fast as possible. If their work is more effective and efficient, the flow of value across the shop floor will be faster. Now, while doing their daily work, people at Layer-0, face obstacles and these obstacles disrupt the flow of value creation on the shop floor. When they face obstacles, either they overcome obstacles themselves or by involving peers. However, if an obstacle excessively challenges their ability or scope of work, they look up to (Escalate/ Inform) their superiors a layer above, i.e. Layer-1.

2. Layer-1: This layer has more capability and a larger scope of work than Layer-0. When an operator in Layer-0, faces an obstacle, say, on his machine and is not able to do his work, he looks up (Escalates/ Informs) to his superior at Layer-1. In turn, Layer-1 *must be available to help and facilitate* Layer-0 in overcoming the obstacle. This facilitation most often, is a Decision required in dealing with obstacles, which helps to move the work ahead at Layer-0.

Figure 6.2 shows the basic element of this behavior i.e. action-escalation-decision (AED).

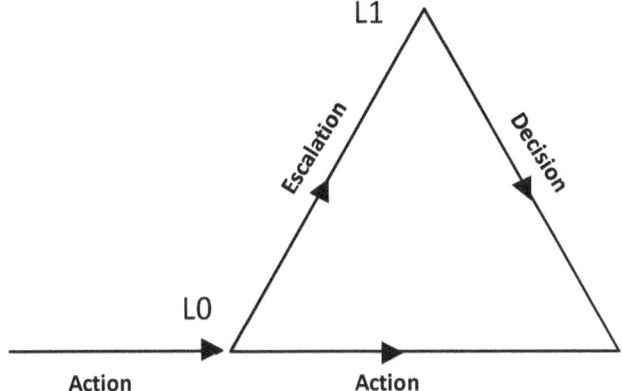

Figure 6.2 Building Block of Action-Escalation-Decision based operating system

And Figure 6.3 shows how, the behavior of following AED elements make things move faster at Layer-0.

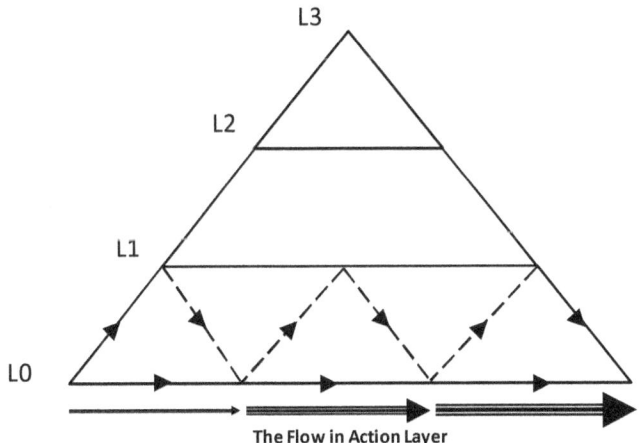

Figure 6.3 The Action-Escalation-Decision behavior increases the flow at Layer-0

Additionally, Layer-1 is also responsible for taking actions within its capabilities and scope of work, e.g. design and preparation of process documents.

Now, while resolving the issues faced by several Layer-0 staff or taking actions within its own scope, Layer-1 would be able to resolve or take action only on certain obstacles. There will be other obstacles large enough to excessively challenge its capability and scope. Under such circumstances, a Layer-1 staff looks up (Escalates/ Informs) to a Layer-2 staff, who is sensitized to be ready to help and facilitate in overcoming the problems faced by the Layer-1 staff.

3. The above *cyclic* process of taking actions (flow) - escalating (informing) - facilitating (decision making/expediting) and then quickly taking action is iterated across the hierarchy of the organization. This cyclic process forms the fundamental way of bringing up and resolving the problems that prevent work from moving ahead in the shop floor. Figure 6.4 shows, how this process maps onto a 4-layer organizational system.

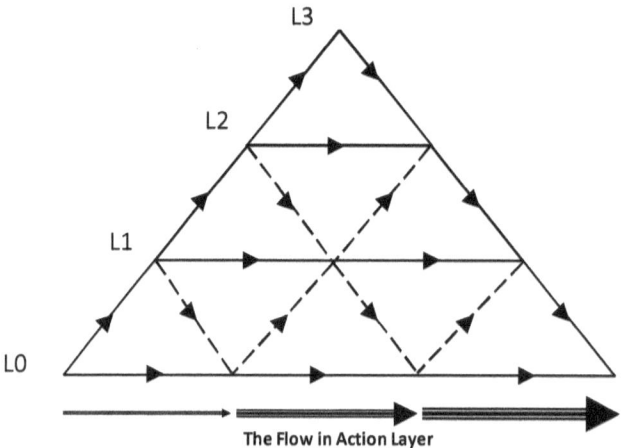

Figure 6.4 Action-Escalation-Decision behavior mapped on a 4-layer organization, increases the flow dramatically

Escalation ≠ Expediting

Ajay's team helped in detailing out the AED based operating system. It was also meant to guide the staff on popping up improvement ideas while they dealt with disruptions to flow at Layer-0.

However, very soon, it realized that a non-trivial part of confusion and noise created in Operations was due to lack of clear understanding of Escalation and Expediting actions. Often, the staff was seen expediting an action that should be escalated, which resulted into false urgency, chaos, higher cost and unwanted delays. On the other hand, the staff was seen resorting to only escalation when an expediting action was needed. This resulted into procrastination, finger pointing, poor quality and emergencies. Hence, in order to provide greater clarity on the behavior needed to work effectively in Life2.0, it came out with a clarification on Escalation and Expediting needs.

Subject Note on Escalation and Expediting

Escalation

Escalation is the act of reaching out to relevant persons in time, who have the authority and responsibility to help on issues that are beyond one's control. In order to make escalation process effective, the plant staff must escalate issues within the desired trigger time.

Table 6.2 Trigger Metrics for Escalation in the Plant

Who	Trigger time for Escalation	Escalate To
Operator	5 min	Shift Supervisor
Shift Supervisor	15 min	Shift In-charge
Shift In-charge	30 min	Production Manager
Production Manager	1 hr	Plant Manager
Plant Manager	4 hr	Head-Manufacturing
Head - Manufacturing	1 day	Head- Operations

Upon receiving escalation trigger, it is important for the superior to acknowledge the escalated item and respond appropriately.

Expediting

Expediting is the action taken to deal with an 'urgent' situation.

Expediting actions, although often, seem to emerge instantly, a vast majority of situations generally considered requiring expediting actions result from inconsistent escalation process. If there exists a stable escalation mechanism, expediting actions would be based upon the need, importance and 'urgency' accorded by management. For example,

1. The 'rushing' or 'chasing' of process orders that are needed in less than the normal lead time.
2. The 'rushing' or 'chasing' of activities, delay of which will result in major loss to performance, quality, safety, health or environment.

Expediting is managed by

1. Building and following through a list of expediting actions.
2. Clearly communicating the expediting actions.
3. Allocating the 'accountability' to right people.
4. Providing the right facilities/help to expedite the actions.
5. Building a system to eliminate seemingly expediting scenarios and converting them into effective escalation protocols.

It must therefore, be understood that Escalation is not same as Expediting, and the two are not interchangeable.

The clarification on the difference between Expediting and Escalation became a historic guideline. It also clarified scope of responsibilities of different levels in the plant.

Thus, Terra Pharma implemented a process to create an Operating System based on the primary AED building block. The Operating System allowed reasons of key disruptions to surface up to the management layers quickly. Higher the layer to which an issue was escalated to, bigger would be the problem. Each significant problem was then taken up at respective layers and started as the trigger for improvement projects. Since, these projects were created from the real problems faced at the bottom of the pyramid, their solutions delivered quick and big results. The warm convection current like culture, also significantly reduced the level of sudden urgencies and brought down the effort and attention otherwise wasted in a large number of expediting actions.

With time, the new framework evolved into a culture of excellence and built a confidence in the staff of Terra Pharma that quick improvements were possible on an ongoing basis. It made the top management available to address the escalated issues and to spend its time in driving improvement proposals emerging from the shop floor. It directly connected the actions in the shop floor to the decision making of the management. This developed significant trust in the staff about the management. Gradually collaborative problem solving became everybody's responsibility.

Reducing Dilemma by Innovating Measurements

A few days later…on a sunny morning, Seth himself was driving the car to the Sanovi Plant, where Amin, the Chairman of Terra Pharma was due for a visit. On the way, he recollected the events that went by Life2.0. His meeting with Amin in the early days of Life2.0 flashed back.

Seth had said, "Amin, we are making fundamental corrections that are like 'Newton's laws of motion', of which everybody seems to be convinced. However, we do not know how to calibrate measurement on these fundamental steps, since it is being implemented for the first time. And at present, it is difficult to mathematically connect it to the outcome, since it is a 'do and learn approach'."

"You mean a bottom up approach!"

"Yes largely. Our intuition and logic tell us that the outcome will only be good. The gap that we have today in our organization, what Ramcharan [13], the famous management guru says, is in 'Execution'. We are suggesting that we will have to walk a distance in order to see the obstacles that will come on our way. And, for the same reason, it may not be wise to work on a definitive and detailed plan".

Amin's eye brows had risen up, but Seth was able to have his buy-in on the promise that his team would be taking small and measurable steps in the right direction; and would do with minimum risk and without costly trade-offs.

The approach was new to Amin also, since moving away from supply based on forecasting to that on actual consumption from stocks, was a paradigm shift. The prevailing notion was that in order to provide good availability of drugs one must keep huge stocks and to have efficient operations of the plant do production based upon quarterly forecasting. Seth's team was, thus working in opposite direction to the norm, i.e. maintain just enough stocks and produce based on daily consumption.

Amin had full faith in the iterative process of 'learning by doing', and therefore, he had backed the initiative fully.

As the things moved ahead, Seth kept control on the outcome, and moved one step at a time, letting the team to discover and improve its solution at a reasonable pace. All this happened without causing costly trade-offs and burn-outs. Amin also realized the change in culture, where people were beginning to look for opportunities to innovate.

It took Seth around 20 minutes to drive into the plant entrance and leave his car at the porch for valet parking. When he reached his office, his secretary informed that Amin had already arrived.

Amin was a gentleman in his early 60s, who was easy going and had no qualms about breaking hierarchy. The Sanovi Plant was his first and the biggest; and his soul belonged here. He would visit the plant quite frequently. He would, normally, take a walk inside the plant and spend some time with operators and supervisors.

Seth always had good time with him. They had first interacted with each other during an inter-ministerial initiative on policy related interventions in the Pharma Industry. Amin was enormously impressed with Seth and picked him from an Innovator Company to lead Terra Pharma.

Seth entered into the Executive suit that was reserved for important visitors. Amin rose to wish him and they shook hands.

Amin said, "I loved my stroll inside the plant. There seems to be so much happening here. You seem to have taken Life2.0 very well."

"Thank you Amin, your encouragement in initiating the project was a big help. I am grateful to you for giving the staff so much independence to experiment. It is coming up good and we are now on a journey that must improve our performance on an ongoing basis. I guess the numbers will follow soon"

"Very Good! I have something to share with you and perhaps, this could further help you," said Amin.

He drew out a sheet of paper from his blazer pocket, walked up to the white board and started scribbling some numbers.

He said, "I got the report of recent internal audit. They are very happy with the changes being brought in and the way SOPs are being built to validate and institutionalize the new system. However, there are some observations and of course, they will discuss with you. I just thought to understand a bit from you."

He continued, "While the fundamental parameters seem to improve and customer satisfaction index is extremely pleasing, our top most index of measurement for the plants, "Number of Pills" delivered per month is quite unstable. The alarming trend is that, while things seem to be very stable everywhere, the throughput numbers have been fluctuating wildly. This is difficult to comprehend. Is there something that is shaking the system up and down, or is this a pre-curser to something which we are not able to comprehend?"

Seth said, while trying to think aloud, "General understanding makes us believe that the volume should go up since substantial improvements have been made in shop floor practice. Perhaps, we are missing something fundamental. I know that some of our products have large batches, while others have small batches. So, when we look it over a short period of time and considering, monthly production to be a short horizon, we do see wild fluctuations in the accumulated output, when product-mix changes."

Amin recognized Seth's comment and said, "You could be right. You know, traditionally managers set a firm target (goal) and then, they frame the rules to achieve them. Though this seems rational, I appreciate your way of thinking in Life2.0."

Then he said, "Your step number one is actually, to identify the rules by challenging the basic assumptions and then to work upward. However, my guess is that once you work bottom-up and set new rules, while the overall objective remains same, you probably need to change the way the progress towards goal is measured. Measurements we do require. Perhaps, you need to have a relook at what you want to measure, so that if people are doing right things and right way, they must be measured on the outcomes that they influence and not on an archaic parameter. It may even mean that all plants need not be measured on raw number of pills produced…, at least people should not be."

Amin spoke so gently, but Seth got it like a jolt of insight.

Seth acknowledged, "That's a revelation, thank you; let me get into it. I guess measuring the plant by 'Volume or Number of Pills' may not be the right index."

Seth knew that Amin already had the answer, but he wanted himself to walk through the solution with his team. The gentlemen spent some time in reviewing other business issues. And then, Amin shook hands with Seth and bid him good bye with a smile.

Seth realized that the staff at Terra Pharma had very well moulded itself into the desired behaviour demanded by the new system. It also made significant contribution to improve performance of the plant. He had also got feelers about the growing expectations of people for reward and recognition. It was necessary that his team addressed critical issues related to people. Thus, the concern raised by Amin was very timely.

"How do we reward people?" Seth asked his team during the following review of Life2.0.

Nobody answered, for a while.

Then, Raman responded, "We review our performance every month and those who contribute good to production are given special rewards and recognition; and on yearly basis, the annual appraisal rewards the good performers."

Ali said, "Good", and then asked, "Can you show the list of people, who got rewards this month."

Ramesh pulled out a Power Point™ slide that displayed top 10 performers of the recent month, their respective functions and cryptic phrases for commendation.

Then, Ali said, "Very Good! Can you show the list of rewards for the last month?"

Ramesh, took a while to search out the file, and then flashed it up.

Perhaps, Seth noticed something, and asked, "How many employees from the other list, appear in this one?"

Ramesh flipped between the slides and then, Raman said, 'One'.

Seth queried, "What does it mean? What happened to the other 9 people?"

Ali added, "Did not they do well during the recent month? Did they perform badly?"

Raman was blinking, and so was everybody in the room.

"Ramesh, just check trends during a couple of months back" Raman said.

They checked the data for 3 months further backward. To their surprise there was hardly any repetition of high performers across months.

"What does this mean?" asked Seth, and continued, "It gives the impression that we do not have any consistent high performer. It is difficult to believe that this is true. I do not think you did anything wrong, but it tells us that there is some gap in the way we measure our performance and the way we reward people. We need to solve this puzzle."

"So, how do we measure people on shop floor? We measure them by number of pills produced. However, our reward system shows that some people perform excellently in one month and not so good in the next month. Is anything wrong with people? Are they so inconsistent?" said Ali.

"That may not be the point," said Seth, and added "Is the demand we place on them and the way we measure them consistent?"

"Oh!" said Ali.

"How have been your plant performing...has the performance been consistently good, month on month?" asked Seth.

"Let's look at our monthly production trend," said Ali.

Ramesh flashed over 12 months of production data. The running average was pretty stable, but the monthly production figures were wildly fluctuating and lately, they were extremely wild. Going twelve months further back, it was as smooth as a goose flight.

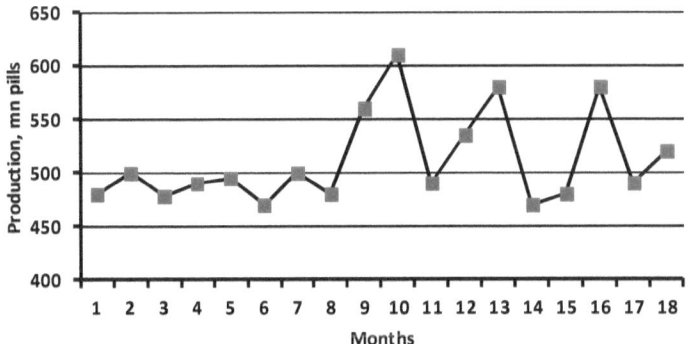

Figure 6.5 Variation of monthly production

Seth said, "Let's try to first answer the question, why was the trend so smooth 9 months back and then turned into wilderness?"

It was time for Raman, he opened up, "Actually, prior to the implementation of the Single Priority System, we knew what to produce much in advance, and we used to produce things in bulk. However, now the priority is based upon actual consumption from stocks that closely follows the immediate market demand. We have too many changeovers too often. Some of our products have each batch of a couple of millions of pills but a good number of other products have batch sizes of just a few thousand pills. Further, we have some products that take a long time to run due to slow recommended speed of machines, while others take shorter time. This means that during the recent times, the *product mix* that flows through the plant is more volatile."

Seth thought that it was a fair explanation from somebody, who was day in day out *pulling* the batches in production.

"Very good" said Ali, and continued, "It means that earlier, the product mix was decided by us and hence, we could choose the products by consolidating demand over a longer period. However, now for good reasons, the product mix is decided by the market."

"We have a feeling that we are not able to control the outcome (influence the outcome) although we are taking the right actions. This is despite all other parameters (including sales) moving in the right direction." said Raman.

"Today, we take a monthly target of 600 million pills and convey this to the staff working on machines. They obediently accept the target, *since people are good*. However, when we monitor their performance against an aggregate monthly target, some time they meet the target and the other time, they do not. This happens because there is a lot of variability in product mix. Further, output per machine or per operator is dependent on the type of the product. Thus, we leave people under constant conflicts, one day patting them on the back and the other day, dumping them down even though they work with equanimity. It obviously means that we are doing injustice to people in the shop floor by including arbitrariness in the way we value their contribution and set the expectations," explained Ali.

At that moment, Rita came forward and prodded Susan to flash her data on the wall. It showed that the product mix had actually changed dramatically. Number of changeovers in certain lines were up by 60% (this was significant, considering that product changeover were often as long as 24 hours). And recently, there were quite a few new products, which needed to be run carefully at lower speeds.

She also projected the product portfolio based on batch size. It validated Raman's intuition and experience.

Then, Rita said, "There is no denying that Volumes (Millions of Pills) is an indicator of the outcome, but when we evaluate performance of operators, it needs to be tempered with factors like product type and changeovers."

Then, she scribbled on the white board to explain how some organizations practicing 'Manufacturing Excellence' resolve the issue. She said that to deal with highly variable environment of product scope and scale, they use a *surrogate* performance measure. And in her views, manufacturing across Terra Pharma's plants could follow a similar measure.

She suggested, "Under these circumstances, the plant would have better control on its outcome, if it is measured on 'equivalent volume' and not on 'absolute volume'."

In her words, 'absolute volume' meant the raw number of pills produced. However, an 'equivalent volume' meant, the number of pills of a reference product, if it were produced instead of all other products during a month."

Then, she wrote the formula for normalizing metric of the plant in terms of equivalent throughput.

For estimating equivalent throughput in millions of pills, she wrote:

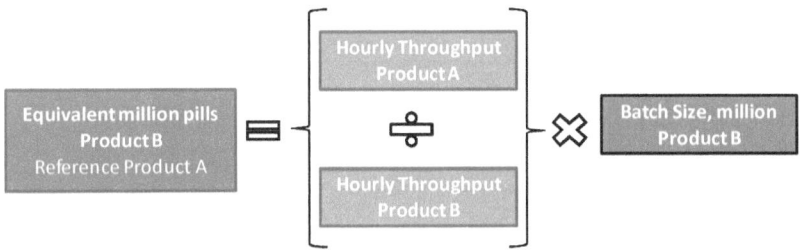

Figure 6.6 Derivation of throughput in equivalent number of millions

Since often, plants measured their throughput in batches, she wrote the following formula:

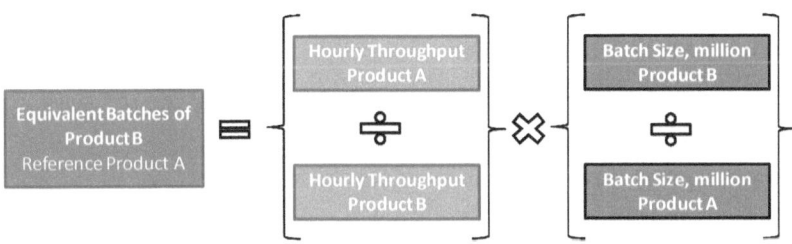

Figure 6.7 Derivation of throughput in equivalent number of batches

She illustrated the calculation of equivalent throughput, in terms of millions of pills and batch sizes for a range of products considering Product A as the reference, Table 6.3.

In the Table, Column 1 represented Product Description, Column 2 represented the rate or millions of pills produced per hour and Column 3 represented the size of each batch in terms of millions of pills. The Column 4 represented the equivalent million of pills of the reference Product A for one batch of the respective product. Column 5 represented equivalent number of batches of the reference Product A for each batch of the respective product.

Thus, for the same effort (machine runtime) in the shop floor, for every batch of product B, 3 equivalent batches of product A would be produced. Similarly, for every batch of product C, D, E and F; 1, 0.5, 1.5

and 2 equivalent batches of product A would be produced, respectively. And also, if 1 batch each of all six products was produced, they would be equivalent to 9 equivalent batches of product A.

Table 6.3: Derivation of Equivalent batch size (Reference Product-A)

Product	Relative Hourly Throughput	Batch size, million	Equivalent Throughput of Product A	
			millions	Batches
A	2	2	2	1
B	1	3	6	3
C	3	3	2	1
D	2	1	1	0.5
E	2	3	3	1.5
F	1	2	4	2
Total		14	18	9

Rita explained further, "The equivalent number of batches (or pills), could be the measure for the plants and the plant managers and perhaps, the production manager. Since the product mix is going to be decided by the market, the products with less counts and running at slower machine speed, will be given due weight in the equivalent batch size calculation. This way of measuring could thus isolate the variability due to product mix. And, it does account for the effort and input of the production staff, who may have to run a slow moving product for longer time."

Ali said, 'Yes, *people working on machines must be measured by the parameter that they can influence.* For example, the operators have great skills in running machines and run time of machines dictates throughput of the plant. Hence, they should influence 'run time' to make their contribution count in the performance of the plant."

But he cautioned, "It also means that linking their performance to the monthly aggregate throughput has no meaning, when product mix changes unpredictably. This is because they will not be able to link their effort to the aggregate throughput of the month. So, they must be measured on how long they run the machine, with respect to the specified product. Their prime role is to ever increase the effective run time of their machines, by running them at right speed and by better maintenance. They can also increase the available run time by working to reduce the changeover time."

"Rita, your approach looks convincing. Let's work on this a bit more. Can you normalize last few months throughput into equivalent batches, and show how the historical trend looks like?" said Seth.

Susan took the lead and said, "Seth, we already have data for these six products; and it validates Rita's hypothesis." She projected the graphs, showing monthly variation of gross number of batches and equivalent number of batches for the product mix. It clearly showed that equivalent number of batches showed direct co-relation to the effort made in improving the flow. It meant that *the effort made in Life2.0 was 'consistently' improving performance of the plant.*

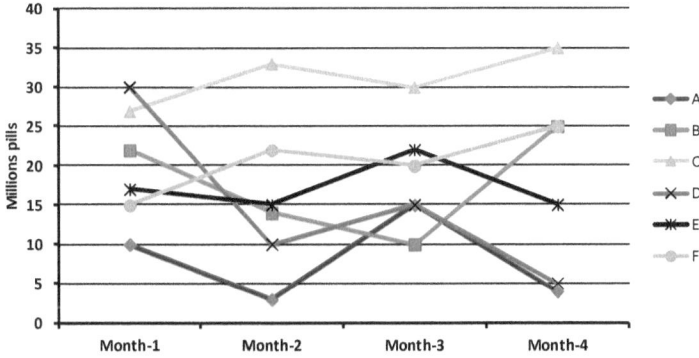

Figure 6.8 Variability in the throughput of a basket of 6 products

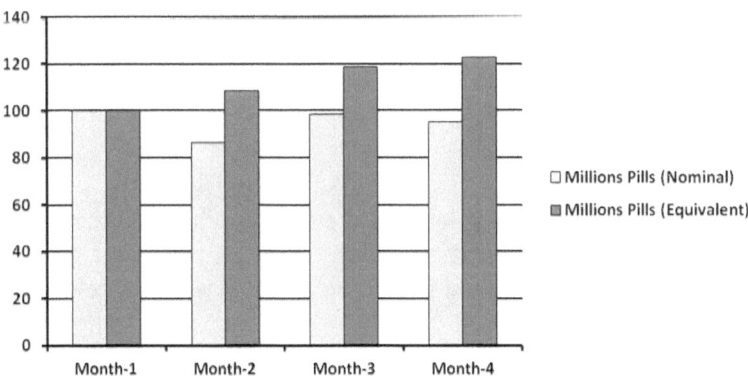

Figure 6.9 Despite the fluctuation in nominal numbers (market based variation), the equivalent number of pills increased month on month reflecting the actual improvements made in the plant

Seth realized that the presentation clarified the need for normalizing effect of product mix on measurement and how it could be made more realistic. He knew that it required further modifications, but wanted to take measurable steps, as his team needed a little more maturity in understanding the cause and effect of changing measurement system.

Clapping his hands, he got up from his seat and then, said, "This looks wonderful. It does enormous justice to the effort of our staff and measures performance of the plant in an unbiased way. Please have a proposal prepared on using new metric, and send it to my office, we will take it from there."

He continued, "But since the change-over time is very high, the market is not going to give us a situation of a favorable product mix. Better we find a way to dramatically reduce the change-over time. We lose roughly 30 percent of our time in changeovers. It is not just about its impact on throughput, it could also be the reason for creating a lot of variability in the flow of batches all along the supply chain. Let's start working on it."

Seth was very well known for providing fair deal to his staff. He realized that in order to make working in Terra Pharma a fulfilling experience, people must go home satisfied, so that they could feel like coming back to work the next day early. This would happen only when employees felt that there was a fair challenge for them to deal with and the challenge was unambiguously defined.

According to Ajay, the latest engagement theory for employee retention revealed that employees would be better satisfied if they saw that they made progress every day. More importantly, they should be able to see that the progress made in their work, contributed to the progress of the company. And, this would be possible if and only if, people were measured by the factors directly influenced by them and their individual metrics were also directly linked to the goal of the organization. It was important that management came out with a metrics, such that the impact of effort made by employees was transparently and unambiguously calibrated, and aligned to organizational goals.

Introduction of the Single Priority System across the flow of process orders meant that everybody in operations followed the same priority system. When an employee would work on a job, it would be clear that one was working on the highest priority work of the organization. This was a big motivation, since the moment an assigned work completed, the company as a whole moved one step ahead towards its commitment made to the market. Thus, it was possible for one to see one's own actions aligned and directly contributing to the goals of the organization.

In that quarter of the year, Ajay launched the review of metrics for the Sanovi Plant. He aligned various external functions by a common priority system and rolled it out with least resistance. People lapped it up full hog, as they were already working in the desired behavior, which the metrics wanted them to adopt. The transition was smooth.

During the next 3 months, a lot of work went into Life2.0 and Terra Pharma did major changes in its policies. Seth himself got involved into establishing collaboration, by bringing together teams from finance, audit, regulatory, compliance, operations and HR. The finance department also agreed to start a pilot, which linked the new metrics of the Sanovi Plant with the financial metrics and framed the rules for audit. These metrics ultimately appeared in appraisal and performance management system of employees through their KPIs (Key Performance Indices). Subsequently, all plants in Terra Pharma were measured by a new *'Operational'* parameter called "Equivalent Millions of Pills" that was insensitive to product mix but reflected the true productivity based on the actual efforts of the people on the shop floor.

Executing the BIG Change

Connecting to the Purpose

Twelve months later… The scene at Terra Pharma had changed completely. The Sanovi Plant had stabilized the consumption based replenishment system and the single priority system, across its product range. Everybody in the value chain knew one's priority and everybody had the same direction on daily basis. When people worked, they knew that they were moving their organization ahead. They had tremendous satisfaction in their work, and it was reflected in their Relay Race behavior. Terra Pharma seemed to have sustained the transformation.

Notwithstanding, the need to ever improve flow in operations, consistent communication from Seth and Ajay on aligning the team around the objective of Life2.0 paid rich dividends. Excerpts of message from Amin, the Chairman of Terra Pharma, during the Leadership Conclave became the anchor for the organization to further accelerate its transformational journey. In his speech, Amin spoke of Terra Pharma's purpose. Here is the excerpt:

".... I am overwhelmed by your collaborative effort in making Terra Pharma a place to work and live. Thanks to Life2.0.

Today, I want to bring all of us to the fundamentals of Terra Pharma, from which our thoughts and actions emerge, i.e. its purpose. Terra Pharma was born out of a purpose. All its strategy and tactics are derived from this purpose, which is of social good to maximize healthy lives.

When we talk about purpose based organization, we differentiate between the *opportunity* to do business and the *necessity* to do business. There may be a huge business opportunity to produce a drug that has high financial benefit but it may have very poor social impact, and *vice versa*. Our drugs have high social impact at the first instance. Although, a large part of our product portfolio does not have high financial benefits, we continue to be committed to produce them and serve the society.

Because of our being a purpose based organization, we make money as an outcome of social good and not the other way. This is a profound commitment in public health context, where a large number of drugs called *orphaned drugs,* severely affecting the wellbeing of selected groups of humanity, have very little commitment from other pharma companies. We constantly work closely with players in healthcare sector like the WHO, Health Ministry, not for profit organizations and other Public Health organizations, in improving health of the society.

Today, we are the largest producer of orphaned drugs and other essential drugs in the region. I think this makes us different and gives us a unique position in the Health Care Industry. This unique position of Terra Pharma is not negotiable, and will never change with time or place.

Having such a strong purpose has no meaning if it is not reflected in our business ambition. Terra Pharma has a global footprint and we want to be a Global Leader. Serving many countries naturally requires meeting so many different regulatory and market requirements. This necessitates an unbelievable variety of products and at any moment, it is very difficult to make all these varieties available at the right place.

Taking such a position and having such an ambition have undesirable effects on our ability to deliver good business results. In the language of economists, our business suffers from the Long Tail effect. This means that over 90 percent of our products have infrequent requirements and that too in small quantities. Delivering Long Tail products creates huge difficulties in conducting our business efficiently. Often, it also disturbs the business potential of our top 10 percent products.

A traditional business approach is to prune the Long Tail significantly on a regular basis. However, for Terra Pharma, the Long Tail is a necessary characteristic than an aberration. It means that the Long Tail is an integral part of our portfolio and Business Model.

Our portfolio management can't always be directed to filter out drugs that fetch low revenues. Rather our effort is to make the Long Tail readily available in the market, while making it profitable for us. Every year, we consolidate our portfolio with an objective to incorporate parameters of our purpose that maximizes our impact on social good. And, we commit ourselves to steer our Business Model accordingly. Yes, we do cut out select products from the tail; but we make sure that somebody else produces it and patients are not left unattended.

In fact, some non Pharma Industries too experience similar phenomenon. But they are able to improvise their Business Model to leverage the Long Tail effect. And, it may not be too difficult for us to do so, as long as we are sincere to our purpose and ambition. We must manage our portfolio, continuously innovate our Business Model to optimize our delivery system and constantly do justice to our purpose.

The message that I have for you is to believe in the 'Long Tail' as a necessary condition, i.e. the Long Tail is integral to our purpose and our business. Given this belief, it is now our responsibility to see how we can maximize our productivity. When the purpose is so clear, I am sure that the methods will emerge soon and we move ever closer to our objective...."

Dealing with the Long Tail

The Long Tail, which only got longer with time, had always been a point of conflict within Terra Pharma. Amin had centered his message on long tail products. It might have meant that some of the products that might have got neglected must have come to his attention. It was also possible that the growing clamor about pharma companies neglecting supply of essential drugs might have rocked some high profile meeting at the ministerial level.

In fact, Sales would always prefer as wide a portfolio of products as possible, so that it could make a stronger pitch to clients and cross sell drugs. Specifically, having a wide portfolio helped in attracting big retail chains. Also, it often brought a level of stability against fluctuating demands in the market.

When the management team of Terra Pharma assembled after the Leadership Conclave, dealing with the Long Tail was the hot topic.

Ranbir, picked up from where Amin had left and said, "The Pharmaceutical Industry works based on a concept called 'basket of supplies'. We need to offer our clients a basket of therapeutic values. Drugs are not always sold one SKU at a time. They are often prescribed in combinations. If we have a large portfolio of associated drugs, sale of one drug automatically pushes sale of others."

Seth could not deny the strong benefit of basket offerings, but he knew that Sales had a tendency to go to extremes to fulfill its targets. Sometimes this could make life of everybody difficult; of course, for a good reason. However, Ranbir always denied any notion of their intention to create trouble in Operations.

Certainly, Amin's message was a shot in the arm for the sales team, and it pounded heavily on Operations to honor the wide portfolio of Terra Pharma.

Ranbir said, "Just have a look at the Long Tail! Look at the area under the curve!"

He went to the flipchart stand and drew the Long Tail curve. He then shaded the areas under the head and the tail, and marked them as A and B, respectively, Figure 7.1.

And said, "Now, if we do the math, we find that the opportunity represented by A and B are comparable."

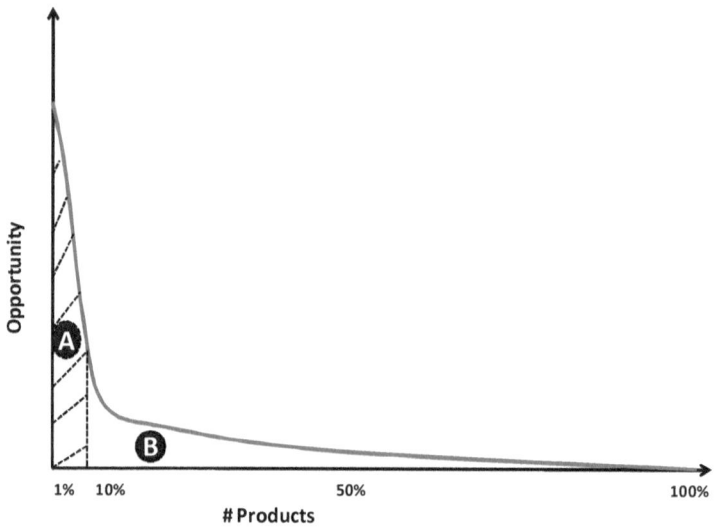

Figure 7.1 Opportunities under the Head and the Tail products are comparable

People knew that the logic was strongly validated by data. It was difficult for anybody to take on the argument.

"Yes, I understand," said Ali and, continued, "The tail is too long, but it forces us to take too many changeovers (setups) in our lines and eats away our capacity. It is not at all profitable to produce the tail quantities."

Seth interjected, "I do not think that the debate is whether we need to produce tail products or not. Produce we must, and deliver them, as Amin said. Being in operations, it is our responsibility to figure out, how we do it more effectively. Though, even today we are delivering them."

Tony jumped in, "Seth, this may not be a typical problem of the Pharma Industry only, although we may be the one to challenge it."

Rita, who was quite till then, said, "Yes, several other industries including FMCGs, have a similar problem, but some organizations are able to handle it efficiently in the plant."

Seth said, "Yes, but the tail there may not be as long as it is here, and they are not obliged to supply all products. For them, only profitability counts."

Tony said, "What I mean is that probably the Long Tail tells us something, and we need to breakdown its characteristics." Tony was in his typical mood of deep diving into the problem.

Then, he said, "Yes, traditionally, all industries which face long tail portfolio have nothing but to cut the tail rigorously. Let's look under part A and part B."

Demand Determines Facility Design

Tony walked up to the flip chart, and asked, "What are the characteristics of products under part A, Ranbir?"

Ranbir said, "These are really fast movers and high gross margin products in the market. They are either our blockbusters or well matured products."

"Alright! If these are our flagship products, how are they being manufactured these days?" asked Tony.

Tony saw the team looking at each other. He asked Ali, "I mean, do we have a specific way of manufacturing this group of products; a manufacturing strategy, technique, flow, layout, routing, scheduling etc.?"

"Inside the plant, most of them flow through the Modules, where flow of their batches have minimum disruptions; they are supposed to be largely dedicated lines," said Rita.

Ali added, "However, over the years, some of the long tail products have found place in these lines. And unfortunately, they often create disruptions to the Fast Movers."

"So, ideally, to meet the demand in the market, the Fast Movers should flow like a nonstop train. Right Ali!" said Tony.

"Indeed!" said Ali.

Ali realized that Tony was facilitating verbalization of the current reality, so that everybody could have clarity on the way the Long Tail was being handled. He always liked Tony's way of bringing people together to solve critical problems.

"So to repeat, the Fast Movers, which have regular demand, must flow like a bullet train and must use module facilities." Tony said briskly and then asked, "Do we have a clear understanding on this?"

"Yes!" everybody said in unison.

"I do not know what we are going to do with products that come from the Long Tail," Tony said, running his fingers through his hair, as if trying to pull out an answer from his head.

Instead, he asked pointing towards area B on the curve, "So, what type of demand do we have in the Long Tail?"

Ranbir prompted, "Most of these are in small number of batches. Generally, they are needed infrequently and often, not required urgently."

"So what problem do we have from production point of view?" he asked Ali.

"It may be better to illustrate the problem," Ali said, as he walked up to the whiteboard and started scribbling.

He said, "These lead to a high number of changeovers. For example, if we produce six batches of product 'A' in sequence, on a compression machine, we could produce all these, in approximately, 72 hrs. Now instead, if we produce six batches, consisting of two batches each of three different long tail products (A, B and C), in the sequence AABBCC, it could take over 100 hrs. The reason being that when we want to change the product being processed in an area, the complete area including machines must be cleaned, sanitized and machine parts changed. The changeover time currently runs as long as 24 hours. Thus, it reduces our throughput dramatically."

"I see," said Tony.

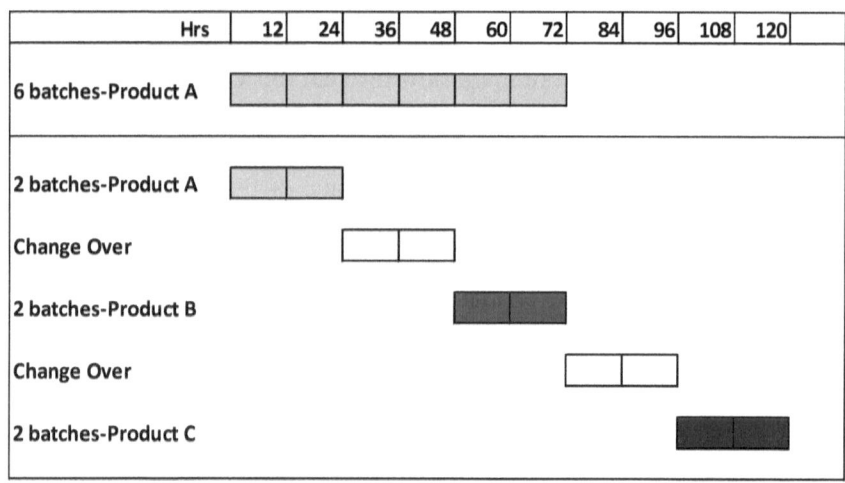

Figure 7.2 Changeovers reduce the throughput dramatically

"And for the same reason, long tail products are, normally, not taken into the Modules, since there…, the cleaning takes too long a time. Rather, they are produced in the Suites, where each process is isolated from the other, and it provides significant flexibility in running different products. However, the flexibility is not big enough to deal with our too long a tail," said Rita.

"So, by design, all machines in the Suites process only long tail products," Tony tried to rephrase Rita's inputs.

"Not really, we also have some Fast Movers, flowing through the Suites, primarily because, when they were launched, we did not expect that their demand would run so high or because then, there was no capacity in the Modules." Thus, Ali added the exceptional element to the discussion.

"I see. So summarizing, ideally we would like the Fast Movers processed in the Modules and the Long Tail in the Suites. Now as the reality has changed since the respective products were launched or validated, the rule is not followed strictly. Probably, we need to review our manufacturing recipe. What do you say Ali?" asked Tony looking at Ali.

"Yes indeed! If we run some long tail products in the Modules, they eat away capacity and unduly delay the Fast Movers. At the same time, some of the Fast Movers are being produced in the Suites, thinking that there is no capacity in the Modules," said Ali.

"This is one major issue that we try to address regularly, through revalidation of products. It includes shifting of products manufactured in one area into another area. Unfortunately, it takes significant time and we have a separate team that helps us in validating alternative facilities. Its job is to ensure that the drugs produced in a new area retain the specified chemical and physical properties," clarified Ali.

Seth said, "It makes great sense to look at the Long Tail as it is, and adopt their routing accordingly. Why can't we speed up the revalidation process?"

Seth was nervous and this was reflected in his tone as he said, "Let's agree to come out with a clear classification of the Long Tail and the Fast Movers, and have a plan to deal with them separately in the Suites and the Modules, respectively. This will immediately release significant capacity."

Tony sensed the urgency in Seth's suggestion but restrained from derailing the ongoing discussion. He said, "Yes, we need to expedite rerouting of the Long Tail and the Fast Movers, separately. But, I think that we have not yet finished with the understanding of the long tail phenomenon. Perhaps, there is something more that we could do."

It looked as if he had some insight. All eyes and ears were on him.

All Products Need Not be Stocked

Tony said in a while, "Traditionally, we stock all of our products in the Finished Goods warehouses. As Ranbir said, most of the long tail products are required infrequently. This means that most of the long tail products are not required to be stocked too much in advance.

"Also, often, we have sufficient time to process them and deliver," said Rita.

Tony said from his experience in delivery management, "Yes. We have the Fast Movers, which move faster and are required to be almost readily 'available' to be shipped. Most of the Long Tail are not needed so urgently, but can be delivered on a sufficiently later date, though must be supplied reliably to the due date."

He added, "The fundamental understanding which we build today is that the tolerance time of customers for the Fast Movers and most of the Long Tail is different. Hence, products for which the customer tolerance time is less than our lead time, we must stock only them. But products, for which the customers can wait and have long tolerance time (longer than our lead time), we must produce them only upon receiving firm orders from the customers."

"Do you mean that we have different ways of promising to the clients, depending upon which product they need?" asked Ali.

"Exactly!" exclaimed Tony. He said to Ranbir, "Is it ok if we keep FG stocks of the Fast Movers and produce them based on the consumption from the stock? However, we produce most of the Long Tail only based on actual orders."

"Yes, of course Tony," said Ranbir.

He confirmed further, "Actually, even today, we supply the Long Tail based on far enough due dates only, although, they are stocked in the warehouses."

"Which means that all along, we have been unnecessarily trying to produce all long tail products in advance, thus creating load and chaos in the shop floor," Ali said and stared at Ranbir. Ranbir smiled and avoided eye contact.

"That is one reason, why we have overstocking and non moving stocks on one hand, while we have stock outs on the other hand," said Seth.

"So, does it mean that changing the way we produce to fill the stock or meet a due date does not create any problem to you?" Tony asked Ranbir.

"I am sure that it would only improve the situation. Our need is to fulfill the promise to supply as per market demanded lead time. Whether it is readily picked up from stock or produced and immediately delivered, is not a concern for the market. But yes, producing most of the Long Tail strictly based on real customer orders would definitely help and would avoid a lot of confusion among production, delivery and sales teams." Ranbir gave his stamp of approval.

"So we have another way to lighten the burden of the Long Tail," said Tony.

"We will have the Fast Movers as Made to Availability i.e. stocked products. Most of the long tail products, will be made to meet a committed due dates, and we can call them Made to Order." Thus, he described the new rule of product classification.

<u>Product Classification Policy:</u> The Fast Movers will be supplied from the Stock and the Long Tail will be largely supplied based on due date of sales order.

While it seemed that the discussion had closed, Ali said, "We have one problem. How would people in the shop floor set priority for long tail products, if they are based on due date?"

"What do you mean?" asked Seth

"For stocked products, by looking at the inventory levels one knows which product is in the danger of being stocked out. Hence, the priority system there is very intuitive. But when we have orders based on due dates along with those based on stocks, there will be confusion in the shop floor in setting the priority."

"Should not be a problem. We will have to redefine 'endangered orders' with reference to actual commitment to the customers," said Tony thoughtfully.

"It means that the orders that are in the danger of missing committed due dates will have higher priority between the long tail process orders!" said Rita.

"Yes, indeed. So, shorter the relative time left for an order to meet committed due date, higher will be its priority," clarified Tony.

"Tony, I think we need written guidelines for managing priority of long tail orders," said Rita.

"Yes, I understand. Till the revalidation of products is completed, we will have both types of products running simultaneously in the Modules and the Suites. We need a clear instruction on how to manage priorities, when those from stock and those based on due date share the same resource," said Tony as if he had forethought the possibilities. (Please refer Appendix- Unambiguous Priority System)

"Will it now help Ali in simplifying manufacturing?" asked Seth.

"Yes, we can start the validation project, since it will help in streamlining the Fast Movers and the Long Tail," said Ali.

But immediately, he pointed to a negative effect, "The Suites will now have more changeovers, and the supply of these products will have poorer lead time and reliability."

"But Ali, we would now produce more in tune with market demand! The new classification of products will help reduce the load and the revalidation must release some capacity," pointed out Seth. "Of course, we now need to find a solution to the increased number of changeovers, and I believe that it is entirely in your domain. Let's think it out loud now."

"Ok," said Ali.

Duty Cycle Reveals Improvement Actions

After a while, Seth said, "We agreed that the Fast Movers will flow in the Modules continuously. It means that there will be fewer changeovers, hence, longer runtimes and better utilization."

"Yes, a Module is like a continuous flow plant. Hence, its duty cycle has relatively longer touch time or runtime," added Ali.

"It means... with other things remaining the same, in order to further improve the flow, the module team must focus on reducing the process time, which is the dominant part of the duty cycle. Isn't it?" Seth asked Ali.

"Yes, it must." nodded Ali.

"The type of expertise we need here is of those, who understand the process, machines and automation. We need collaboration of engineering, maintenance, QA and technology transfer people."

"Let's minute this," said Seth, and Rita jotted down 'improve process time of batches in the Modules'.

Tony raised his hand and said, "That's good for the Fast Movers. Now when we look into the Long Tail, which flows through the Suites; based on what Ali explained, the duty cycle is something like this." He walked up to the white board and drew the duty cycles of the process orders flowing in the Modules and the Suites, which appeared in perfect contrast to each other, Figure 7.3.

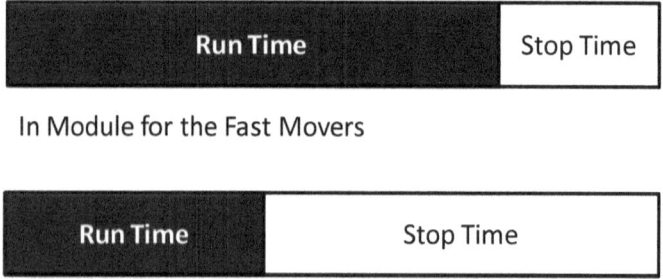

Figure 7.3 The representative monthly duty cycle of facility

Pointing towards the duty cycle of the Suites, he emphasized, "The Suites have touch time of around 30-40 percent and idle time including voluntary stoppages of over 60 percent. Since between process time and idle time, the latter is longer and easy to improve, it makes sense to focus on improving idle time of machines in the Suites."

"Absolutely, if we could somehow reduce the long changeover times in the Suites, it would make a lot of difference to productivity," said Seth.

Tony said, "So, as an immediate action, it makes sense to draw the following improvement rules." And then, he wrote down the rules to improve flow:
- For Modules, focus on reducing process time.
- For the Suites, focus on reducing changeover time.

He then said, "Of course, in both cases, we have unscheduled stoppages due to various reasons. This may include, lunch and tea break, break downs, meetings etc."

"Agreed! Let's minute it," said Ali as he smiled and looked at Seth.

Operational Strategy for Dealing with Wide Portfolio

Thus, the senior management team of Terra Pharma, came out with its new approach to resolve conflicts involved in dealing with the Fast Movers and the Long Tail. The following rules were then agreed and formulated.

Table 7.1 Guidelines for dealing with the Fast Movers and the Long Tail

Elements	Fast Movers	Long Tail
Commitment	Availability	Reliability
Supply	Made to Stock	Made to Due date
Scheduling	Replenishment	Sales Order
Routing	Modules	Suites
Focus	Touch Time	Stop Time
Improvement Elements	Machine Reliability, Process, Automation, Revalidation	Changeovers, Maintenance, Revalidation

While the top four elements were system based, Seth was curious about the bottom two that required significant change in the behavior of the people.

Improving the Process of Improvement

Aren't Big Improvements Overwhelming?

The team at Terra Pharma had agreed to resolve the conflicts in dealing with the Fast Movers and the Long Tail. To deliver all products seamlessly, it chose to rapidly implement following improvement themes:

1. Cross validation of products between the Modules and the Suites
2. Crashing Process time of the Fast Movers
3. Reducing Stop Time (includes changeover time) in the Suites

The Sanovi Plant had over 500 machines and equipments. If each one of these three improvement themes were to be implemented across the plant then, each one seemed like a huge project in itself. It meant involvement of huge resources, effort, time and money.

When the preliminary project plan for implementing the three themes came to Seth, the estimates were mindboggling. The three improvement programs together were going to consume the plant's man power for almost two years, which was close to 2x1500 man years. And, the budget for improvement including training, travel, tools and infrastructure, was almost competing with its operational budget.

Seth was in a tight situation. Although the improvement themes had great potential, the resource commitment was looking daunting. Things looked too complex for his team. Realizing the enormity of the required effort, his team proposed to roll out one theme at a time. It made sense to Seth too. However, no body was sure where to start, so that it could get early win, without shaking up the complete system.

Seth called me and said, "DJ, we have identified at least three themes of improvement. However, deploying these across the plant seems too much complex and it might exhaust us. It might also be risky."

He explained the three areas of improvements, and then asked, "Is there a way out?"

I said almost instantly, "The improvement themes are promising ones and I have no doubt that your team knows the techniques to unleash these improvements.... Now, you need to help it in improving the process of improvement."

"Improving ... the process of improvement!" murmured Seth.

"Yes, there must be an Inherent Simplicity in the plant to allow you to simplify the process of improvement."

I waited a while, and then said, "You told me that the scope of improvement is overwhelming, i.e. it is getting too detailed. This is typical of any major improvement initiative. You have got into a situation of complexity called Detailed Complexity."

"Yes, we are probably getting into too much work of managing details than effecting improvement," said Seth.

"When the details become too much, we need to follow the system's logic. It would help us simplify the areas needing attention. It means that we need to identify the Inherent Simplicity in the plant."

"I see, but where is this Inherent Simplicity?" asked Seth thoughtfully.

"Search for it." It came logically from me.

"Search for what?" asked Seth, as if he lost the track of our discussion.

I said, "Inherent Simplicity."

"Inherent Simplicity! Pardon me! With 500 resources catering anytime to a load of over 1000 process orders across of a wide portfolio, it can only be highly complex."

"The more complex a system, the simpler it is." I said while recalling Eli Goldratt's [14] famous quote, though I did not mean to confuse him.

He kept mum.

I grasped his difficulty and said, "Look, an organization is a system, made of interdependent parts, like... a chain and its interconnected links."

Figure 7.4 An organization is like a chain made of several interdependent links

And then, continued, "You need all the links to make the organization work."

"Yes," said Seth

"So, what is the normal way of improving strength of the chain? Just increase the strength of each link!" I said.

"Of course" said, Seth. He fell into the trap.

"Now, if the Sanovi Plant is made up of 500 resources, then you have so many such links, isn't it?" I further quipped him with a seemingly silly question.

"Yes, indeed, that is why it is very complex." Seth said.

I said aloud, "NO!"

As if he woke up to a shock, and murmured, "What do you mean?"

"All links of your chain are not of the same strength."

"Yes, possibly!"

"No, they are definitely of different capacities."

I said quickly and loudly, "And, at any moment of time, the strength of the chain is determined by the weakest link."

"Oh yeah!" he said softly.

Figure 7.5 Strength of the Chain is no stronger than the weakest link.

Then, I said, "Your organization is made of, perhaps, not one but a few chains. Nevertheless, at any moment, performance of your organization is limited by just one or a few of the weakest links. "

"Oh! All parts are not of the same strength" said Seth, as he grasped the profound knowledge.

I asked, "If strength of the chain is limited by the weakest link, will making improvement anywhere other than the weakest link improve the strength of the chain?"

"No, no! It will be a waste of time, effort and money," he understood quickly.

Then, he said, "At that moment, it is enough to focus improvements on the weakest link, rather than spreading effort on all other links. Any improvement in the weakest link will improve overall performance."

"So, what do you say about the Logical Complexity of 500 interrelated resources?" I asked immediately.

He replied, "The challenge is in finding the Weakest Link or the Constraint that prevents throughput of the plant, when we want to produce both the Fast Movers and the Long Tail."

"And, what do you think about the three improvement themes. How enormous is their implementation?"

"We do not need to drive the improvement themes in all the places but at the Weakest Link(s)." He said.

"We need to identify the *vital few* areas where we can drive the improvement themes. This would be the way to make significant improvement quickly, without taking too much risk and without exhausting costly resources. Now, the implementation of the improvement themes does not look so overwhelming and complex," he spelt out his thoughts.

And then, he asked, "Is this the way, a complex situation becomes simpler?"

"Indeed!" I knew that Seth had the insight.

Identifying the Weakest Link

Throughout the night, Seth was thinking about the possible 'Weakest Links'. In the morning, he went back to his team, replayed our discussion and asked them to search for the Inherent Simplicity in the plant. He told his team, "Let's find the Weakest Link."

"First, what does the Weakest Link mean to us?" He asked, to begin the discussion.

"Something that prevents us from reaching our goal," said Tony. He had always been to the point.

"You mean… the goal of the plant?" asked Ali.

"Yes, for us, it must be the goal of the plant, which must also be derived from the goal of Terra Pharma," said Tony.

"Ok! What is the goal of the plant?" asked Ali.

"Achieving higher throughput," said Tony.

"Yes, but in our case, it is the reliability of the supply coupled with Throughput," said Ranbir.

"Yes! Of course, it means, the effective throughput of the products which is driven by consumption pattern and actual customer orders." Tony corrected himself immediately.

Ali got back to answer the original question on the Weakest Link, "You see, traditionally, we call bottlenecks as the rate limiting elements in the plant. This means that bottlenecks limit the throughput."

He then drew a flow diagram and said, "Actually, a bottleneck is with respect to the flow of process orders. Our process orders flow through a sequence of operations. And, it may just happen that, along one flow, compression of tablets may be the slowest operation. In such a case, compression decides our throughput."

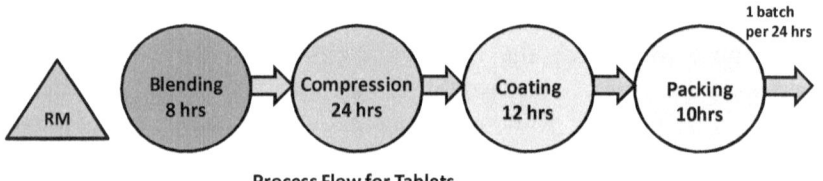

Process Flow for Tablets

Figure 7.6 The slowest operation decides the throughput. Here, compression operation prevents the line from producing more than 1 batch per 24 hours.

"Compression machine is then called the bottleneck, since it limits the production rate of the line," said Ali.

"So if the Weakest Link decides the strength of the chain, then bottlenecks are our weakest links," Tony said emphatically.

"How many bottlenecks does the plant have?" asked Seth.

"Not very sure, but yes, quite a few," said Ali.

"Quite a few! DJ said that there can't be too many," said Seth.

"Traditionally, for each line, we can say that there could be at least one bottleneck, and if we have crisscross flows, then a few more," said Ali.

"Oh! This means that we have more than one chain!" Seth said reflecting on the discussion he had with me.

"You mean, 10, 20....?" he asked.

"Yes, around 15 parallel paths," said Ali.

"But, how do we find the bottlenecks?" asked Tony.

Seth interrupted, "15 chains are too many... it can't be so complex. Wait a minute! These bottlenecks must be preventing us from delivering specific products flowing through them. So, in the near term say today, how many products are in the danger of being stocked out and how many bottlenecks are standing in their way?" Seth was definitely hooked on to the objective of Life2.0.

Tony ran through stock positions on his laptop and said, "We have as on date, 15 products in deep red and they are running into this situation almost chronically and sometimes into stock out." He also spelt out the names of the products.

"It means that often, demand for these products outstrips supply; if we could improve throughput of these products, we would immediately improve our sales," said Seth, while Ranbir looked at him, in agreement.

"Which lines do these products flow through, Ali?" asked Tony

Ali had already an XL™ sheet opened in front of him, and said, "These products flow through, essentially four lines, one Module and three groups of Suites."

"So, do we know the bottlenecks in these four flows," asked Seth.

Ali said, "Not precisely, but standard timings can give us some indication of the bottlenecks."

"So at this moment, we need to focus on these four flows. And any improvement in the throughput of bottleneck machines along these flows, will give us significant improvement," said Seth.

Leveraging the Weakest Link

Seth called me in the night, and said, "DJ, we have found the Inherent Simplicity in our Plant."

"Really! What does it look like?"

"At the moment, we may not have more than four resources that limit our growth in throughput. There may be more, but they may not have immediate visibility."

I said in one breath, "You do not need more visibility, if you are looking at the situation of your stocks and due date performance now. They are good starting points to trace back to the real constraints."

Then, he narrated how his team figured out the flow from endangered products down to the lines; and how they planned to trace out specific constraining operations and machines, the *Weakest Links*. Yes, they knew it, I never had any doubt.

He said, "Intuitively, our people know the bottlenecks, but now we have to validate them with data. It feels good that we almost have the Weakest Links in our hands."

"I see. Remember, these resources may not be bottlenecks yet, they may just seem to be Capacity Constrained Resources because of the way they are operated."

"What is a capacity constrained resource?"

"A machine could become a constrained resource, due to breakdowns, lower skill of people, longer changeover time, lower speed of operations, regular stoppages due to worn out parts or process issues, delay in quality check, starvation etc. Despite this, nothing should prevent you from leveraging these machines to obtain higher throughput." I said.

Seth said, "Now that we may not have more than four resources to improve, we will do everything required to get maximum throughput from these resources."

"Indeed! March ahead and get maximum output from them. Your team must know that an hour of extra work on these machines is an hour of extra throughput from their respective lines. That is, if you improve utilization of a constrained resource by 10 percent, the throughput of the entire line improves by 10 percent. On the other hand, if you lose one hour per day on these machines, you could lose much more than 5 percent throughput of the entire line." I said.

"We will go full hog on this," said Seth.

"Seth! Leveraging the constraint is not trivial. In a vast majority of cases, the possible throughput gain could be much more than your expectations. At the same time, it is not easy to estimate, *a priori,* how much capacity is hidden in the constraint. Through a focused improved program on constrained resource, almost always, you would see an immediate improvement. It also means that you need to guard your team against complacency at early wins. You also need to ensure that leveraging the constraint is not diluted to just another improvement work."

"Anything specific I need to do?" asked Seth.

"Yes, the constraints must get your regular attention. And, everybody in the plant must know that these machines are the leverage points of the plant and they deserve highest priority, should they face any slackness. Such a strong focus is required because these machines are your *gold mines*, and at the moment, they determine how much more the plant can help make more money through sales without incurring too much cost and without spending too much effort." I said.

"Sure," said Seth.

Then, he asked, "Is there any specific recipe for leveraging a constrained resource?"

I said, "Just do it. People dealing with these resources are best qualified to leverage them. However, they would need support from the management and peers."

"OK, I will have a plan and then, discuss with you," he said.

"No, just do it." I repeated.

"Just do it!" he echoed.

I said, "To start with, it may be a good idea to handle one constraint, till we establish the process and behavior of leveraging the constraint." I felt that the team still needed to discover the right behavior for dealing with constraints which was not same as required for managing bottlenecks. Perhaps, the team could do a pilot on one constraint, before moving over to the others.

"Sure," said Seth.

It was very easy for the Sanovi team to identify the exact four resources that were preventing the plant from increasing throughput of their key 15 products.

The team realized that those four resources were *goldmines* for them, as they were controlling any increase in the throughput of the plant. Loss of a single hour on these machines meant loss of an equivalent revenue across the plant. However, as per my discussion with Seth, his team began the journey of leveraging constraints from one resource. It was a compression machine (resource code: CCR) in the Suite area which was serving eight products, out of which six were regularly running into stock outs or failing to meet the committed due dates. To everybody's surprise, most of the products were fast movers.

Once they picked up the CCR, the team found that it already had a pending Capital Expenditure (CAPEX) application, and the shop floor team had been crying for buying a new machine. The machine with an advanced configuration was costing a bomb. It also had a long supply lead time. It was to be fetched from Switzerland, involved testing and validation, and had a gestation period of at least six months. It also meant training of the staff in running and managing the machine. And, once the machine would arrive, it would go through weeks of validation process.

Seth realized, "Six months is a long period and the market would not be the same again. Instead, the team must do what is in its hand, NOW."

He also recalled the saying, "*Capacity of the plant is capacity of its people.* Our people need to search out hidden capacity in the CCR."

He walked up to Ali and convinced him to start exploiting the CCR by the time the Swiss machine would come in. Later, in an afterthought, he suggested Ali, rather not to hasten buying of the new machine and asked him to review the CAPEX requirements for other machines.

In order to start focusing on the CCR, Ali and Raman, ran a session with operators, supervisors, shift in-charges and area managers who were associated with the CCR line. They announced that the CCR was identified as the most valued machine for the plant… the Goldmine.

Ali said, "The CCR is the lever for the plant to demonstrate that there is significant hidden capacity and people can reveal additional capacity."

Given the focus on the CCR, people spoke out and volunteered to improve its utilization. Ali was surprised that his people knew so much. But he realized that he needed a systematic way of exploiting the CCR, as Seth had warned him about the danger of trivialization.

His sensitization of the staff directly working on the CCR was to get the buy in, for starting improvements in the shop floor. The staff knew that its key products were in good demand but their availability was not good. It realized that it was entirely in its hands to increase the throughput of the plant. It understood that any additional throughput of these products would be sold immediately and would give significant benefit to the bottom line.

Ali had used the following explanation to induct the line managers into the rigor of expected improvement process.

"The growth of the company is dependent upon the profit it makes, and this profit must grow with time, so that it can be invested back. For the profit to grow on an ongoing basis, it is necessary that the Margins (and hence Sales), grows faster than the growth in Operating Expenses."

"Let's consider an example (Table 7.2); the Column two, dissects Sales during a period. Now look at the Column three. You would find that just a mere 10 percent increase in Sales, increases Operating Profit by 30 percent. The assumption here is that Operating Expenses do not change much, during the short period of increase in Sales."

Table 7.2 Focusing on Constraint gives significant benefits

Measurement	Mn USD	
Sales	100	110
Material Cost	40	44
Margin	60	66
Operational Expenses	40	40
Operational Profit	20	26

"A constrained resource is the one, where demand is more than supply. Therefore, any increase in its effective utilization will immediately increase Sales. And since, the efforts are focused only on the constraint, the risks are extremely limited and the Operating Expenses do not increase much. Thus we obtain a fast global advantage (companywide benefit), by acting on a very small and local part of the plant. This is the secret of inherent simplicity and focusing mechanism."

Table 7.2 was a very simple and effective way to demonstrate that *any increase in Sales due to a focused improvement on the Constraint provides immediate bottom line benefit.* In fact, the relative increase in profit would be substantially higher than the increase in Sales.

Having sensitized and got buy-in from the staff working around the CCR, it was very important to set the base line. The team found that the CCR, at an average, produced 20 million equivalent pills per month. When, the team worked out details, it was found that this corresponded to an actual uptime of the CCR of approximately 35 percent of the scheduled monthly calendared time.

A number of suggestions that came from the team promised improvement in the utilization of the CCR to almost 50 percent. That was very encouraging.

In his email to Ali and the production team, Seth had written "Since we know that the CCR is a constrained resource, we must eliminate all waste on and around it, and we must improve its overall effectiveness."

Later on, when they met, Ali asked Seth, "Are you hinting at the OEE?"

Seth replied, "Yes Ali. Why do not we follow the template of OEE to exploit the CCR?"

"Sure we will do. OEE is, perhaps, just what is needed now." Ali affirmed.

The Overall Equipment Effectiveness (OEE) is a measurement for indicating the effectiveness of a machine, and is used extensively in validating improvements made on and around a machine. Typically, OEE categorizes losses around the machine as, Downtime Loss, Speed Loss and Quality Loss; and back calculates the OEE factor. The OEE calculation that is followed across industries uses integration of Availability, Performance (Speed) and Quality at the target machines and is stated as:

Seth knew that Terra Pharma was still far from making OEE as a standard parameter for measurement. The availability of machines in Terra Pharma was very low. Hence it did not make sense for it to use all the three multipliers. To start with, the team chose to focus on Availability of the CCR.

The deliberations of the team revealed that the key losses in the CCR affecting its Availability (utilization) were Downtime Losses that consisted of the following:

1. Stoppages: Due to breakdowns, unscheduled maintenance, mal-operations, absenteeism, lunch and tea breaks, utility failure, etc.
2. Setup: Part change over, start-up delay, low operator skills, line clearance delay, non-availability of operators, etc.
3. Cleaning: Line clearance failure, change part unavailability, delay in cleaning staff arrival, non-availability of utility, etc.

However, amongst all the reasons of delay, changeover and cleaning related time dominated Downtime Losses. It amounted to almost 20 hours per product changeover on the CCR. And so, if in a month there were 8 product changeovers, then it meant a loss of almost 7 days of productivity. In fact, in Terra Pharma, changeovers were taking more than 35 percent of the utilization of the machines across the plant.

The 35 percent loss of productivity due to changeovers, was a shaming figure for Seth, not because it was high on its own, but because it was also high at the CCR (where every hour lost was an hour lost for the complete line).

It was just a coincidence that in those few days, Seth's office received an industry wide survey on productivity numbers. It did not surprise him that poor changeover time was identified as the major cause of poor utilization and low operational efficiency in the industry. The report had actually, exhorted the readers to learn from the Automotive Industry. It narrated the amazing story of Toyota, where setup time between two different models of cars, was reduced from 3 days to less than 10 minutes [11,15,16]. Seth learnt that a technique called SMED (Single Minute Exchange of Die), was used to crash the setup time dramatically.

Seth wanted to implement SMED in Terra Pharma. He did acknowledge though that his team might not follow SMED exactly as it was done in Toyota. Specially, since in the Pharma Industry, people could easily get hung up in the physical aspects of rapid changeover and might overlook certain boundary conditions. His team realized that pharma operations included huge paperwork, procedures, presumed regulatory hurdles and bureaucratic elements that must also be addressed. And, these might not allow the level of benefit to Terra Pharma as in the case of Toyota. But nothing reduced his team's enthusiasm to try SMED on the CCR, since 20 hours for changeover was too long a time.

Face-Off with Changeovers

According to Lean Principles (also Toyota Production System), any stoppage of a process order (batch) in the plant is considered a waste, since it does not create any value to the customer. Hence, if an activity related to a machine is a reason for the stoppage (waiting) of process orders, then, anything that can be done to minimize stoppages of machines, must be done.

Lengthy setup times of facilities occurring during product changeovers reduce overall effectiveness of the line, and hence it becomes the prime target of waste reduction. SMED is an important technique, widely used within improvement projects to crash setup time. It is based upon four basic steps:

1. Ensuring external setup actions are performed, while the machine is still running,
2. Separating external and internal setup actions, ensuring proper functioning in efficient ways,
3. Converting internal setup actions into external actions,
4. Improving all setup actions.

Identifying and Observing Activities

As a starting step, Ali and team mapped out the activities carried out around the CCR during product changeover. Incidentally, the CCR was one of the largest equipment not only in the Sanovi Plant, but also in Terra Pharma. The activities involved in a product changeover were normally carried out in a sequence, as shown in Figure 7.7.

The gamut of activities was not exhaustive but included enough steps to cover the duration of downtime due to product changeover. Also, these activities were often not as sequential as shown. Rather they sometimes overlapped, took place in parallel and would get into a loop. But the team felt that to start with, it was better to take up an actionable approach than trying to make it precise and laborious.

The activities would start immediately after the collection of last compressed pill of the previous batch. The product changeover process involved the following.

Once compression of a good batch is completed, the containers are moved to the Material Out-Gate, where they are weighed, recorded and labeled. Then the supervisor prepares the documents to confirm standard operating procedures, machine operating conditions, ambient conditions, estimation of the yield as per the batch manufacturing record, pasting of sample labels, etc.

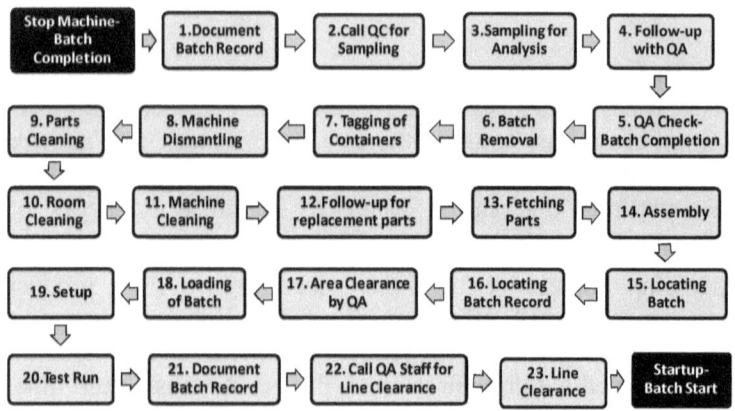

Figure 7.7 Workflow during the changeover

By then, the record is almost complete and the QC staff is intimated to pick up samples of pills for analysis. The QC staff comes, opens the lid of a container, draws out a measured amount of pills, records details and closes the lid of the container. Once the QC staff leaves, reconciliation of pills in the batch record is completed.

Afterwards, the QA staff is called to clear the batch. When the QA staff arrives, it checks the batch record, and if everything is found in compliance, it applies tags to the containers allowing them to be moved to hold area for the next operation (coating or packaging). Should there be any non compliance including error in calculation of the yield, the QA staff suggests the supervisor to call them again when full compliance is done or to file a CAPA (Corrective and Preventive Action) report.

Once the QA staff completes its work, the batch is moved out of the area.

Then, the operator goes around the tool room to collect tools and infrastructure needed for dismantling and transporting the used parts of the machine. Upon return, along with the support staff, the operator dismantles the machine and sends the changed parts for cleaning to the Parts Wash Room. Then, the operator calls the cleaning team, to clean the whole area and the machine, with sanitized water. When the cleaning team arrives, the utility team is requested to normalize the ambient conditions. Once the HVAC is brought to the normal condition, cleaning and drying of the room (including HVAC filters) and the machine is completed.

After the machine and the area are cleaned and dried, the supervisor calls the QA Staff for area clearance. The QA staff checks each and every corner of the room for any stray tablet or dust, and approves clearance or raises objection.

Once the QA team gives clearance for the machine and the area, the Supervisor checks description of the next product and follows up with the tool room to get the change parts and tools.

Once the change parts and tools arrive, the operator with the help of the support team assembles the machine.

Then, the operator searches around for the location of the next batch and guides the housekeeping staff to locate and bring the batch. Along with the batch, the relevant batch manufacturing records are also traced out and brought along.

In the meanwhile, the utility team is signaled to bring up the HVAC to the recommended operating ambience.

Once batch records and the in-process batch are available in the compression area, the operator contacts the QA staff to give clearance to materials. The QA representative comes to the area and checks with a hawkish eye, the labels on the batch material, records of the batch at previous stage and confirms or otherwise the goodness of the incoming batch.

After the area and the materials are cleared, the operator loads the batch (or lot) into the machine, does the setup, takes the help of the supervisor to ascertain that the setup is correct, records the environment, utility and machine parameters and conducts a brief test run. Once the test run is satisfactory, the QA staff is called to give the line clearance.

The QA staff comes, looks at the batch record, looks at the environment parameters and machine parameters, and if things are found ok, gives the go ahead to start the operation. The moment the operator presses the start button, the machine starts processing the batch.

Usually, when one asked a general question, "What is the work breakdown of a product changeover process?" the standard answer would be, "Dismantling, Cleaning, Assembly and Start-up." But when the steps were detailed out as above, it already looked a big process in itself. With so many steps involved, there was a fair possibility that a significant time was also spent on waiting, following up, locating, re-working, documenting, delegating etc.

Then, the team identified the activities that could be done during running of the previous batch, but were being done when the machine was stopped. Eight out of 23 activities were supposed to be done during the running of the previous batch. The team sharpened its observation to ensure that these activities were done in parallel with the running of previous batch. The mere *identification and observation* of these activities, led to a reduction of almost 3 hours in the changeover time of the CCR. This was in fact, Step-1 of SMED.

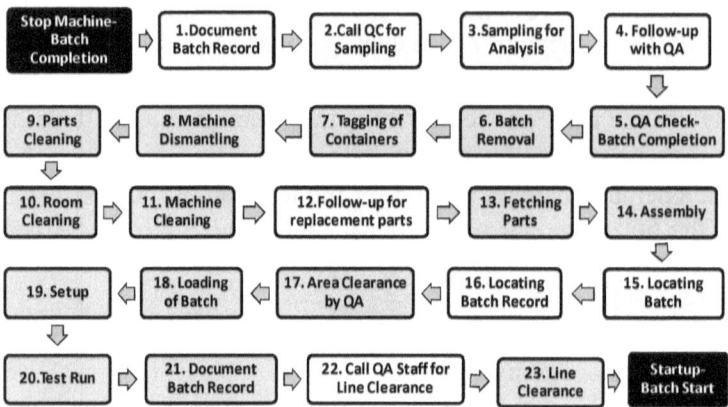

Figure 7.8 Eight of the 23 steps performed during the product changeover time were identified to be performed while the machine was running the previous batch.

Separating Internal and External Activities

In the previous step, the activities were classified and *separated* into External and Internal activities. External activities were the ones that could be done whilst the machine was still running. Internal activities were those that could only be carried out when the machine was stopped.

And then, the respective activities were performed as efficiently as possible.

The identified activities were scheduled and aligned to serve the CCR team rather than being done at the spur of the moment. This eliminated significant time spent in following up and rushing at the last minute.

It meant that much of the work related to the batch record documentation, was done during the progression of the previous batch and not solely at the end of the batch. QA, QC and Tool Rooms would get advance intimation of tentative finish time of the batch in progress so that they were well prepared. It reduced the follow up time required by the operator and the supervisor of the CCR for activities 2, 3, 4 and 12.

Batches and their records (activities 15 and 16, respectively), were traced out while the previous batch was running. Taking these small measures to improve information and co-ordination further reduced the changeover time.

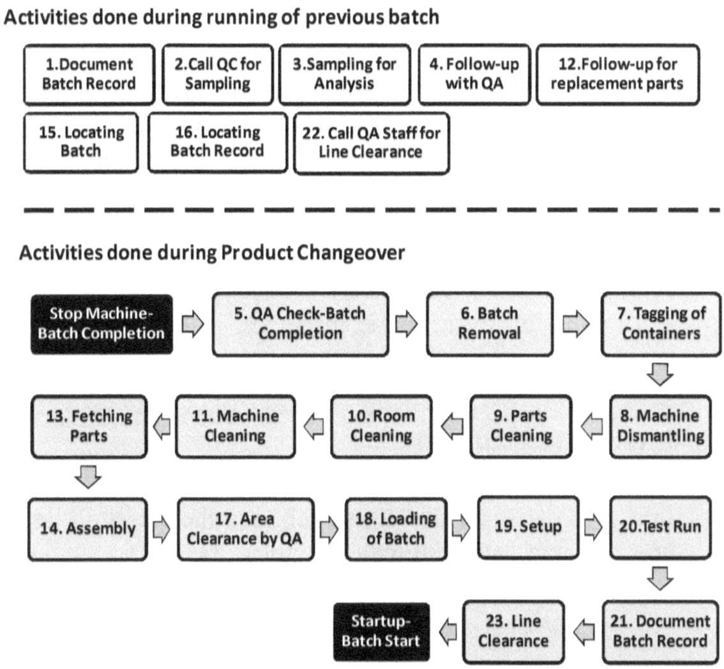

Activities done during running of previous batch

1. Document Batch Record	2. Call QC for Sampling	3. Sampling for Analysis	4. Follow-up with QA	12. Follow-up for replacement parts
15. Locating Batch	16. Locating Batch Record	22. Call QA Staff for Line Clearance		

Activities done during Product Changeover

Stop Machine-Batch Completion → 5. QA Check-Batch Completion → 6. Batch Removal → 7. Tagging of Containers

↓

13. Fetching Parts ← 11. Machine Cleaning ← 10. Room Cleaning ← 9. Parts Cleaning ← 8. Machine Dismantling

↓

14. Assembly → 17. Area Clearance by QA → 18. Loading of Batch → 19. Setup → 20. Test Run

↓

Startup-Batch Start ← 23. Line Clearance ← 21. Document Batch Record

Figure 7.9 Separation of activities done during the run of previous batch, dramatically reduced the total activities to be handled during the product changeover

Then, spare tools and change parts were procured to prevent waiting of the CCR assembly due to cleaning of repeatable parts and tools.

Subsequently, the team implemented a visual mechanism, which automatically prompted QA, QC, Tool Rooms and other support functions, well in advance about the progress of the batch and changeover schedule at the CCR.

The support functions made their own arrangements to see that they attended the requirement of the CCR without delay. This actually meant redefining role of support functions and transferring responsibility for reducing delays during changeovers to them from the manufacturing team. The commitment of the team to reduce changeover time led it to look deeper into internal activities. It shared details of 'changeover time reduction' project with specialists at the Regional Productivity Council. To the surprise of the team, there already existed a number of efficiency improvement tools that the team could employ in further reducing the changeover time.

As a result of brief orientation with the members of the Regional Productivity Council, the team employed 5S tools to organize the tooling in Tool Rooms and reorganized the process of managing tools. This also led to the moving of some critical tools into the CCR area, thus reducing delay due to their transportation and readiness.

The team employed Poka Yoke (a Japanese term for 'mistake proofing'), to identify mismatch and misconnections at the startup stage. For example, during the cleaning of the room, three phase wires of the blower would be unplugged. However, after cleaning, often, these connections would be fitted back with wrong polarity. This would result in tripping of the blower at the startup, necessitating a cumbersome and external intervention to correct the polarity of electrical lines. The team implemented Poka Yoke in several other instances, including the design of toolsets to avoid mistakes in picking up the tools.

Converting Internal to External

Once the activities were performed more efficiently, it was time to look deeper into internal activities to search out the possibilities of converting some of them into external activities. This was Step-3 of SMED.

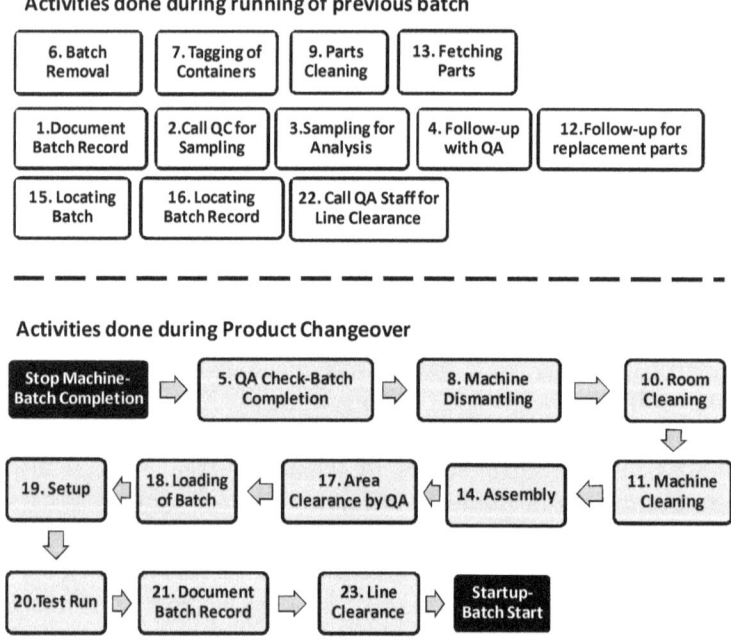

Figure 7.10 Step-3 of SMED, 4 Internal activities were converted into external activities, which further cut down the activities carried out during changeover

Step 6, 7, 9 and 13 were identified and the team began the work to convert them into external activities. Earlier, the Batch Removal (6) activity would wait for the QA staff although it was not mandatory. In the new scheme of things, it would be done as soon as each container filled in. Earlier, Tagging of Containers (9) was done by the QA staff. Before the QA staff could come for batch completion clearance, it would pick up tags from stores, register the identification number for the respective lots and then tag them to the filled containers. The responsibility of tagging was transferred to the machine supervisor who would tag a container and make note of the tag number on the batch record, as soon as a container was filled with tablets. This allowed for the tagging of all containers but the last to be done while the machine was still running.

Step number 9, Cleaning of Parts, was made redundant by using spare change parts; while the responsibility of Fetching of Change Parts (13) was given to the tool room staff, which based on the progress at the CCR, ensured on-time availability of change parts at the work center.

Activities 8, 10, 11 and 14 involved a lot of physical as well as coordination work. And these were of different nature from that of running and maintaining the machines. The team suggested instituting a separate crew (called the Changeover Crew), dedicated for removal of parts, cleaning and assembly activities. The concept of the crew was similar to the concept of Pit Stop Crew in Formula-1 Race.

In this concept, based on the requirements of the CCR, the Changeover Crew would arrive well in time with its paraphernalia of changeover and cleaning; and wait outside the CCR room. As soon as the batches moved out, the crew would rush in pounding on the machine and spread across the room to do its work quickly.

The involvement of Changeover Crew reduced the in changeover time significantly, giving a benefit of over 3 hours per changeover. The Changeover Crew concept worked well for Terra Pharma. Since it had a large number of changeovers taking place daily, a separate dedicated function was created for managing changeover activities across the plant. Incidentally, the Changeover Crew was created from internal resources and benefits were obtained without causing any extra expenses.

Stabilizing the Improvement Process

Once, a significant number of the activities was done offline and some Internal activities were converted into External activities, the team needed sometime to allow the new workflow to stabilize. In due course, each activity was fine tuned, and Steps 1 to 3 of SMED were revisited regularly, which was the Step-4 of SMED.

The improvements made at the CCR actually had spin off effects on other machines of the plant. Some of the key improvement steps brought in as a result of the SMED pilot at the CCR were the following.

1. Automation of documentation work
2. Real time tracking of batches
3. Standardization of tools
4. Improved stock management of tools
5. Skill development of operators
6. Formation of new function - Changeover Crew
7. Revision of roles and responsibilities
8. Installation of checklist culture
9. Implementation of full kit based batch release

Within a few weeks of starting SMED pilot, the team significantly reduced the changeover time. While immediate benefits were derived from the first three steps of SMED technique, Step-4 provided stabilization and process innovation that went beyond the CCR. Within three months, the changeover time on the CCR reduced from over 20 hours to less than 8 hours, Figure 7.11.

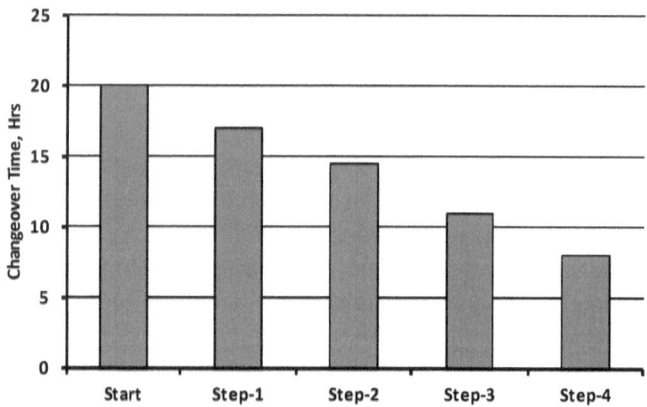

Figure 7.11 Trend in changeover time of the CCR, as each step of SMED was applied.

The focused work on the CCR had a viral effect on the rest of the plant and people worked voluntarily to improve changeover time in other areas.

The reduction in changeover time by employing SMED technique had a profound impact on the overall ability of the plant to deal with product mix as well as the Long Tail, which is worth noting.

Campaigning-The Holy Grail of Operations

In the facilities of the plant, where long tail products were produced, significant number of product changeovers caused huge productivity loss, whenever a shorter Campaign was worked upon. In Terra Pharma, the back to back processing (run) of a number of batches of the same product was called Campaigning.

Before the SMED pilot was implemented, the dataset on production time of the CCR looked like this:

Table 7.3 Effect of changeover time on the operation time (before SMED)

Changeover time, hrs	Campaign size, # batches	Process time per batch, hrs	Operation time per batch, hrs
20	1	6	26
20	2	6	16
20	3	6	13
20	5	6	10
20	10	6	8

For a product that took 6 hour process time per batch, the changeover time before starting another product was 20 hours. As a result, if one had to produce one batch without any campaign, the operation time was 26 hours. Even for a Campaign of 3 batches, it was 13 hours per batch. However, if the team did a Campaign of 10 batches, the average operation time per batch went down to as low as 8 hours. Traditionally, with Throughput being a key metric, there was a belief that large Campaign size was good. There was, in fact, an established (and acceptable) behavior of producing more number of batches than required or delaying processing of a product till sufficient number of orders were accumulated.

In those facilities, the staff normally avoided changeovers and ran longer Campaigns. A longer Campaign helped in reducing the average operational time per batch and getting higher monthly throughput. However, when a product was run on longer Campaign (say, 10 batches or more), it often jeopardized availability of other products as those would have to wait too late to be delivered on-time. And so, the staff would be in a dilemma as to whether to run longer Campaigns to achieve higher throughput or run shorter Campaigns to achieve better availability (reliability) of supply.

Figure 7.12 Campaign size was a recurring dilemma for the production team.

This dilemma existed on a day to day basis and the solution, normally, was a compromise. When somebody was watching for good availability and reliability of the supply, the team would painfully run short Campaigns and carry out changeovers. However, when nobody was watching or the pressure of throughput was high, they would run long Campaigns. Of course, this would often result in some products running with higher than required stocks, while others stocked out or delayed inordinately. This behavior was clearly evident in the weekly changeover data. The staff would diligently try to provide good availability and reliability in the first two weeks of the month. But, it would run long Campaigns in the last ten days of the month. In fact, in most organizations, peaking of volumes in the last ten days of the month was normal.

In ensuring that the plant produced as per the changing demand in the marketplace, it was important that it developed an ability to deliver small quantity of drugs quickly, as and when required. While the system of production based on consumption and real customer orders was implemented, it was also important to create a change in the underlying belief that small quantities (or number of batches) could be delivered quickly, while obtaining significant gain in throughput. The SMED pilot gave an experience in this direction.

Situation after the Pilot at the CCR

When the team applied SMED technique, and dramatically reduced the changeover time to eight hours, it had a game changing impact on the operation of the plant.

The operation time for even a 2-batch Campaign was cut down to ten hours per batch. This experience built the belief that small number of batches could be produced with improved productivity. The SMED pilot brought down the changeover time to such a level that the team became willing to take shorter run of batches and abolish long Campaigns. As a consequence, it helped the team achieve higher throughput and better reliability simultaneously. Actually, the team had started feeling that *it had more incentive to do smaller campaign than the longer ones*. Thus SMED changed the thinking of the staff of Terra Pharma and brought in a fundamental change in the culture of the organization.

Table 7.4 Effect of Changeover Time on the Operation Time (After SMED)

Changeover time, hrs	Campaign size, # batches	Process time per batch, hrs	Operation time per batch, hrs
8	1	6	14
8	2	6	10
8	3	6	9
8	5	6	8
8	10	6	7

SMED played a big role in overcoming the conflicts on the shop floor and gave the team much shorter operation time per batch. The team that had earlier hesitated to take shorter Campaigns now daringly took even one batch run without jeopardizing its promise to the market, while simultaneously achieving the desired throughput. And, before the team could realize, the new behavior also resulted in lower working capital and better quality of products. The team also felt that the wide portfolio of Terra Pharma can now be very well exploited.

The team obtained marvelous results by stabilizing SMED in a short time. The performance of the CCR improved by an order of magnitude. The review of pilot projects in the Operation Board of Terra Pharma gave a 'go ahead' to Ali's team to implement focused activities on other constrained resources. This subsequently led to significant improvement in the performance of the Long Tail as well as the Fast Movers.

Seth knew that although, SMED was not implemented by the book, conceptually it worked. It was a commendable achievement, since it raised the enthusiasm of his team in seeking new ways of improving productivity. It also meant that there was a lot to be gained by further improving the changeover process.

The SMED thinking was specifically important for Seth's team, since changeovers included not just the change of parts. It consisted of setting up of process variables, running and testing of sample lots, re-certification and retraining of operators and requalification of machines. It needed generation of several reports, preparation of quality records, carrying out analyses, doing data verification, labeling, sign-offs and everything else that was almost like revalidating the process. In the process, the team picked, verified, validated and used a variety of process improvement tools (Lean Tools) to reduce waste and employed Six Sigma technique to reduce variability, on and around the constrained resources. The plant staff also found the whole exercise fulfilling, since it provided them with a focused way of learning new techniques and methodologies that got them the desired results, quickly.

The team knew that all the non-Toyota stuff (typical of the Pharma Industry), really slowed down the plant. But it demonstrated that by quickly adopting concepts of SMED, these issues too could be re-organized for improving flow, obtaining higher throughput and delivering higher quality. It, of course, meant often crossing organizational boundaries to get buy-in on expectations, goals, roles and responsibilities. It also meant to give an equal delay weight to activities in Safety, Quality Control, Quality Assurance, R&D and Regulatory, if they took weeks and months.

Given all that pharma operations consisted of, the team at Terra Pharma was able to reduce changeover time from almost a day to a shift. It realized that the Pharma Industry, perhaps, couldn't meet the 10 minutes changeover norm of Toyota; but one shift changeover was no less challenging. This led to adopting a new term for changeover reduction in Terra Pharma. A Terra Pharma wide competition led to coining of a new acronym, SSEP (Single Shift Exchange of Product). And the Sanovi team was proudly honored for this innovation by the Regional Productivity Council. Across Terra Pharma, soon it became a golden rule to ensure that no changeover took more than a shift. In fact, teams competed with each other to reduce several changeover times to less than half a shift. Thus, the team simply focused on changeover time, which is the total time between the last good batch of the previous product and the first good (100 percent quality met, safely deliverable and legitimately legally saleable) batch of the next product. And in doing so, the team progressed closer to using OEE measurements on the constraints, by improving speed and quality parameters, as well. It included dealing with the following additional issues:

1. Reduced Speed: Untrained operator, worn out parts, unstable process, etc, often resulted in running the machines at lower speed than they were designed for. It directly affected the throughput.
2. Start up Rejections: Wrong setup, untrained operator and unstable ambience, meant that an unacceptable number of pills was being used for testing the machine before the operation stabilized to produce the first good pill.
3. Running Rejects: Unstable process, incorrect assembly, faulty material and unstable ambience, often led to reduced yield of the process.

In fact, the team realized that focusing on just the constrained resources not only improved their stop time, it also developed ability in the staff to question process time of machines and quality of product. In one instance, the machine centre team collaborated with the engineering team to reduce the process time on a constrained coating machine by over 15 percent.

As a result of intensive engagement of the teams to make the best use of constrained resources, a new set of guidelines was discovered for obtaining quick and significant improvement in the flow, without making costly trade-offs.

<u>Guidelines for Unblocking the Flow:</u> Some products will become endangered chronically, indicating capacity of the plant falling behind the demand for such products.

The slowest resource or process along the flow (routing) of the product could indicate a blockage to the flow. In the plants, such situations exist regularly. Hence,

    i. Plants must develop a mechanism to regularly identify flow blockers.
    ii. Increase the focus on flow blockers to identify reasons for the blockage.
    iii. If the reason that prevents improvement in flow through the resource is the resource itself, then
        1. All efforts must be made to improve productivity of the resource (constrained resource), while closely monitoring and analyzing its process and non-process time.
        2. All other resources, including support and management functions must protect the constrained resource against starvation and give its requirements the highest priority.
        3. All upstream resources, must avoid overproduction and flooding the resource with excessive inventory.
    iv. Several times, the reason for a resource blocking the flow may not be the resource itself. A detailed analysis of the working on and around the resource will indicate an outside root cause (constraint).

In just over a quarter of the year, the Sanovi Plant saw a significant improvement in its throughput, lead time and product availability. When the finance department worked out the numbers, the calculation of return on investment became redundant, since the improvement of over 15 percent in throughput of the plant was obtained with hardly any additional expense.

Thus, Terra Pharma conceptualized and improved the performance of its main plant by identifying the inherent simplicity and zeroing down to just the few critical resources that dictated its throughput. It allowed the teams to increase their attention on those few resources, involve people in improving utilization of these few machines, learn new tools on the go and reveal significant hidden capacity. All these benefits were obtained without taking too much risk and without succumbing to costly trade-offs.

How do you Set Improvement Targets?

Seth and his team got a stable grip on dealing with disruptions as well as on opening up capacity at the flow blockers. Seth realized that improvements were becoming more predictable.

Till then he had resisted the temptation of setting a long term and big numerical target for Life2.0.

But very soon, Ajay insisted, "Data and numbers lend transparency and objectivity to management. We must start setting metrics for Life2.0 before subjectivity overwhelms the team [17]."

Seth said, "Intuitively I agree, but, however logical and objective the metrics be, expected target numbers are often full of conflicts, confusions and suspicions. Unfortunately, this creates a lot of noise in the system."

Ajay said, "Yes, there are likely to be some problems, but we need to find a way out, because we are on a mammoth drive of improvement. I am more confident of data making sense now than ever. Actually, we now have a pretty stable system and predictability of performance is very high. Data will help us in obtaining the right information that we and our people need to take validated decisions. It is time to scale up improvement efforts."

"Agreed, but we can't set improvement targets the way we set the budgetary targets. We need a more coherent measurement system at each levels of Terra Pharma," Seth put forth his reservation and condition.

He spelt out his gut feeling, "Probably it is because of the way people are forced to accept targets..."

"I fully agree that we need to be sensitive to the likely adverse effects of measurements on people." Ajay said cautiously.

Subsequently, Ajay and Seth agreed on the need to work with the team to *change the way of deriving improvement targets,* and planned to take it up in the following Operational Board Meeting, that was due very shortly.

The Operational Board Meeting, in fact, had a bigger than the usual quorum. Teams from all the plants of Terra Pharma had assembled.

One of the teams presented an attractive improvement idea. It became very clear that there was a huge hidden capacity in the plant and it was possible to improve utilization of critical machines by an order of 30 percent. Even domain experts vetted the improvement opportunity.

However, when specifics of the implementation plan were being discussed, the plant manager said, "It looks nice. Let's take an improvement target of two percent initially and continue to add two percent every month thereafter."

"Ultimately, it will accumulate to a large number of 20 to 25 percent, by end of the year."

Mathematically, it looked straight forward (dividing a large number into smaller ones and applying the rule of 'sum of parts equals to the whole', 7.13).

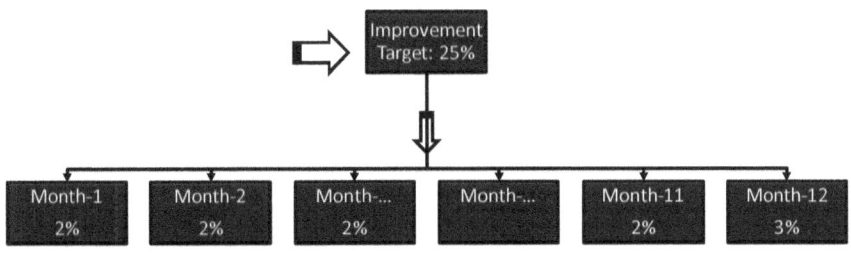

Figure 7.13 Yearly improvement target broken down into average monthly improvement targets, a 'sum of parts equals to the whole' approach.

Ali was not convinced though. In fact, he was surprised to hear the comment, especially because his teams had achieved unbelievable results during Life2.0. He then realized that perhaps people were not so comfortable in setting targets. He looked at Ajay, who gestured him to be cautious.

He said, "I understand the logic of averaging, but I am not sure if it is applicable in this case and if we need to do a time averaging. It means that we fix, *a priori,* a two percent improvement target per month and then, try to figure out what actions to take to achieve the two percent improvement in results. It does not seem to be a natural direction for improving the system."

"But what's wrong with this? This is how we have been setting all targets!" said the Plant Manager as Seth, Tony and the rest of operations team from different plants looked on.

Ali's spelt out his logic:
 1. Targets should not be set by projecting historical levels, but must be derived from the proposed actions, i.e. the numbers are subservient to actions and not the other way.

2. Targeting a two percent improvement would not take the plant anywhere, since a two percent improvement is too tiny and would be lost in the noise (inherent variability in the system).
3. If a threshold of two percent is fixed, people would then have to search for the actions they need to take, in order to get two percent improvement, which is not easy.
4. When numbers are given as targets and people are asked to propose actions, there would be a tendency to cap improvement effort to two percent and limit the possibility of achieving higher performance levels.
5. Growth could only be achieved by surpassing and not by reaching the target.

Of course, reluctance of the Plant Manager was not without justice. He did not want to over commit and fall flat, since the plant had never *formally* taken such a big improvement target (30 percent) *without exhausting resources and without taking too much risk*. And, he was suggesting the approach that was followed by most of the plant managers across industries.

Seth had to pitch in because being the CEO, he owned the responsibility for the existing approach, "I think that we need to understand what it means to divide a target. We have been doing this for ages, but perhaps, the time has come to take a step back and correct our assumptions. I think Ali has a point, but you are not entirely wrong...Ali, would you like to explain it a bit?"

Ali said, "Let's understand it better. When an entity is a simple aggregation of *mutually exclusive parts*, it is possible to distribute a bigger number into the constituents. This works very well, say, in the case of sales from different customer segments, revenues from different therapies, independent cost of different functions etc. This concept is called 'the whole is the sum of its parts' or 'managing by division of parts [18].'"

He continued, "We tend to over simplify the logic of 'sum of parts' by applying it to mutually interdependent parts also. We must know the pitfalls in distributing yearly improvement targets on cost, quality, safety, lead time etc., across functions (Figure 7.14). For example, we can't give an open ended target of cost reduction to Purchasing Department without worrying about its implication on Quality, Production and Sales. The concept of division of parts is based on the thesis that the parts are mutually independent and therefore, making improvement in all areas *locally*, would add up to give the total organizational improvement. Similarly, trying to think that benefit of each month will accumulate is not that straight forward."

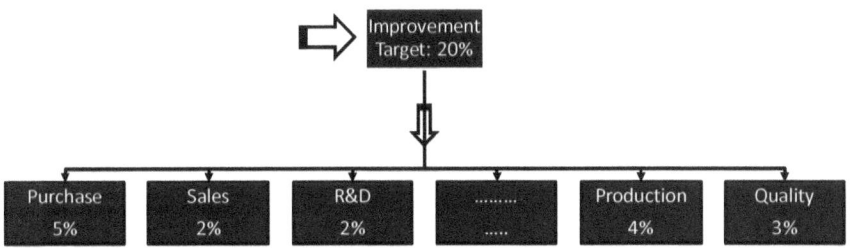

Figure 7.14: Yearly improvement target broken down among functions, 'a sum of parts equals to the whole' approach

"But what's the alternative?" was the genuine query from the Plant Manager.

Seth said, "We learnt a great deal about it during the past few quarters.... You see, we work in a system, where different functions are interdependent on each other. An activity performed in one part of the organization has an impact on the outcome of activities in other parts of the organization. Which means that our organization is not just a sum of the parts; it is much more than that. Just recall the Business Model Canvas."

"Does it mean that if we reduce the cost of input materials too much, our quality deteriorates and throughput also slows down?" said the Plant Manager, as he tried to figure out the new approach.

Ali said, "Yes... Given that our organization is made up of several parts that interact with each other, we need to use 'cause and effect' approach rather than 'sum of parts' approach. We must first identify the few core issues that inhibit us from achieving the desired results."

"But how do we do that?"

"For this, we must be able to understand working of the system, and identify the causality, i.e. cause and effect logic. This will help us in identifying the core issues inhibiting growth of the plant. Figuring out solution to these issues will take us towards the desired results. Within operations, once the solution is known, it is quite possible to calibrate the results with respect to the extent of actions," said Ali.

The Plant Manager looked confused, and Seth realized why. He got up and drew a cause and effect based logic tree (Figure 7.15).

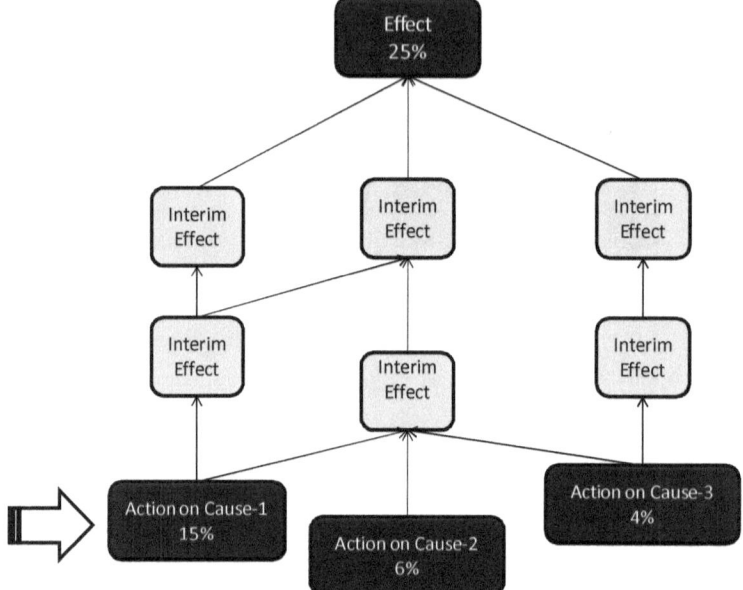

Figure 7.15 A good way to set operational improvement targets is by identifying the root causes (and actions) that contribute to significant benefits

Then he said, "Believe me, we know the problems faced by our teams and also the solutions. We just need to reorient ourselves a bit." He explained, "…It is good to have an objective, but it is not advisable to set a numerical target on the objective without clearly identifying the actions (or causes) that would take the team towards the objective…"

"But, this is quite a different way of thinking and visualizing. For years we have started with numbers and worked backwards!" said one of the plant managers.

Seth said, "Yeah, we know this is different. However, interdependencies and interactions are the reality, and we must recognize the need to see things as they are. We will need to slowly build our competency in thinking this way." He looked at Ajay, who nodded and made notes in his diary.

Tony said, "I have a feeling that when people know what actions to take, it is often possible for them to identify the impact on the objective. Under such a situation, and especially, with regard to improvement projects in operations, bottom-up aggregation approach would be important."

"Yes, we know that it works superbly," said Ali.

Ali was not sure if the discussion was conclusive. He did not want to leave this important subject to doubts. He said, "Let's get into a real example… For years, Lead Time has been our important operational metric which we have been trying to improve. However, the measurement of lead time has been very cumbersome and we have not progressed beyond report generation." Then, he walked up to the white board, and drew a sketch, Figure 7.16.

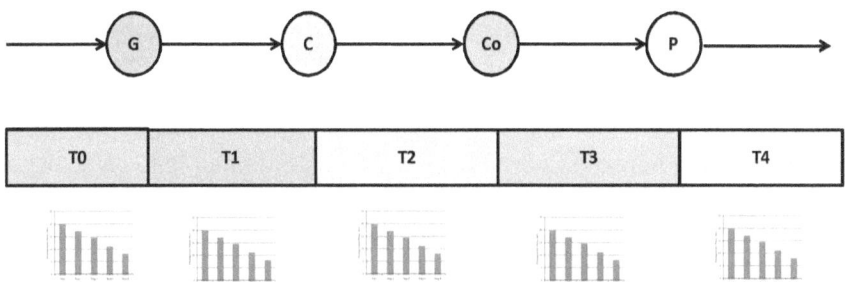

Figure 7.16 The traditional heavily loaded approach to crash Lead Time.

Then, he said, "See what our approach has been, which was based on 'the whole is the sum of parts' philosophy. We would normally divide Lead Time into 4 parts, as Granulation Time, Compression Time, Coating Time and Packaging Time. Subsequently, we would conduct an elaborate exercise of collecting the number of days spent by each batch at each stage. People would be asked to collect reasons for delays in the movement of batches. Then, we used to hire special data entry operators to just key in the data of Lead Time at each stage. These data sets would then be collated and presented in a series of Pareto Charts to obtain key reasons of delays at each stage. Now think about this exercise being done for each line, each stage and each product, and then, think about the amount of data that you need to handle to just know what's happening to Lead Time. What a waste of effort and time…"

"No wonder, we could never get hold of Lead Time… and nobody had the patience to follow through its measurement. This was the approach of 'the whole is the sum of parts' applied in the wrong place," commented Tony.

Ali added, "Knowing what direction of results an organization needs to achieve, the thought process of operational improvement starts at the bottom of the logic diagram. People have a lot of intuition and experience. And then there are some basic laws of operations which are generic in nature, like the Newton's Laws of Motion. These together allow them to establish cause and effect relationship between the needed actions and the desired results very well. They know what prevents them from achieving the result."

"But how do we do it in the case of shrinking Lead Time…?" The Plant Manager was interested in finding the alternative way to set targets.

Before this could be answered, somebody from the group asked, "Do we have a natural Law for Operations?"

"Yes, of course, it is called the 'Little's Law', which says that for a constant WIP, throughput is inversely proportional to cycle time of flow." said Tony.

"Let's answer the main query...For example, people know that Lead Time elongates due to high WIP. They also know that if a resource has long queue of batches to be processed, then speed of the resource determines Lead Time of the complete flow. And day in day out, they see the adverse impact of unstable processes and running long campaigns on Lead Time. They are able to infer that they must control the load on the plant, avoid local optima and manage their bottleneck better, in order to reduce WIP and long queues in front of bottlenecks," said Ali, as he illustrated the way to work backward from actions to target, Figure 7.17.

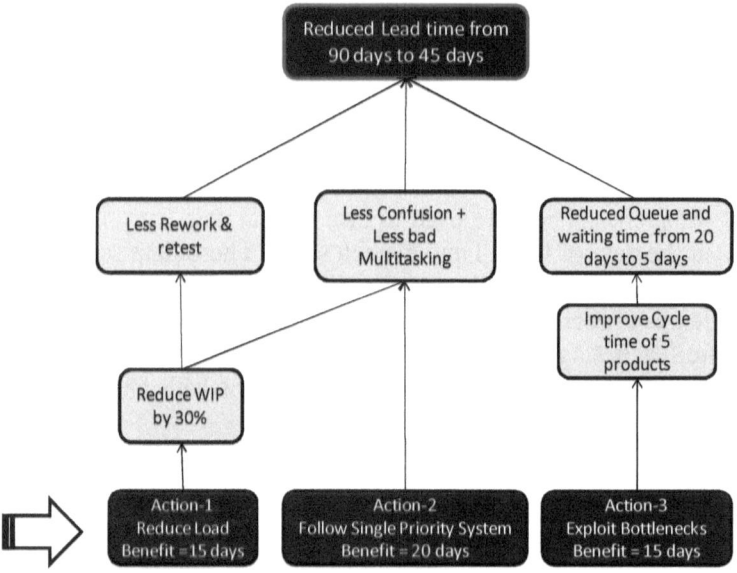

Figure 7.17 A cause and effect based actionable way of setting improvement targets in Operations.

He said, "Let's read it from the bottom... Since we want to reduce Lead Time significantly, people came out with Action-1 (Reduce or Regulate Load), Action-2 (Use Single Priority System) and Action-3 (Exploit Bottlenecks). If load on the plant is reduced, it shrinks WIP that in turn reduces defects and chaos in the shop floor. Similarly, following a single priority system reduces chaos in the shop floor. And finally, focused exploitation of bottleneck reduces waiting time of batches in the queue. The intermediate effects of reduced WIP, reduced chaos and reduced queue in front of bottleneck machines, result in reduced Lead Time. This way, linking actions to results, allows people to figure out exact actions they could take and how much improvement they would trigger. The idea is to allow people to connect cause and effect, to innovate themselves, set their metrics, develop ownership and move ahead with actions, on an ongoing basis."

There was far deeper importance of the approach Ali was propounding. Seth therefore emphasized, "We must understand why we want to set *operational* improvement targets based on actions that come from bottom and not from the allocation of numbers from the top. It is quite possible in certain cases that our effort may not yield expected results. Getting into the habit of understanding such deviations will allow us to initiate the process of improvement and bring innovation into operations. When we continue to take up new actions based on effect of our previous actions, we start relating (validating) our understanding of cause and effect better, and we improve robustness of our improvement process. And this is the key to long term business success."

He added, "Taking a numbered target and trying to measure against it is one thing. But identifying the inputs (actions) that give those numbers is paramount and must become a way of achieving our operational goals. As long as we know that there is a big opportunity out there, we must identify the key actions that will deliver those results and then focus on these actions without becoming overwhelmed and paranoid about the overall grand number."

"Numbered targets are of operational importance only when they are driven from clearly drawn actions; and pursuing these actions gives us the numbers which could be 2, 5 or 10 percent. But within Operations, *a priori*, we can't fix these numbers as targets, without taking appropriate actions as the basis of the improvement activities. However, if we know that an action can deliver a 30 percent improvement in throughput, we must go ahead with it." Thus, he repeated his advice.

The discussion in the Operational Board Meeting came out with a different way of setting targets for improvement projects, and the team agreed to adopt bottom up approach to frame improvement projects. The new approach to set targets for improvements was then drafted, which was as given below.

1. Figure out the actions needed to improve performance in those areas, where it is needed the most, i.e. find the core problem causing poor performance.
2. In an organization consisting of interdependent parts, core problem can't be identified easily by division of parts or using the Pareto

Principle. Rather, managers must resolve to use cause and effect based tools.

3. Generally, the areas needing improvements will be very few since an organization is a system comprising interdependent areas with just a few independent value streams and degree of freedom.
4. The actions (improvements) needed to resolve the core problems must be identified by people who work in the specific areas.
5. Some of these actions could be directly implementable, while others might require system based solution.
6. Organize these improvement actions in the order of their impact. Pick the top few and each one of these will generally give much more than an improvement of low single digit percentage.
7. Once it is known, which actions will give how much benefit, drive the improvements around the most prominent actions.
8. Manage the improvement process to achieve the likely benefits, which could be 2, 5, 10 percent or more.
9. All the big ticket improvement actions must be presented in the Quarterly Meeting of the Operational Board, for reassessing the organization's growth.

The Impact

With time, as improvement potential became more visible across the plants, action based target setting became ingrained into the performance management system of Terra Pharma.

People collaborated voluntarily to work on priorities and deal with obstacles that came in the way. Each time they faced an obstacle, they would walk up to seek and give support to quickly solve problems rather than bypass and accept them as given. Finger pointing became history. The process of transformation developed strong team spirit within Terra Pharma.

The pattern of market demand and therefore, constraints would shift in the plant. However, at any moment, the number of resources that needed management attention would be very few. It was not too difficult for Ali's team to identify constraints and focus there. The systematic way of identifying constraints and working on them changed the way Terra Pharma spotted areas of improvements. Seth's team moved from trying to improve everything everywhere, to improving just the few constraints that dictated capacity of the plant. As a result, the plant had just a few urgencies, and everybody had sufficient time to work on priorities with ease.

During this period, the team changed several policies and beliefs, and invented several methods. Each one of them improved performance of the organization significantly. The new culture brought in the resilience that also helped in commercializing new products faster. Further, the support functions, including Finance, Human Resource, IT, Regulatory and others in the Corporate Office were aligned to ever improve the flow of process orders.

The best practices at the Sanovi Plant were extended to other plants of Terra Pharma. The teams further innovated the measurement system and incorporated effect of changeovers, machine condition and product quality into a single metric of plant performance. Its participation in industry forums led to adopting Overall Equipment Efficiency (OEE) as the major metric for plant performance. This normalized all possible variabilities in production at source and measured machine level performance on an unambiguous parameter.

There was a distinct character to the improvements made at Terra Pharma. These improvements were not just to improve performance of Terra Pharma by one notch. Rather, the pace of improvement kept building up, one over another, and unleashed a strong culture of ongoing improvement. Every time, the team achieved one success and stabilized the process, it would already have the next opportunity in sight. Every new improvement thus kept building on the former base that was only getting bigger and bigger. In turn, it provided *sustainable growth* to Terra Pharma (Refer Appendix- Inside the Growth Curve). In fact, the approach of dealing with constraints gave it a growth trajectory that was *scalable*, i.e. the quantum of growth increased with every new step.

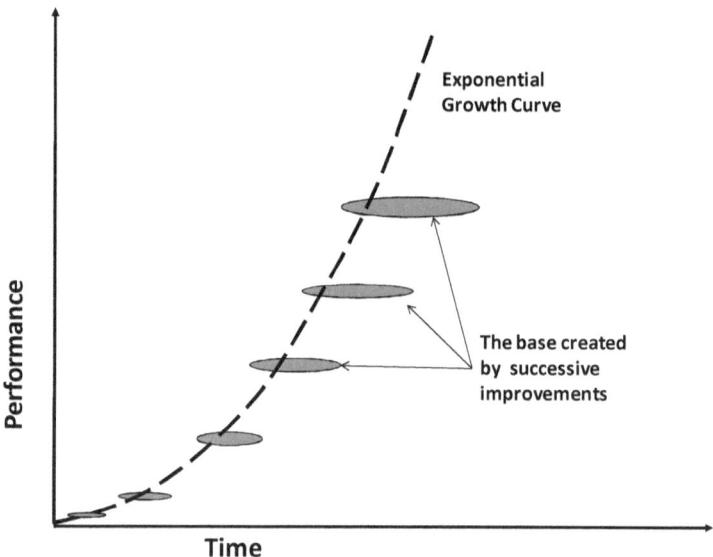

Figure 7.18 The improvement culture at Terra Pharma was characterized by growth with stability

Supplying drugs based on actual consumption from stocks and as per the committed due dates, became a standard practice. Mid way in the second year since the implementation of Life2.0, the response time of the Sanovi Plant had improved dramatically and the customer satisfaction index zoomed up. Its sales orders were moving faster across the supply chain, with a guaranteed availability and reliability of above 98 percent. And, Seth was very happy to see his YOY Sales up by 55 percent.

All this, with an inventory level that actually went down by one third and the WIP of the plants reduced to less than half of that a year back. Most of its operations were working in two shifts, people were relaxed, they knew their priorities and they had good balance between family and work life. To everybody's surprise, the operating costs were not more than they were a year ago.

The lead time (the prime measurement of plant's responsiveness) had already come down by more than half. The load on the plant had reduced substantially, while its monthly equivalent output had increased by more than half. Realizing that the plant had not only built but also sustained over 20 percent reserve capacity, its sales team started taking orders at challenging terms that fetched much higher margins. That year, Terra Pharma was accorded the highest Corporate Social Responsibility Award for its superlative commitment to ensure high availability of essential and orphaned drugs.

Clients started recognizing the benefit of short response time and high reliability of Terra Pharma's supplies. They could keep low inventory per SKU and add more variety to their portfolio. Increasingly, clients also started relying on Terra Pharma to meet their urgencies. Thus, Terra Pharma not only built, 'rapid and reliable response' as a decisive competitive edge, it helped improve business results of its clients as well. After gaining significant confidence in reliably supplying drugs to its main customer segment, Terra Pharma added new and emerging customer segments and innovated its supply chain further.

It was no wonder that the terrific transformation of the Sanovi Plant became a case study in leading MBA schools and a much talked about operational excellence story in the media.

Terra Pharma's staff, its key stakeholders in the plant got interim bonus twice in the year, a first in the history of the company. Workers' Union became a part of the operational innovation team, it came forward to seek ongoing improvements and.... Terra Pharma became the darling of the stock market.

The Larger Effect

In the first quarter of 2010, Amin got a call from the Health Ministry to lead a ministerial level discussion on 'Innovating Health Care for Masses'. During the lunch, the Minister approached Amin and congratulated him for improving reliability of drug supplies in the market and providing high availability of essential and orphaned drugs. He conveyed his pride for Terra Pharma's efficient supply chain and the rapidly building story of its plants. The young minister wanted Amin's team to help his office in assessing the medicine procurement and delivery system of the Government.

Within a month, a delegation from the Ministry visited Terra Pharma's plants and warehouses. It also went around the distribution centers. The team was surprised to see the *high availability of drugs, with such a low level of inventories.*

Subsequently, the delegation made a presentation on the distribution chain of drugs owned by Government agencies. Thereafter, the Health Secretary described the challenges faced by the Government in ensuring its 'Health for All' program. At the end, the Secretary invited Terra Pharma's team for a working session on streamlining the drug supply chain of the Government.

He said, "The cost of medicine, specifically in our country is becoming a dominant part of the growing health care burden. Our hospitals and dispensaries face severe shortages of essential drugs, despite the purchase of millions of dollars of drugs every month."

Recently, the ministry had suffered a massive blow to its image when the media exposed heaps of expired and outdated pills in government hospital stores. The expose confirmed the gross ineffectiveness of the government's supply chain.

The ministry was under pressure to urgently act on the *paradox of stock-outs and expiries occurring at the same time*, and respond to the queries of tax payers.

The secretarial team displayed the graphic of Government's drug supply chain, which spread wide and massive, from national warehouses through intermediate storage points to tens of thousands of dispensaries in the remote villages. It was clearly one of the largest and most complex supply chains in the world, with innumerable supply nodes and a mind boggling variety of SKUs.

Rita's algorithm showed that the level of aggregation of the supply chain held huge advantage for the ministry. It revealed that if right rules were placed, it would make the chain very lean, with consequent benefits. The proposed design of supply chain would provide high availability of drugs with lower stocks (cost). The Minister immediately took note of their observations and expressed intention to upgrade the supply chain.

By the middle of 2010, Life2.0 had established the process of ongoing improvements across all the ten plants and things looked all set on autopilot at Terra Pharma. Rita's team had whirlwind tour across locations and built a strong base of facilitation teams at each plant. Her core team had already moved back to Seth's office. Each plant had started showing initial improvements and the respective teams showed tremendous commitment to transit to the culture of ongoing improvement.

In mid 2011, Seth called Rita and showed her a letter from the Government. Signed by the Minister of Health on a thick white matt paper, it carried an embossed emblem of the nation and was addressed to Amin.

It was an official letter formally seeking help from Terra Pharma to handhold the Secretariat in redesigning the supply chain of drugs across the country, under its 'Health for All' program.

On the letter head, Amin had scribbled, "I recommend Rita to join the ministry on sabbatical for 18 months."

Rita was speechless for a moment. Seeing her silent, Seth said, "Get ready for the endeavor."

She said in utter disbelief, "It is too big a job...!"

Seth said, "You have already done a much complicated job here... very successfully. The Ministry's work may be large in scale but the rules of the game are not different. Keep faith in the fundamentals of Inherent Simplicity. Actually, larger the supply chain, simpler it is to improve its effectiveness. Focus on the objective and the task at hand; and it will be completed in no time."

"In this case, they will need you at the level of program management and you will not have to be stationed in plants. This must suit you very well. Your previous work with the WHO will help immensely. The Minister's team is young and dynamic; you will have fun and will get a good perspective of the national health problem. The problem is big and therefore, I felt that it is worth taking it up," he completed his brief.

"Great! I can't refuse your offer. Thank you... I enjoyed Life2.0, nothing has been better than this in my career. I came to know people better, and understood why it is said that people are the core assets of an organization. I also realized the meaning of 'time is money'. Indeed, today we sell time and make money. Our drugs are readily available and our clients get drugs on time, specifically because process orders move faster across our supply chain. Our clients pay us for availability and reliability of supply, in addition to the drugs we make. And, this is done at far lower cost than anybody else. For me, time is the key driver of business. Our only job is to shrink the time it takes us to fulfill market demand, while other things tag along." Rita said, as she kept staring at the letter.

She knew that the job at the ministry would have its own challenges; but she was ready to get going. She had a few known faces in the Ministry to help her catch up quickly with the nuances of working with the bureaucracy.

Consolidating the Change

Business Model Innovation

Terra Pharma's way of doing business created a number of innovations that went beyond its traditional engagement of bringing-out Generic drugs. Several industry players began making Operational Excellence central to their core strategy and they started preparing to adopt its agile Business Model. Interns from one of the world's leading management schools spent a full summer at Terra Pharma to capture its story of transformation. The complete case study appeared in the 2011 winter edition of a premier management review journal, under the heading "Operational Excellence for Accessible and Affordable Medicines." Below is the excerpt from the publication.

.......While, it would take writing a full doctoral thesis to describe the remarkable transformational journey of Terra Pharma, it is important to provide an intuitive view and clear description of the gamut of innovations carried out by its team. Such a view and description would provide a pathway for the creation of best practices and new knowledge for the whole industry. In order to achieve this objective, a model based on logical flow of business value is presented here. This model of innovation, used by the Management Team of Terra Pharma, is adopted from the Business Model Canvas that was proposed by its Executive Coach, Adam Weisner.

The Business Model Approach

For starters, a Business Model is best defined as, "The rationale of creating, delivering and capturing value of a business."

Adam starts with a four block model of value creation (infrastructure side), value proposition (the value), value delivery (customer side) and value capture (financial side), as shown in Figure 8.1, [4].

The arrows show how 'value flow' can be modeled. It is the prime responsibility of the Operating System of an organization to make flow of value as fast as possible. For this flow to be faster, it is important that the key blockers of flow, wherever they occur along the line of flow, are dealt with effectively.

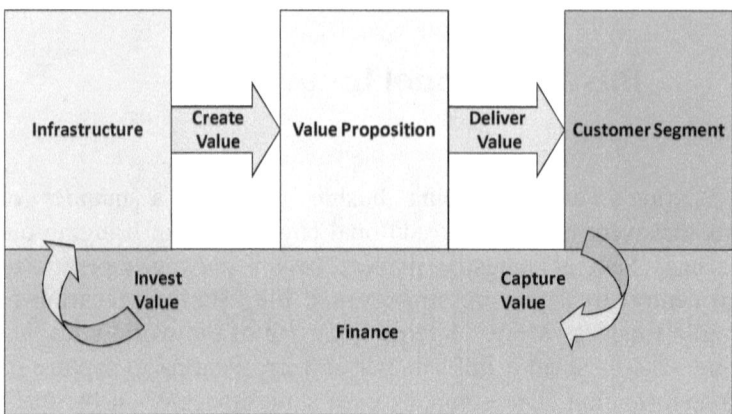

Figure 8.1 Four Block Business Model Framework

Subsequently, Adam breaks down the model into nine blocks [4] and lays them into a graphic called Canvas (Figure 8.2) that further improves comprehension and visualization of the Business Model.

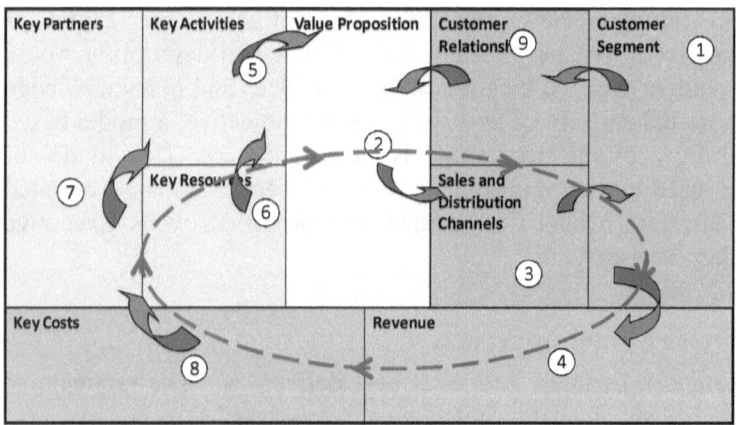

Figure 8.2 The Business Model Canvas

Here is how Business Model can be described, based on the guidelines provided by Adam.

"A Business Model can be described fairly through 9 basic building blocks that provide the logic of how a company intends to fulfill the necessary conditions of making money faster in a sustained way. In fact, it represents the blueprint of a company's logic of doing business that is then implemented through organizational structures, processes and systems."

From Figure 8.2, the nine building blocks of a Business Model can be described as:

1. The target *customer segments* and their clearly identified significant needs. An organization must play in large enough customer segments. In order to have a sustainable growth, other things remaining the same, the business must fulfill at least one significant need of its each customer segment like no other competitor could and would.
2. The *value proposition* of what is offered to the target customer segments. It is a value affixed product, service or solution, offered singly or in combination. The qualifying value could be quality, variety, availability, accessibility, price, safety etc.
3. The communication and distribution *channels* to reach customers, make sales and deliver the value proposition. This block has an interface to the value proposition block and the target customer segment block. The value delivery arrow therefore, flows from the value proposition through the channels to the customer segments.
4. The *key activities* to implement the Business Model. Key activities are derived from the value proposition and when they are *executed*, they create value. Hence, the value creation arrow goes from the key activities block to the value proposition block.
5. The *core capacities (resources)* are needed to enable key activities of the Business Model. Key resources provide the capacities to conduct and facilitate key activities. The value creation arrow therefore, goes from key resource block to key activities block, and delivers value proposition all the way to the customer segment block.
6. The *key partners* and their motivations come together to make a Business Model happen. In today's complex world, not all activities are doable by an organization itself and hence, some of the resources and therefore, activities are performed by key partners, who become part of the value chain. The value creation arrow goes from the key partners block to the key resources block and the key activities block.
7. The *revenue streams* of the Business Model constitute the revenue model. When the value proposition is delivered to the target customers, the value is captured through revenue streams. The value capture arrow goes from customer segment block to the revenue stream block.
8. The *cost structure* to support the Business Model. An organization invests in creating resources, doing activities and managing the partners. In a stable and growing business, operational cost structure is supported by the revenue streams. The value investment arrow flows from the revenue stream block, through cost structure block to the resource block and the partners block.
9. The *relationships* established with customers form the basis of *long term viability* of the business. The business is an ongoing entity and must be built to transform. This will happen if and only if significant needs of customers are fulfilled the way no other significant competitor can. The organization therefore needs to build a customer relationship block that constantly upgrades the value proposition based on the feedback derived from the strong relationship with the customers. The long term value creation arrow flows in a direction opposite to that of

other arrows, i.e. from customer segment block to value proposition block; and then merges and reinforces the cycle of value flow.

A Business Model is best presented in a visual format and its logic is articulated in a clear description (read-out) to enhance grasp of the big picture.

Terra Pharma had never been an Innovator Company in a true sense. Like most of the native companies from emerging markets, it had been at the periphery of drug re-engineering. Till recently, it enjoyed huge margins in pure Generics business, not because of any low cost strategy, but because of having low cost structure in an emerging country. And within the local market too it was protected by favorable market and IPR related policies of the government.

The management understood that developing a wide range of products through rapid re-engineering was a necessity. However, a lopsided attention on development was not only increasingly becoming insufficient advantage, it was actually adversely affecting its operational performance. It found that the reliability of supplying even the existing portfolio was very unsatisfactory due to increasing fragmentation and volatility in the market. It meant that improving the response time to the changes in the market place was more than a necessity.

Terra Pharma's search to deal with rapid changes in the market forced it to adopt 'agility' as its key tactics, and make creation of this capability central to its strategy. The team at Terra Pharma also understood that low structural cost must transcend to low cost operations 'by design'. This, it thought to be the natural course of its strategy, and decided to prepare itself well in advance.

Terra Pharma went through the process of Business Model Innovation. To start with, it took one step at a time in innovating its own system, through rapid cycles of experimentation, process design and implementation.

Visualizing Innovated Business Model

While the staff in its plants was working on action based innovation, Terra Pharma's Top Management was constantly juggling blocks of its Business Model to create seamlessness in the flow of value. The team had conducted an elaborate exercise to redesign the Business Model. It scrutinized the emerging Business Model with proven analytical tools like, SWOT analysis and the 'Blue Ocean' framework of Kim and Maubourgne [19], to increase the value while simultaneously reducing the cost. Figure 8.3, shows the Canvas for the Innovated Business Model of Terra Pharma.

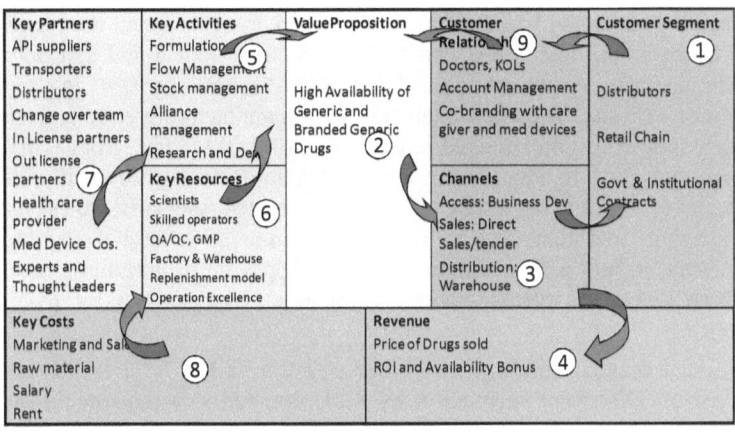

Figure 8.3 The Business Model Canvas of Terra Pharma after transformation

Read-out of Innovated Business Model

The read out of the innovated Business Model of Terra Pharma, is as given below:

1. Customer Segment: In order to align itself with regularly shifting needs of the market place, Terra Pharma defined its market more sharply. It segmented its market into Distributors, Retail Chain and Government Procurement. Its empathy analysis of customer segments revealed different significant needs of these slices of the market. For example, for distributors, the significant need is the return on investment (ROI). The opening up of retail industry in the regional markets and the trend in group or aggregated buying led to inclusion of separate focus on retail chain. Also, since the future is going to be constrained by government regulations that will force the prices to be driven down, it included government contracts as a separate segment.
2. Value Proposition: It is now articulated in terms of specific value proposition that meets significant needs of each segment. Hence, high ROI, high availability (reliability) and low price are the value propositions for the three segments, respectively. Terra Pharma realized that when the changes in the market are unpredictable, *high availability and reliability* of drugs are pre-requisites for all the segments.
3. Channels: Value proposition to each client segment demanded a distinct promotion, sales and distribution approach. Terra Pharma built its delivery side as an autonomous center through account managers, who managed the end to end delivery activities for these segments.
4. Key Skills: In order to offer the value proposition to the targeted segments, Terra Pharma needed exceptional skills in managing the stocks that would not only result in high inventory turns but would also result in high availability and reliability of its supplies. It created specialized skills in stock control to monitor and regulate the flow of the sales orders into the supply chain according to the market pull.

Deciding to supply based on priorities set by market, meant the plants to be agile and fast. Terra Pharma's production team found that poor manufacturing practices contributed to over 60 percent loss in production time. The team interacted with manufacturing experts from other industries and engaged practitioners of TQM, TPM, Six Sigma, Lean and TOC, to adopt best practices in manufacturing. Gradually, its employees picked up these skills, and created specialist roles for managing operations better. In a major innovation in the Pharma Industry, it built a team similar to the Pit Stop team of Formula-1 race, which helped its plants increase runtime of its machines by 15-50 percent.

Since, it decided not to give lopsided attention to R&D, Terra Pharma hived off Discovery segment of its R&D division as a separate entity, with a goal to work on long term objective. This permitted its management to focus its attention on market led operations. Further, this also reduced the variability in business performance due to offloading of highly volatile nature of Discovery process. It then restructured the Development segment of its R&D as operations focused innovation arm, with a clear focus on bringing Generic drugs faster to the market. However, to ensure its future and its strategy to move closer to customer side, it decided to in-license drugs from Innovator Companies, who need to enter the regional market. In the same vein, it out-licensed part of its Long Tail products to those players who either have better benefit of aggregation on these products or are at a vantage position in alien markets. Thus, it added 'alliance management' as a new functional area to its organization, and committed to build deep skills in industry knowledge, business relationship, contracts, regulatory framework and legal strategies.

5. Resources: Beyond its physical resources, Terra Pharma built Structures, Systems, Processes and Tools that helped it master pull based production, follow market based priority and rapidly improve utilization of its plants. This also forced significant changes in the way Terra Pharma manufactured drugs. Terra Pharma introduced a new flow based manufacturing architecture for all its plants.

Its incessant search for ongoing improvements led to development of a new operating system that allows its teams across the hierarchy to collaborate in quickly identifying and solving operational problems. In fact, it turned its staff into operational scientists, who are involved in day to day hypothesis and validation of their improvement ideas, while performing their daily work of moving process orders.

Its team's investigation into manufacturing practices had initially revealed a severe scarcity of basic manufacturing expertise. So much so that most of its manufacturing staff were earlier from pharma background rather than being from manufacturing domain. Actually, they found that this was not so only in their organization, but was an industry trend. Somehow, even today, most of the manufacturing staff in pharmaceutical companies tends to be graduates with pharmaceutical degrees. The team then went on a recruitment spree to enroll staff from manufacturing background in order to build a solid manufacturing base. Following this, Terra Pharma brought in new specialist positions demanded by its manufacturing architecture such as, Production Planning and Control Manager, Industrial Engineer, Stock Controller, Flow Manager, Changeover Crew Member, etc.

Terra Pharma now has a new set of efficiency resource set called 'the manufacturing tool box', that contains best practices from different industries, ready to be deployed in its own context, as and when the need arises. Needless to say, training of its staff on new practices is, now more than a routine.

To manage development of new products and the alliance of in-licensing better, it introduced an intelligent portfolio management and analytic software framework. It brought the future pipeline of products map closer to changing therapeutic needs of the market and gave a high ROI to its alliance partners.

6. Key Partners: In order to meet the new definition of value proposition, the company needed a capability to supply small batches of drugs faster. For this, it negotiated an availability based bonus with its material suppliers, transporters and distribution partners, who agreed to reconfigure logistics to meet the need of moving smaller dispatches faster.

   Activation of its Alliance function, similarly converted its competitors into partners, in a win-win relationship.

   While most of its partners were earlier based on transaction based relationship, Terra Pharma entered into collaborative partnership by strengthening its knowledge of industry wide best practices and created a strong network of experts not only in manufacturing and supply chain, but also in other functional areas. There is now an increasing level of engagement of its staff with external world in continuous benchmarking its processes and moving to the next level of performance. Today, in the global benchmarking study on Operational Excellence conducted by Europe's leading institute, only Terra Pharma features from the region in the top quartile of best global operating pharma companies.

7. Revenue Streams: Terra Pharma's clear focus on significant needs of individual market segments was received very well by its clients. Then, it started topping up its traditional revenue model with a bonus clause on performance that was linked to inventory turns, product availability and on time delivery. By choice, its plants retained more than 20 percent reserve capacity; which allowed Terra Pharma not only to quickly respond to unexpected volatility in demand, but also grab umpteen urgent opportunities created in the market.

8. Key Costs: Contrary to expectations, its overall cost went down. A significant reduction was in Marketing, Sales and Distribution cost. Its cash flow increased dramatically due to release of cash from lower WIP

and inventory. And as a consequence, Terra Pharma became the most cost effective drug maker as well.
9. Customer Relationship: Account management went extremely well with each customer segment and individual clients, where each team tried to maximize the targeted value proposition to the clients. Better customer relationship started showing up in terms of preferred supplier status for an increasing number of clients. And, clients started increasing the portfolio of products from Terra Pharma.

The above renewed Business Model of Terra Pharma is a result of clearly describing each of its building blocks and connecting them logically, from customer segment to value proposition, through delivery channel to revenues, and developing its infrastructure accordingly. Terra Pharma's team understood what's in its hand and what's not in its hand, developed new policies, built core skills and nurtured relationships across the value chain. The new Business Model positioned it uniquely and decisively amidst the chaotic marketplace, where its competitors are struggling to survive, and most of the first generation entrepreneurs are succumbing to market pressure and selling off their businesses.

The biggest innovation brought in by Terra Pharma was the cultural change that moved its organizations from number or dollar based target chasing organization to a purpose based and action driven organization. Emanating from one objective, each element of its supply chain is remarkably synchronized with market demand based on a single priority system. Having a single priority system, across the organization, helps it to quickly resolve conflicts and avoid local optima. Today, the organization works with unbelievably high synchronism and harmony, and thus marches ahead on the path of ongoing improvement.

If the original canvas of Terra Pharma's Business Model is juxtaposed with that of its renewed Business Model, it will be a magical realization on how many innovations Terra Pharma did in its Business Model. Table 8.1, lists some of the key innovations in its Business Model.

Seth the CEO of Terra Pharma says, "All these innovations came one step at a time, but at an amazingly faster pace." He attributed these innovations through Operational Excellence to the guidelines that were discovered by his team.

Table 8.1 Comparison of Traditional and Innovated Business Models

Elements	Traditional Business Model	Innovated Business Model
Client Segment	Focus on Distributors	Distributors, Retail Chains, Institutions
Order Classification	Made to Stock	Made to Availability & Made to Order
Value Proposition	Large Portfolio of low cost Drugs	High Availability of Generic Drugs
Channel	Doctors, Conferences, Sales Reps	Doctors, Account Management, Sales Reps
Supply Chain	Push System	Pull System
People profile	Pharma Graduates	Manufacturing, Pharma Graduates, Industrial Engineers, PPC Engineers
Planning	Monthly and Quarterly	Real Consumption and Order based
Internal Alignment	Multiple Priorities	Single Priority System
Partners	Material Suppliers	Suppliers, Transporters, Innovators, Competitors, Industry Experts
Revenue	Price of Drugs and Discounted Sale	Price of Drugs and Bonus
Key Costs	Sales, Raw Material, Inventory	People, Raw Material, Sales
Culture	Student Syndrome, Procrastination	Relay Race, Problem Solving
Improvement Process	Sum of Parts, Arbitrary, Incremental	Focused, Cause and Effect based, Action Oriented, Transformational
Metrics	Revenues, Million of Pills, Utilization	Revenues, Lead Time, Availability, Inventory Turns, OEE @ Constraints

Guidelines for Operational Excellence

Objective of Operations: Ever improving flow of process orders to fulfill the promise made to customers is the prime objective of operations.

Promise to Customers: High Availability and Supply Reliability of Drugs

Key Metric: Availability (MTA) and Due Date Performance (MTO)

Lead Indicators: Lead Time, Inventory, Urgency, Improvement Projects

Prime Guidelines: In order to fulfill its responsibilities, the guidelines for the team are as given below.

1. Do not work on a process order that is not triggered by the consumption of stocks or by a customer order.
2. Work only on those process orders that are triggered by consumption of stocks or by customer orders.
3. If multiple process orders compete for the time of a resource, then an order that is 'Endangered' to miss the promise made to the market must be given preference.

a. When a product is stocked out at the warehouse, it is an emergency and highest level of expediting must be used to pull the batches through the system. *This situation (of stock out or an order missing due date) must always be avoided.*
   b. When process orders are in RED zone (with less than 1/3rd safety left), ensure that they are either being worked upon or they are in front of the queue for working and are given the priority to jump the queue at each process stage.
4. A low priority does not exclude any order from being worked upon; all open orders must be worked upon.
5. Once a process order is in hand, it must be started as soon as possible, and once the order is under process, it must be processed as fast as possible (baseline speed).
6. While work is being done only on orders that are triggered by consumption or customer orders, and "Endangered Orders" are given priority, these process orders will often get stuck and will be delayed for various reasons.
   a. Since, time is the key constraint, trying to improve everything will dilute attention and exhaust the scarce human resources. Hence a focused approach must be adopted, to systematically address the reasons of delays.
   b. If there is a delay (disruption) in processing an order due to an assignable cause, then pause for a while, use local ingenuity to solve the problem, otherwise summon seniors or domain experts to seek quick solution.
      i. All improvement programs related to Operations must be those that come up while following the priority across the supply chain.
      ii. The problems that are in the hands of Operations must be promptly dealt with.
      iii. In order to rapidly come out of disruptions, an effective escalation and expediting procedure must be followed.
      iv. For each disruption, the reasons of delays are collected, and analyzed on a periodic basis. Improvement teams are created to tackle the problems, one by one starting with the most prominent ones first.
      v. The Plant Management must monitor, review and manage the portfolio of these improvement projects.
   c. Not so less often, the reasons for delays would not be readily assignable. Such delays would be caused by systemic issues. During such a situation, an approach must be adopted to identify the core problem and a robust solution must be implemented. This may often require consulting with cross functional teams.
7. Some products will become endangered chronically, indicating capacity of the plant falling behind the demand for such products. The slowest resource or process along the flow (routing) of the product could indicate blockage to the flow. In the plants, such situations will exist regularly. Hence,

      i. Plants must develop a mechanism to regularly identify indicators of flow blockers.
     ii. An increased focus must be brought onto the indicators of flow blockers, to identify reasons for the blockage.
    iii. If the reason that prevents improvement in flow through the resource is the resource itself, then
        1. All efforts must be made to improve productivity of the resource (constrained resource), by closely monitoring and analyzing its process and non-process time.
        2. All other resources, including support and management functions must protect the constrained resource against starvation and give its requirements highest priority.
        3. All upstream resources, must avoid overproduction and flooding the resource with excessive inventory.
8. Several times, the reason for a resource blocking the flow may not be the resource itself. A detailed analysis of the working on and around the resource will indicate an outside root cause (constraint).
9. For problems that need deep investigations and systemic corrections, the best of the brains in the company must take up these problems and include them as high impact improvement projects into their KPIs.
10. The top management of the Organization must monitor, review and manage the portfolio of systemic improvement projects.

When asked, "How long could you maintain this competitive edge?" Seth replied, "My team has not just found new rules, it has found a new way to discover the rules to improve performance on an ongoing basis. Of course, other organizations are welcome to visit our plants. If they wish, they can adopt our techniques. The truth is that *every organization is unique and, in the long run, it has to find its own way of excellence.*"

Seth was right. To the onlookers, it seemed as if Terra Pharma has built skills in using an assortment of tools and adopted a quick reactive system that fixes the broken things faster. However, on looking deeper, it becomes evident that the reality on the ground is something different, which would not be easy for any outsider to know or replicate.

The working of Terra Pharma has evolved into a participative operating system called the AED (Action - Escalation - Decision) model that helps its plants in constantly *reducing the disruptions to flow* and shrinking lead times. It reduces the internal source of variations, whether it is due to skill, quality, process issues, raw material, breakdowns or forecasting based planning. This is, of course, a Bottom Up initiated convection current system.

However, the management of Terra Pharma has built a complementary Top Down system that dramatically improves the effectiveness of its AED based operating system. The management constantly steers the plants towards market needs and operates a management system that *identifies flow blockers* on an ongoing basis. These blockers are necessarily the big stones that dictate the growth of Terra Pharma at a given moment. They are resources, policies, people competencies, portfolio, legacy systems, suppliers, environment conditions, etc., each one of which has huge potential to improve performance of Terra Pharma. *These flow blockers are not the same as the day to day disruptions.*

Once flow blockers are identified by using a systemic focused approach, it provides people down the hierarchy a clear direction to focus their improvement efforts in these vital areas. This allows Terra Pharma to make quick and big jumps in its performance, without taking too much risk and without exhausting its costly resources. This is quite the opposite of 'carpet bombing' approach traditionally followed by several organizations in pursuing continuous improvement programs. Such organizations often try to improve everything everywhere and undergo painful, costly and long drawn experience that often creates backlash to improvement culture.

In essence, the AED based operating system and the Focused approach to identify flow blockers, complement each other to give Terra Pharma an unbelievably effective and efficient framework of excellence.

Seth's journey has not ended yet. "We have set up our system and teams to achieve better effectiveness and efficiencies in operations within the plants. Now, we can get into new products and see what sort of issues we have to deal with while making them flow smoothly… The complexity of new products is mind boggling, it injects not just variety but inconsistencies and unpredictability in the process of formulation. Adam was here a few weeks back to help us understand what seems to be a much bigger challenge. But we are confident to take it on and achieve a level of breakthrough that is unheard of in the industry." Seth said about what's his team was up to.

Terra Pharma has already launched a new wave of transformation called Life3.0 and its team is back to what it is good at: *crashing the time taken to change performance of its organization* to dramatically higher levels. And, as Life2.0 proved, it wants to achieve the audacious objective of Life3.0 without shaking the boat, without major trade-offs and without causing burn-outs. Sure, it will with the focused approach!

Appendix

Unambiguous Priority System

The subject of 'Operations' covers a wide area from order creation, raw material procurement, manufacturing to distribution.

Depending upon the perspective it is seen from, Operations can be defined accordingly. The definition could become complex when one tries to consider improvement of operational performance. It suddenly looks consisting of so many parts, each with its own importance, disparate looking agenda and conflicting goals. And each part would claim itself as the most important element of Operations.

Never the less, all the parts of Operations must be connected by a single thread. It must be possible to identify this thread, and perhaps, give it a practical definition such that all parts feel belonging as well as contributing to. The importance of having a clear definition is the first step towards integrating teams by actions as well as by thinking. Such a definition must be actionable and directly related to what people actually see and do.

Let's try one here.

'Operations' is a noun form of the verb, 'Operate'. It means that if you got a system, you operate it; you work with it, on day to day basis, every moment. At this level, it means moving things or service, i.e. creating value every moment. But since, to sustain a business, the value proposition must improve with time, more value must be delivered in a given time, i.e. things must be moved *faster* in a supply chain.

Thus, *the role of Operations is to ever improve flow of things (value) which the organization intends to sell*. And for people on the shop floor, it means improving the speed of 'process orders'. The level of flow is measured by Lead Time, which is defined as the time Operations takes between the creation and delivery of a process order.

Operations handles products and SKUs, machines and people, processes and procedure, SOPs and protocols but each person in Operations, on day to day basis, talks about status of 'Process Order', 'Work Order' or 'Sales Order'. The *lingua franca* of operations is dominated by key phrases like, receipt of order, status of order, dispatch of order, completion of order, delay of order, stuck order, in progress order, etc. A 'Process Order' is, therefore, considered *the least denominator* on the shop floor, to which all operational activities are related to. People in the shop floor live as if process orders run through their blood; and serial numbers of process orders delivered years back remain permanently etched into their memories.

Process Orders are created, released, processed, dispatched and delivered. All activities in Operations are therefore rallied around the status of process orders. If any process order is stuck somewhere, it is a cause of concern, since it is supposed to move faster.

Considering 'Orders' as the least denominator in Operations is critical; since it gives transactional orientation, and transaction means speed. More predominantly, it helps in connecting the organization directly to customer requirements at its lowest granularity. The quality of this connection is what customers value beyond products.

Although faster speed of supply is good and essential, at a moment neither all products are required to be supplied fast nor all customers have a need to receive goods very fast. But they must be supplied as per promised due dates. Depending upon the products, customers actually have different level of tolerance time (requirement of lead time). It therefore, behooves on Operations to reframe its promise to customers based upon their tolerance time.

Promising Availability and Producing to Stock are Different

Some products are very competitive and could also be commoditized. These products are generally available in abundance. It also means that customers consider these products to be readily available, and factor their high availability into supply chain planning. Thus, for such products, tolerance time of clients to wait for shipment could be low. So low that it becomes much shorter than the supplier's lead time to produce plus deliver. It becomes necessary for the supplier to maintain stocks of these products, so that customers could be served immediately or within a competitive lead time.

Traditionally, such a system of supply has been called Made to Stock (MTS), although, terminology wise, 'Made to Availability (MTA)' suites better. The difference between the two is that while in MTS, stocks are *kept in anticipation* of sales; in case of MTA, the supplier specifically *promises high availability* all the time. Further, MTS is based on forecasting while MTA is based on replenishment as per consumption.

In MTA model, the complete supply chain gets the advantage of better availability of products at comparatively lower cost. Thus, an organization that supplies MTA products is considered higher on the relationship and performance maturity curve, compared to an organization supplying products based upon MTS. Indeed, it requires special commitment, system, effort and culture to fulfill the promise of high availability.

When a high availability is promised, unknown variability is factored in the demand. If a plant has a tendency to work at 100% load, then an upward variation in demand would overload the plant. Any overload on the system would increase its lead time and prevent it from ensuring availability. From operations point of view, it is critical that the plant always has a spare capacity to take care of the variability in demand. Such a capacity is called protective (reserve) capacity. Since having a reserve capacity is costly, one must be particularly sure that there is a definite need of having products categorized as MTA. More importantly, customers must have a need for better availability.

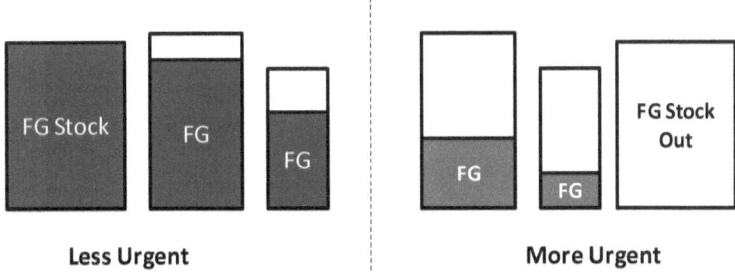

Figure A1-1 For MTA products, priority of process orders on the shop floor is based on the urgency to avoid stock-out of respective products

Once a supplier is adept at offering MTA products as above and the plant has enough reserve capacity, one can further leverage superior supply performance. If there is a benefit of aggregation among clients or products, it makes an even stronger sense to offer high availability of products that traditionally have long lead time (tolerance time), and thereby change the game in the market place.

A production line that serves several MTA products, must give priority to those products that are in the danger of stock out. In Terra Pharma, the MTA orders that were much late and the respective products were in the danger of being stocked out, were distinctly marked with red color, and identified as 'endangered orders'. Performance of its plants for such products were, therefore measured by availability. This ensured that the production operated on right priority.

Non Stock Products

Products which are not commoditized or are known to have difficult processes or are away from competition; the market would generally wait for longer than the lead time of the plant. Orders of such products, are traditionally given a date by when they must be delivered and the suppliers promise to deliver the orders as per the due date.

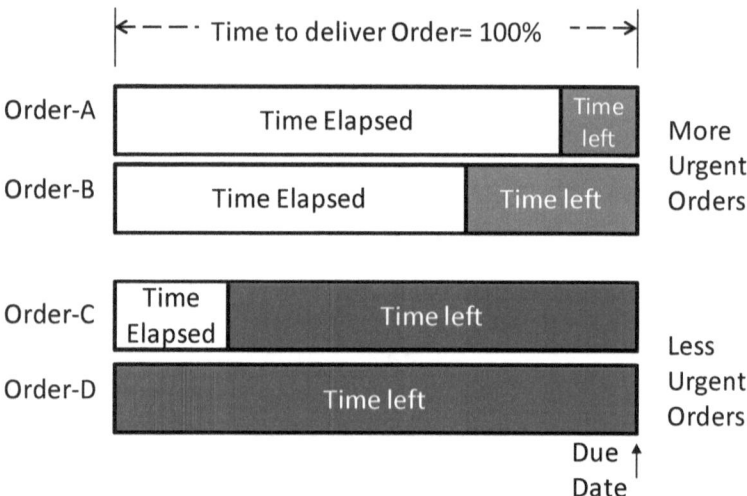

Figure A1-2 For MTO products, priority of process orders on the shop floor is based on the urgency to avoid missing the committed due dates.

The group of products that are supplied against a strict due date, are often called Made to Order (MTO) products. Some of these products which are supplied frequently may already have stock of raw materials, while others that are required too infrequently, might require procurement of raw materials just before they are produced.

When a plant has several MTO products sharing a common line or resource, the needed behavior is to give priorities to those orders that have a higher danger of missing the due date.

So for MTO orders, the relative duration left to meet the due dates is the parameter of urgency. In Terra Pharma, MTO orders which were in a higher danger of missing the due dates were flagged with red color and were identified as 'endangered orders'.

The performance of the plant to deliver MTO orders is measured by the term Reliability of Supply, which is the percentage of MTO orders delivered in full, within the committed due dates.

Single Priority System

Before Terra Pharma had started Life2.0, it was usual for the staff in the planning and as well as in the shop floor, to receive multiple priorities from different people, locations and customers. In fact, most of the time, the planning team was busy in juggling between different priorities leading to bad compromises. And the shop floor staff was never at ease with the arbitrariness in the priorities. In fact, all orders seemed hot urgent. There was no clear classification of MTA and MTO products.

Rather, Terra Pharma operated with a rather confused environment of MTS and by chance sometimes MTO.

After reclassification of the orders into MTA and MTO, roughly, 40% of Terra Pharma's sales comprised MTO orders. This meant that often, some orders of MTA and MTO products were sharing common resources. However, a consistent priority mechanism of MTA and MTO products provided a non-conflicting single priority system. For the staff on the shop floor, it did not matter whether it was an MTA or an MTO order, it just had to go by the single priority system, i.e. giving high priority to 'endangered orders'. And irrespective of the type of order, 'endangered orders' had consistent priority (indicated by red color). Having a single priority system thus, significantly reduced the daily conflict and confusion that the staff across the supply chain went through earlier.

Thus, the staff in the shop floors of Terra Pharma had only to deal with process 'orders' (the least common denominator) as per single priority system.

Inside the Growth Curve

Increasingly it is being felt that a vast majority of organizations has huge hidden capacity, and a good process of improvement could help in achieving more on the existing resources quickly, without taking too much risk and incurring costly trade-offs. Let's dwell on this aspect by getting inside the growth curve.

Case studies as well as popular non-fiction management books on business transformation often depict significant improvement in organizational performance as given in Figure A2-1. Of course, such a growth curve would be an abstraction of the claimed growth over a reasonably long horizon of time.

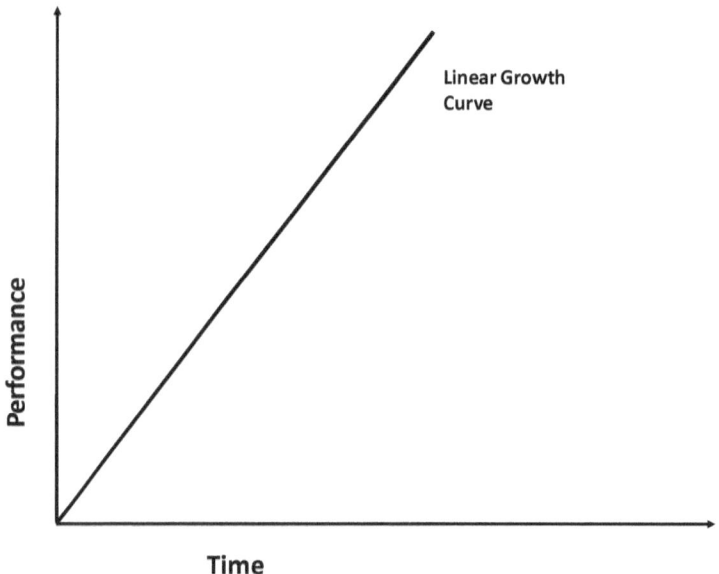

Figure A2-1 Highest level of abstraction for representing growth

Subsequently, an algorithmic methodology of excellence is explained and a step by step growth of the organization is presented, which would look like Figure A2-2. It would give the impression that the growth is so systematic and achieved perfectly as per design and plan.

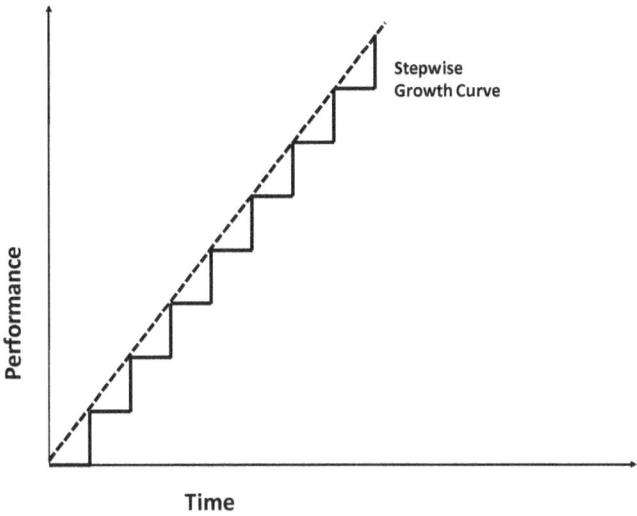

Figure A2-2 Most often stepwise growth of an organization is shown as if the growth follows a systematic, by design, a well planned approach

However, a vast majority of managers are used to commit their efforts to a growth curve, as given in Figure A2-3.

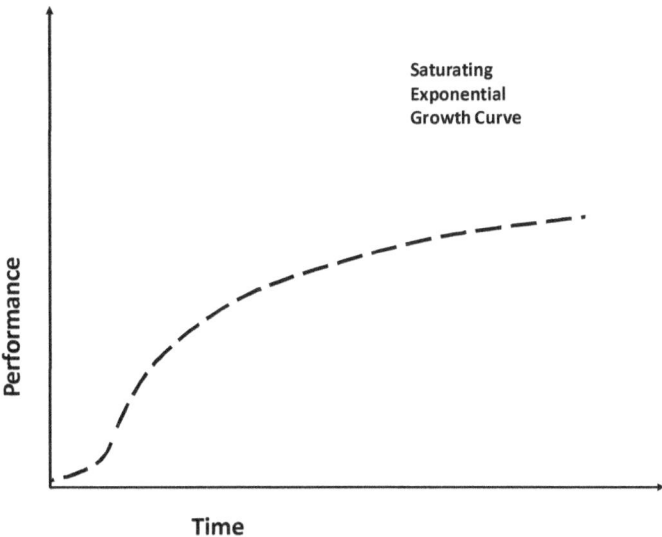

Figure A2-3 With time, the growth rate slows down and is often assumed as a natural growth characteristics

Initially, the growth is faster but settles down to a slower rate as the time progresses. People often relate the initial part of the curve to the 'start up' and 'early stage' entrepreneurial culture. The subsequent part is related to a matured organization, with well laid out structures and procedures. There is a belief that this is a natural phenomenon. In fact, this assumption is also supported by physical phenomenon of saturation, which exists in the material world. Think about growth of human body with age, saturation of a solution with the quantity of solute or change in magnetic field of an electromagnet with current.

However, growth specialists often question sustainability of this pattern of organizational growth, since organizations are living entities, and are resilient enough to jump out of saturation. Actually, organizations are started up with an intention to live longer than one human generation.

Some organizations understand the danger of stagnating growth and initiate actions well in time. For example, if the challenges in business environment cause significant fluctuation in input cost, employee retention, price etc, it is imperative that an organization must improve its performance faster than the effective system variations. Otherwise, its growth would be 'lost in the noise'. It is not difficult to identify organizations with stagnating growth, suddenly succumbing to the external noise and variability, and falling down as shown in Figure A2-4.

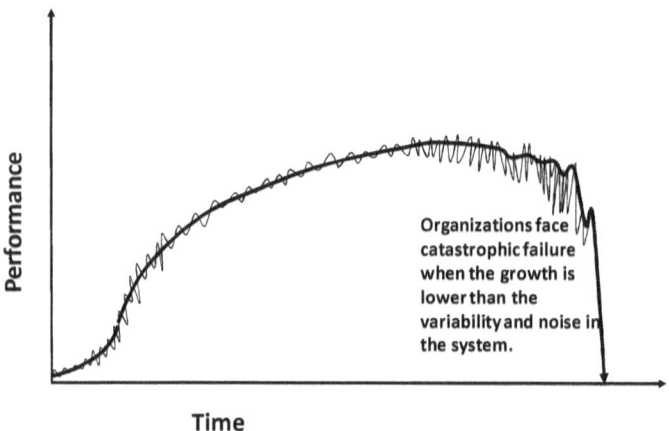

Figure A2-4 If the growth of an organization is less than the noise and variability created in the system, it runs the risk of catastrophic failure

Of course, a vast majority of organizations can be found located on the upper plateau of the S curve. And mistakenly, people believe that this represents stability. In the garb of stability, it actually represents constrained performance. The issue with this condition of an organization is that the capability of the organization that would have fetched great growth in the early part of its life cycle is no more sufficient to maintain the desired growth trajectory. It is wise to assume that some big constraint prevents the organization from growing. And it is this aspect that makes progressive organizations focus on managing the constraint better and improving its performance.

Actually, if you look at the growth curve of successful organizations that are built to transform, you would find that the growth curve is more of an upward exponential nature, Figure A2-5. Just do internet download of past 15-20 years data of companies like GE, Microsoft, HP, Shell, Infosys, TISCO, ABB, IKEA, Pfizer, GSK etc., to validate that it is indeed so.

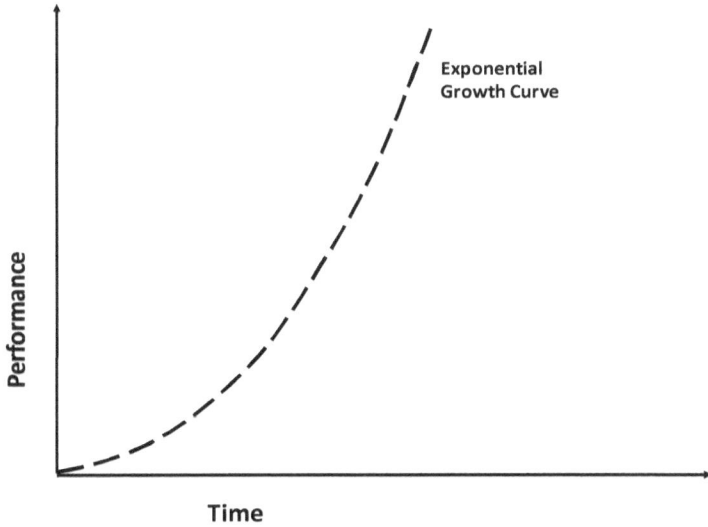

Figure A2-5 A progressive organization actually has an exponential growth curve

Of course, every entrepreneur and business chief aims to follow on this curve of exponential growth. However, this curve is also an abstraction of an ever flourishing company over a long horizon. And it is important to further understand the underlying construct of this characteristic.

Because an organization has high ambition but operates under limited resource environment (including management attention), prudent organizations take up limited growth initiatives at a given moment. So an initiative that is started today, actually would have an S curve in terms of its contribution to the organization's growth. The top tapered part of the S curve actually shows the maturity or stability or institutionalization of *the new ways of doing things*, for that particular single initiative. The responsibility of the organization is to see that this stability is built and strengthened, by an ongoing process that institutionalizes the new rules. The institutionalization of the new rules emanating from any improvement initiative must get into the culture of the organization. Once the new culture is built, it consolidates performance into a strong base. Now, the next improvement initiative, much larger than the previous one, can be built on this strong base, without allowing the organization to slide down on its growth curve, Figure A2-6.

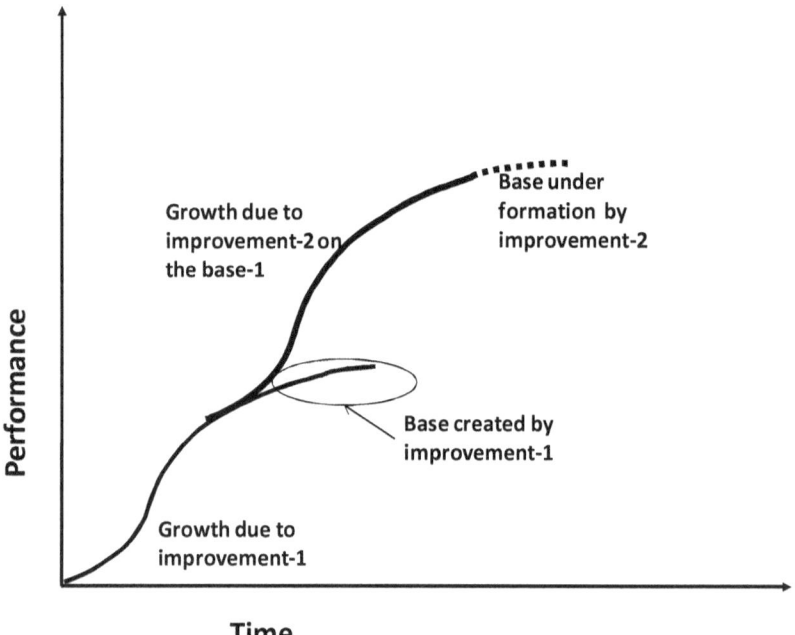

Figure A2-6 The S curve is the fundamental element of organizational growth. Each S curve builds a stronger base for further growth, as the rules of the initiative are institutionalized.

Often organizations try to start too many initiatives when those in hand are mid way or waiting to be stabilized. This only has the undesired effect of not realizing enough benefits of the existing improvement initiative, as it leads to creation of immature base. Often, it leads to conflicting interactions between different initiatives, which jeopardize the prospects of most of the initiatives. It is estimated that a vast majority of failures of such improvement initiatives is linked to running too many of them at once than the organization can manage.

For an organization to grow on an ongoing basis without sliding down dramatically, it is important that it continues to build the base (stability) bigger with just the few initiatives and builds new initiatives on the ever more solid base.

Therefore, when a series of growth initiatives is built on previous base, the concatenation transforms the growth curve of the organization into an exponential curve, with distinct build up of the base, as shown in Figure A2-7.

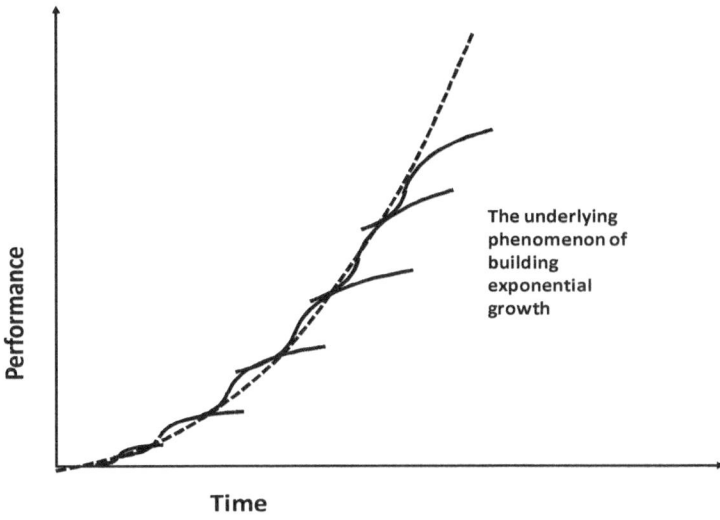

Figure A2-7 Concatenation of growth curves leads to exponential growth

A better representation of such a growth curve is as shown in Figure A2-8, where every new growth is achieved on a higher and stronger base.

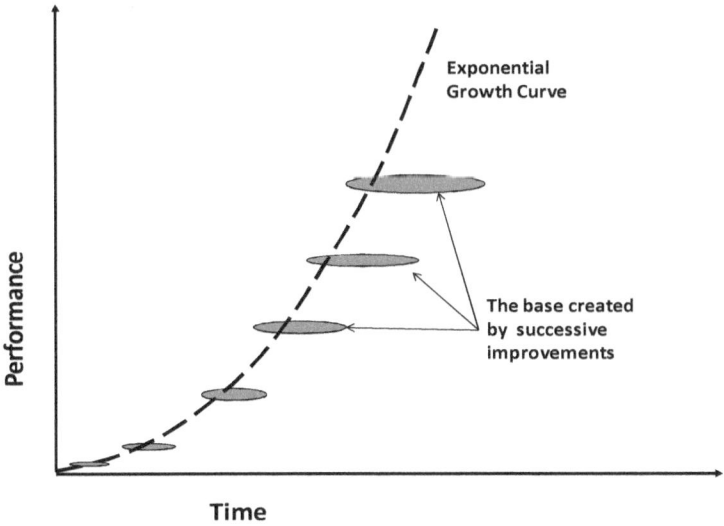

Figure A2-8 The natural growth curve of progressive organizations is an exponential curve with distinct build up of base or shoulder, on which successive growth is built.

This curve is also important for the change agents to acknowledge that every claim of a new initiative offering significant benefit is built only on the shoulders of giants (strong base provided by the previous good initiatives).

The underlying construct (S-curve) of the exponential growth curve has next level of details.

Each level of growth or improvement does not follow a smooth S curve, but within each S curve, there is a process of iterative maturity to build the base (stability). This phenomenon is well detailed in TQM (Total Quality Management [20]).

Any particular object or system taken for improvement, passes through a series of cyclical progression, and gradually builds along concept, actions and standardization. Each iteration of the cycle is called a PDCA cycle (Plan, Do, Check and Act cycle). As an initiative moves from one PDCA cycle to the next one, it moves from initial concept levels to standardization of operating procedures. It then becomes the way of life for the organization, which is analogous to building a stronger base, as shown in Figure A2-9.

This process of iterative progression in seeking improvement through each small but significant initiative is fundamental to the culture of TQM. And Terra Pharma's team entered this level of behavior in their quest for excellence. The behavior of following a process of ongoing improvement was embedded in its DNA, and thus created a long term and decisive competitive edge that was hard for its competitors to perceive and replicate.

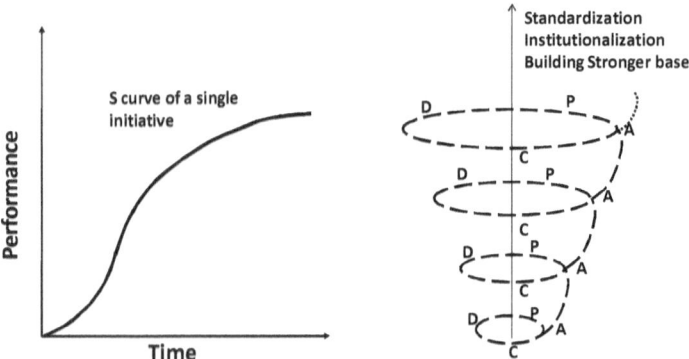

Figure A2-9 The DNA of exponential growth is built iteratively in cyclic progression within each improvement initiative

This is the way, the growth curve of a progressive organization shapes up into an exponential curve.

For those who have spent reasonably long time in the process of ongoing improvement in any organization, the growth curve would consist of a number of iterations and loops, crisscrossing each other, as shown in the Figure A2-10; and they would acknowledge that it is never smooth.

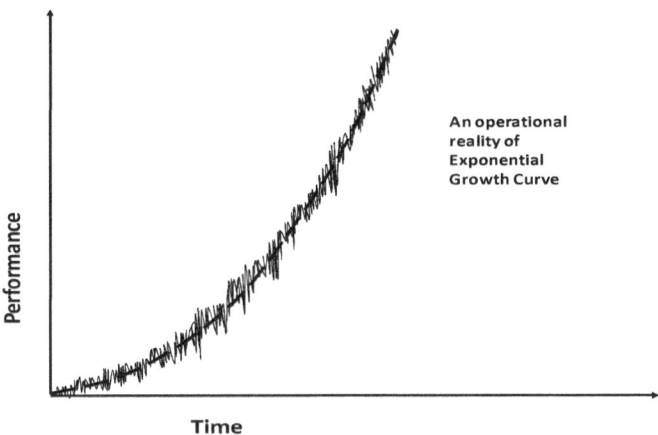

Figure A2-10 The actual operational growth curve of a progressive organization

We do see this pattern of growth in Terra Pharma, Figure A2-11. There were moments of dip in performance as obstacles and constraints popped up during Life2.0. The disruptions to the flow in business are inevitable but it is the ability to figure out the way of dealing with them keeps an organization on the path of sustainable growth.

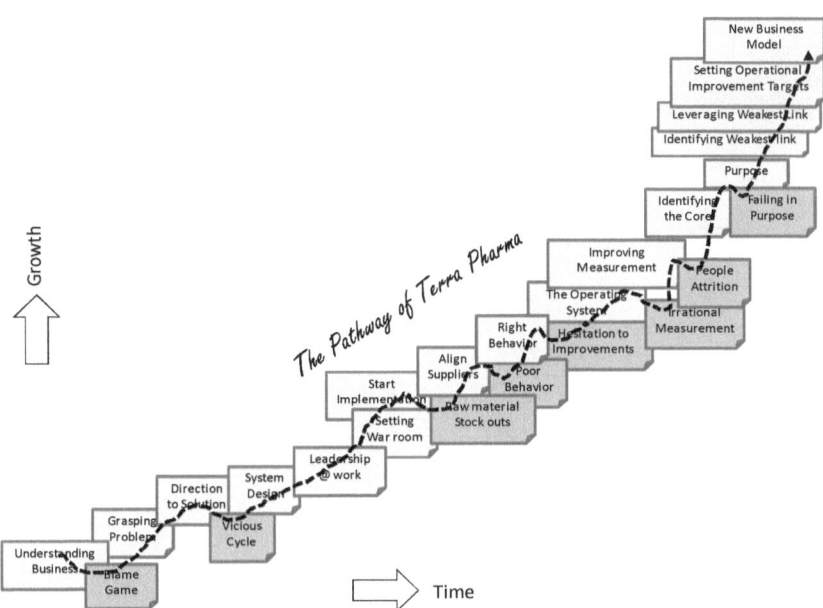

Figure A2-11 The pathway of Terra Pharma during Life2.0

Key References

1. Juran's Quality Handbook, J. M. Juran & A Blanton Godfrey, McGraw-Hill Professional
2. The Role of the Business Model in capturing value from Innovation: Evidence from XEROX Corporation's Technology Spinoff Companies., H. Chesbrough and R. S. Rosenbloom, Boston, Massachusetts, Harvard Business School, 2002
3. Seizing the White Space, Mark W Johnson, Harvard Business Press.
4. The Business Model Generation, Alexander Osterwalder and Yves Pigneur, John Wiley & Sons
5. Beating Low Cost Competition - How Premium Brands can Respond to Cut- Price Rivals, Adrian Ryans, John Wiley and Sons Litd
6. The Long Tail, Chris Anderson, Random House Business Books
7. Sense of Urgency, John P. Kotter, Harvard Business Press.
8. Factory Physics, Wallace J. Hopp and Mark L. Spearman, Waveland Pr Inc
9. Slack - Getting past burnouts, busywork and the myth of total efficiency, Tom Demarco, Broadway Books
10. The Fifth Discipline - The Art and Practice of The Learning Organization, Peter M Senge, Random House Business Books
11. The Machine that Changed the World, James P Womack, Daniel T Jones and Daniel Roos, Simon and Schuster UK Ltd.
12. Standing on Shoulders of Giant, Eliyahu M Goldratt, A Whitepaper.
13. Execution- the Discipline of Getting Things Done, Larry Bossidy and Ram Charan, Crown Business
14. The Goal: A Process of Ongoing Improvement, Eliyahu M Goldratt and James Cox, North River Press
15. The Toyota Way, Jeffrey K Liker, McGraw Hill
16. Lean Thinking, by James P. Womack and Daniel T. Jones, Simon & Schuster, Inc
17. The 4 Disciplines of Execution, Chris McChesney, Sean Covey and Jim Huling, Simon and Schuster UK Ltd.
18. The Wealth of Nations, Adam Smith, Bantum Dell, 2003
19. Blue Ocean Strategy, W. Chan Kim and Renee Mauborgne, Harvard Business School Press
20. Management by Quality, Hitoshi Kume, Productivity and Quality Publishing.

Co-creation of The Path

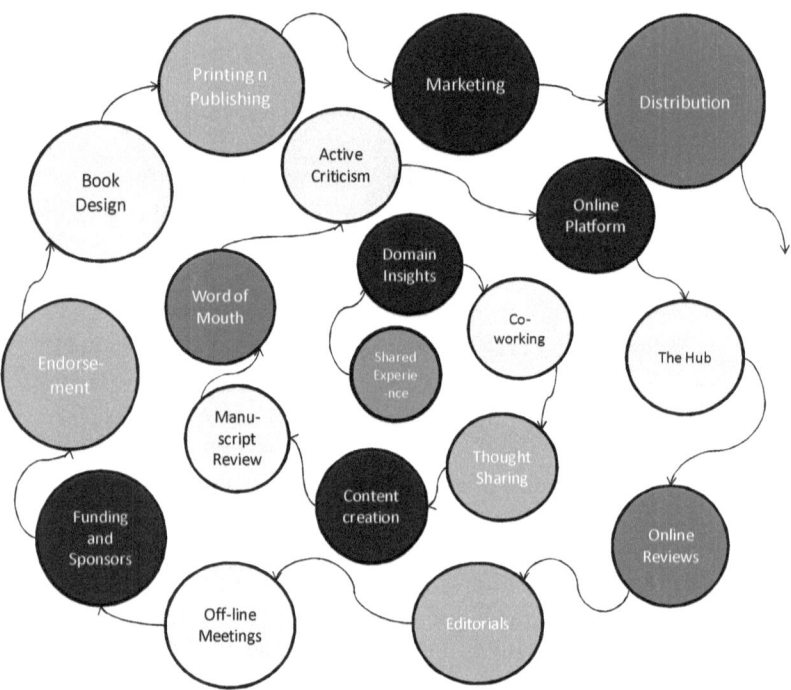

Co-creation of 'The Path' took place online at http://time2change.co.in, the Hub of Operational Excellence. In fact, activities of co-creation spread beyond reviewing and adding content online. Interactions through offline meetings, email exchanges and telephonic conversations played major roles in offering a more realistic and interesting book to the readers. Indeed, co-creation of 'The Path' is about participation of the practitioners in a whole gamut of activities to translate the idea into the Book and place it in the hands of readers.

Results of Co-creation

118 Co-creators
256 Online comments
790 email comments
1280 telephonic conversations
77 offline reviews

\# Industry represented 23
Cumulative professional experience behind the co-creation: 1300 man years
Average time per co-creator= 18 hrs

1st Chapter Uploaded: 30Jun2012
1st Copy of Book Dispatched: 7Nov 2012
Time to co-create the Book: 130 days

All copies of the first print sold out before it appeared In Book Stores

About the Author

Shridhar Lolla is a practitioner of Business Model Innovation, Focused Execution and Operational Excellence. He handholds business leaders in creating 'built to transform' organizations.

Shridhar is an engineer by qualification and holds a PhD degree from IIT Delhi, Masters from IT BHU Varanasi and Bachelor degree from MANIT, Bhopal, India.

Early in his career, he worked with Tecumseh, Kirloskar Electric, ABB and SIFY. His longest stint was with ABB, the Swiss power and automation technology leader, where he got his grounding in business management. In his last assignment, he was the Head of Applications and Solutions Group at its Corporate Research Center in India.

Since then, he has gained extensive experience in achieving breakthrough performance in Engineering, Product Development, R&D, IT Services, Software Development and Manufacturing Industries.

In the summer of 2012, he completed one of the longest direct engagements in operational excellence, which led to creation of 'The Path'. At the time of writing 'The Path', he was visiting, listening, conversing, observing and advising teams across Operations. The book contains insights from handholding professionals across multi-locations, in their journey to ever improve impact of operations on business performance.

Shridhar is an application expert of Theory of Constraints (TOC) and shares his time with Goldratt Consulting in implementing principles of TOC. He is also the author of the book, "Building Manufacturing Competitiveness - the TOC Way."

Shridhar is a recognized coach for first generation entrepreneurs and is a part of Indian entrepreneurship ecosystem.

Spending the day with operational teams and conducting walk through programs is Shridhar's calling. He lives in Bangalore, India, and his email id is lolla@cvmark.com

www.ingramcontent.com/pod-product-compliance
Lightning Source LLC
Chambersburg PA
CBHW021811170526
45157CB00007B/2540